Contemporary History in Context Series

General Editor: **Peter Catterall**, Lecturer, Department of History, Queen Mary and Westfield College, University of London

What do they know of the contemporary, who only the contemporary know? How, without some historical context, can you tell whether what you are observing is genuinely novel, and how can you understand how it has developed? It was, not least, to guard against the unconscious and ahistorical Whiggery of much contemporary comment that this series was conceived. The series takes important events or historical debates from the post-war years and, by bringing new archival evidence and historical insights to bear, seeks to re-examine and reinterpret these matters. Most of the books will have a significant international dimension, dealing with diplomatic, economic or cultural relations across borders. In the process the object will be to challenge orthodoxies and to cast new light upon major aspects of post-war history.

Titles include:

Oliver Bange
THE EEC CRISIS OF 1963
Kennedy, Macmillan, de Gaulle and Adenauer in Conflict

Christopher Brady
UNITED STATES FOREIGN POLICY TOWARDS CAMBODIA, 1977–92

Roger Broad
LABOUR'S EUROPEAN DILEMMAS SINCE 1945
From Bevin to Blair

Peter Catterall and Sean McDougall (*editors*)
THE NORTHERN IRELAND QUESTION IN BRITISH POLITICS

Peter Catterall, Colin Seymour-Ure and Adrian Smith (*editors*)
NORTHCLIFFE'S LEGACY
Aspects of the British Popular Press, 1896–1996

James Ellison
THREATENING EUROPE
Britain and the Creation of the European Community, 1955–58

Helen Fawcett and Rodney Lowe (*editors*)
WELFARE POLICY IN BRITAIN
The Road from 1945

Jonathan Hollowell (*editor*)
ANGLO-AMERICAN RELATIONS IN THE TWENTIETH CENTURY

Simon James and Virginia Preston (*editors*)
BRITISH POLITICS SINCE 1945
The Dynamics of Historical Change

Contemporary History in Context
Series Standing Order ISBN 0–333–71470–9
(*outside North America only*)

You can receive future titles in this series as they are published by placing a standing order.
Please contact your bookseller or, in case of difficulty, write to us at the address below with
your name and address, the title of the series and the ISBN quoted above.

Customer Services Department, Macmillan Distribution Ltd, Houndmills, Basingstoke,
Hampshire RG21 6XS, England

British Politics since 1945

The Dynamics of Historical Change

Edited by

Simon James

and

Virginia Preston

palgrave

First published 2001 by
PALGRAVE
Houndmills, Basingstoke, Hampshire RG21 6XS and
175 Fifth Avenue, New York, N. Y. 10010
Companies and representatives throughout the world

PALGRAVE is the new global academic imprint of
St. Martin's Press LLC Scholarly and Reference Division and
Palgrave Publishers Ltd (formerly Macmillan Press Ltd).

ISBN 0–333–67511–8

This book is printed on paper suitable for recycling and
made from fully managed and sustained forest sources.

A catalogue record for this book is available
from the British Library.

Library of Congress Cataloging-in-Publication Data
British politics since 1945 : the dynamics of historical change /
edited by Simon James and Virginia Preston.
        p. cm.
Includes bibliographical references and index.
ISBN 0–333–67511–8
    1. Great Britain—Politics and government—1945–
I. James, Simon, 1960– II. Preston, Virginia, 1967–
DA566.7 .B666 2001
941.085—dc21

                                                      2001021870

10   9   8   7   6   5   4   3   2   1
10   09 08 07 06 05 04 03 02 01

Printed and bound in Great Britain by
Antony Rowe Ltd, Chippenham, Wiltshire

Contents

List of Tables

General Editor's Preface

What happened in postwar British history? How should it be conceived? By the end of the 1980s it was sometimes tempting for those inclined to see the past through the prism of contemporary politics to regard the period as a whole, consisting of the story of the forging and falling apart of a political consensus, with the Attlee and Thatcher governments acting as convenient bookends. But is this to privilege the roles of particular actors? A different periodicity might emerge if different questions were asked. It might, for instance, be argued that postwar Britain itself ended at some point after the Suez Crisis in 1956, whether in 1961 with the first bid for entry to Europe, after 1968 with the withdrawal of troops from East of Suez or, as Keith Middlemas argues here, with the industrial travails of the late 1970s. During this process austerity and postwar rebuilding were replaced by anxieties about both Britain's international role and her economic performance that, in the case of the latter at least, were to dominate the politics of much of the next 20 to 30 years. A focus on the management of political economy might therefore suggest a number of different staging posts in the journey from 1945, whilst a focus on international relations might emphasise 1973 and the decision to join what was then known as the European Economic Community as a key turning point. Then again, from the standpoint of a globalizing post-cold war world in the late 1990s, the significance of any or all or these events might change or diminish. It might be argued that continuity as much as change is evident, from the 1999 reworking by Blair of Churchill's 1953 evocation of Britain's place at the intersection of the 'three circles' of the United States, Europe and the Commonwealth, to the persistent political significance of a much changed City of London. But it also might be argued that some form of continuity is evident in a different sense, as the state and particular institutions, such as political parties, have steadily diminished in significance since the early 1950s as civic culture, whilst still engaging the energies of large sections of the population, has privatized or particularized its concerns.

It was to debate the trends, the periodicity, indeed 'The State of the Art' of postwar British history, that the conference which produced these papers was held. The issues raised, both in the conference and in this book, cover everything from the dynamics of historical change to the sources and methodologies for the writing of contemporary history. The need to guard against the ahistorical triumphalism of politicians of all parties claiming either the novelty of their views, the intellectual bankruptcy of their predecessors and opponents or, more often, both, was very much in the minds of the founders of the Institute of Contemporary British History. The need to guard against the decontextualized unconscious Whiggery of too much of the writings on postwar Britain has been a *leitmotif* of the Institute ever since. And the need to guard against the polemic distortion of history for the sake of present concerns by a Corelli Barnett or a Will Hutton was also to be very much emphasised at the conference. At the turn of the century the risk remains as great as ever that history will be ignored by amnesiac politicians or selectively distorted by polemicists – one group claiming too much for their place in history whilst the other claims too much for their reading of history. At the same time, historians need to guard against an unconscious selectivity of their own. Privileging any set of sources runs the risk of decontextualising one's subject, of producing institutional biography rather than history, leaving untouched the questions of culture, structure and interactions which need to be explored to produce more textured accounts of the past. Through the range of essays offered here, this book avoids these pitfalls, instead offering a fresh set of readings on the whats, hows, whens and whys of postwar British history.

Peter Catterall
Queen Mary and Westfield College
University of London

Notes on the Contributors

Samuel H. Beer is Emeritus Eaton Professor of the Science of Government, Harvard University, author of numerous influential books including the classic *Modern British Politics: A Study of Parties and Pressure* (1965), *To Make a Nation: The Rediscovery of American Federalism* (1994) and *Groups After Pressure*.

John Barnes is Lecturer in Government at the London School of Economics and author of 'Education: the Changing Balance of Power', in D. Gladstone (ed.), *British Social Welfare* (1995), and 'Ideology and Factions' and 'Making of Party Policy' in A. Seldon and S. Ball (eds), *Conservative Century* (1994).

Jenie Betteridge is a Research Fellow at the Centre for Communication and Information Studies, University of Westminster.

Michael Cockerell is a senior BBC political reporter, author of books including *Live from No. 10* and (with Peter Hennessy and David Walker) *Sources Close to the Prime Minister,* and award-winning maker of documentaries including *Blair's 1000 Days* and *Alastair Campbell – News from No. 10*.

Simon James is the author of *British Cabinet Government* (1992, revised and updated version 1999) and *British Government: A Reader in Policy Making* (1997).

Kevin Jefferys lectures in modern British history at the University of Plymouth. His publications include *Retreat from New Jerusalem: British Politics, 1951–64* (1997) and *Anthony Crosland* (1999).

Keith Middlemas is Emeritus Professor of Politics at the University of Sussex and author of many books including *Power, Competition and the State* (3 volumes), on Britain in the postwar period, and *Orchestrating Europe* (1995).

Virginia Preston is Deputy Director of the Institute of Contemporary British History, Institute of Historical Research, University of London.

Peter Riddell is political columnist and commentator of *The Times*. He is the author of *The Thatcher Era and its Legacy* (1991), as well as *Honest Opportunism: The Rise of the Career Politician* (revised edition 1996) and *Parliament under Pressure* (1998, and in revised form, *Parliament under Blair*, 2000). He is Visiting Professor of Political History, Queen Mary College, University of London.

Ken Young is Professor of Politics at Queen Mary and Westfield College, University of London. He has long-standing academic interests in political culture, public policy, local government and urban affairs. He is author, co-author or editor of many books, papers and research reports on these topics. He writes regularly for the British Social Attitudes series, and is a member of the advisory committee of the Centre for Research into Elections and Social Trends at SCPR/ Nuffield College, Oxford.

1
Introduction

Simon James

The essays in this volume were first delivered as papers at a five-day conference organized in July 1995 by the Institute of Contemporary British History (ICBH) to mark the 50th anniversary of the end of the Second World War. In parallel with this volume, which concentrates on British political history, the Institute has published a collection of papers concentrating on social policy entitled *Welfare Policy in Britain*, edited by Helen Fawcett and Rodney Lowe. A number of other papers given at the conference have also appeared in the Institute's journal, *Contemporary British History*.

It is unusual for an historical conference, even one lasting five days, to publish so many papers. This event, however, was deliberately designed as a showcase for the breadth, depth and diversity of historical scholarship on the postwar period. It certainly succeeded in this: over 100 papers, 15 plenary sessions, and a variety of topics ranging from incomes policies to science policy, from the London Olympics of 1948 to the media barons of the 1990s, from political culture to youth counter-culture, from Hungarian refugees to the Rhodesian rebellion. *The Times Higher Education Supplement* devoted a 12-page special feature to the conference. Perhaps its most encouraging characteristic was the diversity of participants, from graduate students through to eminent professors, with many participants from beyond academia: journalists, civil servants, broadcasters and politicians, including one former prime minister. If the contributions in this book and the companion volume tend to be from longer-established academics and outsiders, a number of excellent papers by postgraduate students given at the conference have subsequently reached the wider world as PhD theses and/or books.

The barely coded message that the conference sent out was: contemporary history has arrived. And a touch of triumphalism was permissible for, in truth, a number of historians had been rather sniffy about the Institute of Contemporary British History when it first came into being in the early 1980s. 'History from newspaper clippings' and 'current affairs dressed up as scholarship' were the kinder forms of disparagement from some academics who, it seems, never bothered to consider how miscellaneous and bizarre is the meagre source material from which medieval historians so confidently weave their scholarship, or how much easier it is to apply the cool detachment of the historian to the dusty archives of Mr Gladstone than to the still-glowing embers of the Callaghan government.

That kind of snooty reception had not helped the Institute in its early years: from its inception as a glint in Peter Hennessy's eye and a cardboard box in Anthony Seldon's spare room, it forever had to justify its existence. In the event, it did so handsomely, blossoming into a respected institution with an impressive publishing record and a substantial international reputation. The queue of major publishers willing to put into print works prepared, commissioned or fostered by the Institute suggests that it has tapped a deep vein of interest in the history of modern times. And the variegated cast of scholars, politicians and policy-makers who appear at the weekly seminar at the Institute of Historical Research demonstrates an interest in contemporary history spreading far beyond the conventional frontiers of academia.

There is, however, another way of looking at this new acceptance of contemporary history which, if correct, might concede some ground to the sceptics. For could it not simply be that as time passes, the study of the 1950s and 1960s becomes more acceptable, not as contemporary history, but as history in the 'conventional' sense? Of course, a significant factor is the 30-year rule, which dictates that government papers are available only up to 30 years before our date, which at the time of the conference was the mid-1960s. But there may be a more significant consideration that accounts for the relatively greater volume of study of, say, 1955–65 compared with 1975–85.

This factor is the concept of a turning point, falling some time between the mid-1960s and the early 1980s, when the politico-social character of Britain changed markedly: a pivotal time before which the political quintessence of Britain could be encapsulated by Rab Butler addressing an attentive House of Commons, and after which it was more aptly symbolized by Mrs Thatcher stepping out of Concorde towards the television cameras. If there was such a turning point, can we still talk of the Butler era as 'contemporary history'?

Here we are not just playing with words: it is not a matter of categorising decades for the sake of categorisation. A recognition that we are addressing two different epochs has significant implications. Firstly, it may change the light in which we examine these two epochs. Secondly, if the emphasis of scholarship is falling unduly on the earlier of them, it raises questions about the way in which those who style themselves contemporary historians should focus their attention and energies. Thirdly, might the different political character of the later epoch not call for different research approaches, especially given the rapid evolution of communications technology?

Here the devil's advocate might justifiably ask why, if this concept of a turning point is so significant, there has not been much debate about it. In part, the answer must be: because the question is so difficult to answer. A symposium on the subject convened by the ICBH in 1992[1] seemed to generate more answers than there were participants. Another part of the explanation may lie in the development of the Institute of Contemporary British History itself, whose work has done so much to set the framework for examination of the postwar era. When the Institute was created in the early 1980s, the Second World War had ended only 35 years earlier: a self-contained span of time. Twenty years later, with not only the commemoration of VE day but also now the millennium behind us, the flickering image of Mr Attlee on a British Gaumont newsreel seems terribly remote. And besides, 50 years is a period of time more easily amenable to segmentation.

A further consideration could be that the study of contemporary history is a relatively fragmented activity: while many people beaver away at individual projects, there are relatively few people who stand back and take a broad view of the period as a whole. In part this is the product of Britain's native approach to history, which tends to the empirical rather than the theoretical. In part it can be attributed to the fact that most of the academics in the field are in the earlier stages of their careers, when one tends to study a brief period in depth; only later in their careers do historians move on to broader studies, examining a longer period in synoptic fashion.

Possibly the principal reason for lack of concentration on this 'turning point' issue, however, is that it has been masked by the (seemingly interminable) debate on the existence or otherwise of a postwar political consensus. This has soaked up to an extraordinary degree the energies of many contemporary historians. The consensus debate is certainly relevant to the concept of a turning point, because if a postwar consensus did exist, its termination would have constituted a significant point of transition. But historical turning points may be defined by many different types of change. At most, the consensus debate is a subset of the turning-point question.

Whatever the reason for its previous neglect, the concept of a significant turning point is present in a number of the essays in this book. Keith Middlemas's penetrating essay 'When Did Postwar Britain End?' identifies a series of possible periods of transition. He argues convincingly for the mid-1970s as the point that marked 'the loss of innocence and confidence on the part of the postwar meritocracy'. The chapter by Sam Beer identifies a longer process beginning in the 1960s, and other essays – Barnes on the premiership, Betteridge on broadcasting, James on judicial attitudes – all point to substantial changes in attitude in the 1960s, although these are likely to have been contributory elements of dissatisfaction whose confluence in the 1970s produced the damburst described by Middlemas. And perhaps these changing attitudes were themselves prompted in part by evident turning points in overseas affairs which lie outside the scope of this volume: the Suez crisis, decolonisation, and the withdrawal from east of Suez. But whenever the pivotal point in postwar history occurred, a pivotal point there was. There may have been a defining moment, or it may be more fitting to talk of a period of transition. But the general perception – expressed in this volume by Peter Riddell's chapter on Mrs Thatcher – is that from the early 1980s, at the latest, we were in a different epoch, with a distinctive political character. For all we know, indeed, the election of the Blair government in 1997 may come to be seen as a further turning point in postwar history.

Confining ourselves to the period 1945 to 1995, however, it is worth making a stab at defining the points of difference between what we might term the 'postwar' epoch and the 'current' epoch, because they have considerable implications for the future focus of historical research and, possibly, of its methodology.

To start with, the most obvious change in the character of the British polity was the demise of Britain's half-hearted flirtation with corporatism. So completely has it been eradicated that it seems almost otiose to dwell on it: yet the reasons for its failure deserve a few paragraphs of reflection, if only because for two decades successive Conservative and Labour governments devoted great energy to making some variant of it take root. The demise of the trade unions' role as serious players in the shaping of national policy was largely their own doing. Beyond question in the 1970s they had ambitions to extend their sway beyond the narrow compass of pay deals; resolutions on nuclear weapons and South Africa were regularly passed at annual conferences. The Social Contract, which helped propel a rather surprised Wilson back to Downing Street in 1974, was a concrete expression of this trade-off, and yielded to the unions at least one substantial gain outside the bounds of industrial relations: a substantial increase in the old age pension. But the unions could never really bring themselves to surrender that element of industrial freedom which had to be traded in exchange for true political power – in part, because shop-floor militants would have overruled their leaders. In truth, the impossibility of such a bargain had been made clear in the 1969 crisis over *In Place of Strife*; the 'winter of discontent' a decade later was merely the playing out of these underlying realities. It was significant, in the closing years of the Callaghan government, that the only political concession agreed with the General Council of the Trades Union Congress (TUC) was the abolition of the House of Lords – scarcely a practical proposition for a minority government – and that Callaghan was himself responsible for shelving the controversial recommendations of the Royal Commission on Industrial Democracy to write unions into the decision-making processes of companies.

The high-profile involvement, and subsequent marginalisation, of the unions has tended to mask the equal reluctance of employers to snuggle into the corporatist embrace. Although the Confederation of British Industry's (CBI's) relations with the government have always been less transparent than those of the unions, the same rifts of opinion existed amongst industrial leaders as existed amongst Conservative politicians over Macmillan's creation of the National

Economic Development Council (NEDC) or Heath's Industry Act. Business opinion has always been sensitive to the commercial consequences of social disharmony, and opportunistic enough to snap up government grants when offered. Yet business valued the liberty to praise or blame government as it saw fit. Its leading lights did not necessarily want to be drawn into a pale reflection of a corporatist state; and, even if they had, the diffuse structures and diversity of views in the business world allowed its leaders to exercise over their members even less sway than was the case in the unions. And just as the interests of Labour governments and the unions diverged, so Conservative politicians did not always regard the interests of business as at one with those of ministers: at different times Macmillan, Heath and Thatcher all railed at the boneheaded refusal of businessmen to cherish and exploit what they saw as the excellent opportunities offered by their governments' policies.

In short, corporatism failed because two of the three social partners, surprisingly, were not sufficiently committed to it. Next to this, the failure of central government – pointed out by Middlemas – to provide the necessary support machinery for the corporate effort, along French or German lines, was only a secondary failing. The abolition of the Manpower Services Commission and, subsequently, of the National Economic Development Council in 1989, was merely a switching-off of the life-support mechanism which ended a prolonged coma. Vestigial tripartite arrangements persisted only in such useful but marginal activities as industrial tribunals.

What, then, has taken the place of corporatist government involvement in economic life? The original answer from Mrs Thatcher's government was abstention from involvement, but this self-denying ordinance did not endure. Anything but. There was certainly a significant redrawing of the frontier between public and private provision, to the latter's great advantage, through privatisation and competitive tendering of public service provision. And much of this shift seems permanent; the Labour government elected in 1997 may have pledged itself to reverse certain elements of the new system, notably the internal market in the National Health Service, but it is a commonplace of political commentary that the socioeconomic assumptions on which government is based had shifted permanently towards the free market by the mid-1970s. Yet what surprises in retrospect is that the shift from public to private provision has been confined to the commercial sphere: industry, services like cleaning and building, some white collar 'fringe' services in local government. Attempts to extend it to the sphere of welfare and education have been vehemently resisted. Some peripheral welfare services have undergone quasi-privatisation – notably dentistry – but even pensions, an area where private provision has been expanding apace since the 1950s, has not been transferred wholesale to the private sector.

Three factors appear to have set parameters to this revolution. The first is the reluctance of the private sector to develop substitute services in certain areas – e.g. the difficulty in persuading the banks to take on student loan provision – or to cater for citizens with relatively low incomes, as in the case of health or pensions. Secondly, there is a strong public attachment to the welfare state – a point repeatedly made in various chapters in this volume. The cry 'The National Health Service in danger!' evokes today the strength of reaction that 'The Church in danger!' provoked in the seventeenth century, and that protective instinct asserted itself vociferously in the 1990s when funding was reduced in such areas as education and legal aid. Thirdly, a point made by Kevin Jefferys, in his essay on class attitudes in the 1950s, still holds very much true today: many of those who had achieved economic status in the postwar order did so as office-holders on the public sector payroll, such as doctors, nurses, civil servants and teachers. And many private sector workers had a substantial holding in the new social economics, none more so than the south-eastern commuters who reacted so violently to increases in the cost of their railway season tickets.

Furthermore, where services were privatised, the result was not a contraction of the state but a change in its *modus operandi* from provision to regulation. At national level retreat from provision resulted not only in the abolition of the national corporations that had run nationalised industries, but also in the withering away of the organs of government that had overseen them – of which the 1993 abolition of the Department of Energy was a deliberately dramatic expression. In their place emerged a new species, the regulator, whose activities – well publicised on the television news – deeply affected the lives and pockets of the public.

Indeed, the concept of government by regulation at national level may be leading if anything to an expansion of state activity. The

substitution of regulation for ownership not only left central government with substantial control over the services it previously owned,
but also offered a mechanism by which government could extend its
control over areas in which previously the state's control had been
weak or non-existent – an obvious example being the regulation of
the City and personal financial services. While the sphere of national
activity directly controlled by the state has shrunk, there has been a
compensating extension of indirect control into new areas, and
future governments minded to extend the reach of Whitehall's arm
might find regulation an effective and inexpensive way of doing it.

There was in any case a tension between the philosophical intention to draw in the horns of the state and the very real public demand
for a reassertion of the authority of central government. The sense of
crisis in the mid-1970s had been almost palpable: as Sam Beer puts it
in his essay, governments were seen as losing control. And, while it is
impossible for a country to maintain a sense of enervation for years at
a stretch, at the end of the decade these same fears came to the
surface again at the time of the 'winter of discontent' that dealt a
mortal blow to Callaghan's sickly government. Even though in retrospect the Thatcherite revolution did not hit its stride until the mid-
1980s, from the outset the rhetoric of the new government was
designed to reassert political control over events. And, in time, rhetoric became reality. Individual achievements – the checking of inflation, the debilitation of trade unions and left-wing councils, defiance
of terrorism at home and Argentina abroad – were important not only
in themselves, but also as part of a greater psychological phenomenon: the sense of strong government, in control of events.

One facet of the reassertion of the power of national government
has been the reduction of the powers of sub-national government – a
term used here to cover not just local government, but also the health
service and other 'quangoid' forms of life. This need not have been an
inevitable consequence: any tighter controls over public spending
were necessarily going to involve some restriction of regional and
municipal discretion, but much of the wing-clipping was inspired
more by the political antagonisms of the mid-1980s between a radical
Conservative government and radical Labour councils. The councils
turned it into a fight for primacy, overplayed their hands, and lost.

The debilitation of sub-national government has been widely – and
correctly – seen as a major constitutional shift. But not all of the

means by which this has been achieved are understood: it has been due to a combination of six factors (some all but ignored by commentators), each with implications for the study of this period. One factor, beyond question, was the extension of direct controls by central government, both financial – notably the capping of local authority budgets – and institutional, such as central control of the memberships of health authorities and police authorities. A second was the remodelling and de-layering of sub-national government, in particular the abolition of upper tiers of local government in Scotland, Wales, the metropolitan counties of England and London – a development mirrored to some extent in the governance of the health service.

Thirdly, a number of activities were taken away and confided to other bodies: for example, the transfer of many housing functions to housing associations, and the transfer of further education colleges to a separate funding council. Fourthly – inspired in part by commercial experience – a great deal of power has been compulsorily transferred downwards to smaller local units. This has proved true of schools, which have been given control of their own budgets and encouraged – particularly by the Major government – to opt out of local authority control entirely; and of hospitals, which were enabled to acquire considerable autonomy through trust status. Fifthly, and linked to this, privatisation at national level of public utilities was reflected at lower levels of government by compulsory competitive tendering, which in a piecemeal but effective way forced large stretches of public service into the private sector. Even those many Labour-run local authorities who contrived to keep many, if not all, services in-house did so within a radically changed relationship, a new world of contract specifications and trading accounts.

Finally, there was the effective imposition of central government policies and standards through the activities of inspectorates – of schools, police, fire, pollution – and of auditors, whose remit, under the aegis of the Audit Commission, has been extended from simple probity into the vast field of efficiency and effectiveness. These bodies tend to impose on local authorities a combination of their own values – since no system for inspection can be value-free – and a framework imposed by central government. The latter is a particularly underestimated facet of the extension of central government influence. While secondary legislation – regulations made under statute by ministers – tends to deal with procedures, circulars of guidance from central government tend to deal more with the substance of service provision. While non-statutory, this guidance tends to be used by inspectors as a template to judge local policies, gradually inducing at local level a convergence towards a common norm encouraged by central government. In this way, such circulars and models of good practice are effectively being turned into a form of tertiary legislation.

However, the reassertion of state power has been in one direction only – downwards. It is offset, even outweighed, by the shift of power upwards towards the European Union. The potential for this transfer of power was enormous from the moment the United Kingdom joined what was then the European Economic Community (EEC) but was disregarded – deliberately or otherwise – until the impact became impossible to ignore. Predictably, perhaps, whether politicians favoured this shift depended on whether they approved of the ends to which Brussels was turning its power. When the EEC was seen primarily as an economic enterprise, opposition came mainly from the left, who suspected capitalist hegemony. Now that the European Union (EU) has developed a strong social focus, the left is reconciled to it (proponents of women's rights woke up to its egalitarian potential earlier than most) and more substantial opposition comes from the right. Today, perhaps the best index of the transfer of power is the extent to which professional lobbyists are increasingly focusing their attention on Europe, especially those dealing with monopolies and mergers. Local authorities, too, have shown a keen appreciation of where the power will lie by increasingly invoking the EU's principle of 'subsidiarity' – delegation of power to the most local level possible.

Yet if awareness of the impact of Europe is now keen, the focus of scholarly attention remains mistaken. There is too much concentration on the policy outputs, and too little on the inputs. Linked to that, the wrong bits of the machine are being subjected to scrutiny. Too much attention is devoted to the European Parliament, which is at present of little real importance; some attention, but far from enough, is paid to the Council of Ministers and the Commission, which are hugely important; and minimal attention is being paid to such shadowy bodies as COREPER (Committee of Permanent Representatives) and the Secretariat-General, which are crucial components of the machine. The same deficiency is true of the study of the changes being wrought to the *modus operandi* of British ministers and Whitehall. There is little study of the new mechanisms of government created to deal with European matters, such as UKREP (UK Permanent Representation to the EU) and the European Secretariat of the Cabinet Office, or of the ways in which longer-established institutions of government have adapted to a radically different pattern of policy-making – although some of these are touched on in John Barnes's essay on the premiership.

What is the relationship of citizens to their changing system of government? The answer to that question, for many decades after the war, would have been sought in electoral behaviour. That in itself was never quite straightforward, as Kevin Jeffreys' essay on the 1950s shows. Yet in the 1970s the electoral and party system was still seen as the main outlet for public dissatisfaction, the more so since, under the pressures of that decade, the stable two-party system seemed in danger of breaking up. In the 1980s the position unexpectedly stabilised: fragmentation was not reversed, but it was checked, with the evaporation of the National Front, the disappearance of the SDP (Social Democratic Party), the plateauing of the Scottish and Welsh nationalist vote, and the entrenchment of the Liberal Democrats predominantly as a regional party in south-west England.

Instead, the citizenry appear to be looking increasingly outside the party system; there is a greater diversity of modes of political expression. Sam Beer provides in his chapter a catalogue of social changes which he considers – controversially – to be more important than economic factors in the 'loss of control' by governments in the 1970s. Whatever their significance in that crisis (and the argument is surely not whether they mattered, but how much they mattered), the cultural upheavals that overturned so many accepted social, sexual, racial, religious, moral and economic standards had their mirror image in the political culture of the time. Not only did they manifest themselves in the corrosive cynicism about politics and politicians that Beer charts, but in a considerable assertiveness and rebelliousness.

As Ken Young's chapter on cultural change points out, there was a strong culture of protest demonstrations in Britain throughout the postwar period, although violent dissent was rare. But we have seen in recent decades not only dramatic instances of social disobedience – notably the backlash against the poll tax, and the refusal of teachers to implement testing in schools – but, probably more significant in its impact upon government, a greater willingness of articulate citizens to argue the toss with the powers that be. The proliferation of ombudsmen and the willingness of citizens to sue for poor performance by public authorities are matched by media attention to the rights of the consumer. Perhaps the underestimated phenomenon of recent decades has been the willingness of the professional classes to complain at the closure of their local casualty ward or cuts in the funding of their local school. The dramatic rise in the incidence of judicial review and appeals to the European Courts are only the formal legal expression of this querulousness.

The decay of faith in the traditional political process has found its counterpart in the growth in activity of pressure groups – and here the term is used to describe bodies pursuing objectives for idealistic reasons, such as penal reform, rather than interest groups representing people with entrenched interests, such as doctors or business organisations. It cannot be coincidental that the memberships of pressure groups have risen as the memberships of political parties have fallen. They are not necessarily more effective than they were, because since the 1970s governments have become more ruthless about riding out storms of protest than they once were. But they are more numerous, more active and more professional. They tend to take three forms. The first is the traditional single-issue pressure group, like the Child Poverty Action Group and Shelter, which have acquired many of the skills of professional government lobbyists. The second category is of voluntary service providers: worthy, altruistic bodies like Age Concern and Victim Support. As they have been drawn further into the national network of service provision, so they command national attention when they choose to speak out on behalf of their clients. Thirdly, there are groups which, to a greater or lesser extent, are willing to step outside the traditional framework of political campaigning and take direct action – for example the blockading of ports and attacks on scientific laboratories by animal welfare activists.

All of which has been made easier by the proliferation of information technology and the ease of desk-top publishing, which make it possible to gather and process data, and produce and distribute widely and swiftly documents which challenge government. These find a ready market in the ever-expanding media outlets. And media workers, themselves sharing the sceptical attitudes described above, will willingly refer these criticisms to 'established' political actors like governments and parties. Indeed, a large component of many serious news programmes seems to be debate between campaigners and ministers. (Campaigners are perhaps chosen by the media because they are better informed on their subject than Opposition MPs.) It is an interesting question to what extent the steady expansion of government public relations activity is as a response to this, but undoubtedly the two feed upon each other. Media skills are now an essential part of the political tool kit; presentation has become an integral element of policy-making. Today, the '14-day rule' and the refusal of 1950s governments to allow ministers to take part in broadcast debates with the Opposition, both described in Betteridge's chapter, seem ludicrous – although Harold Wilson banned his ministers from writing letters to the press as late as the 1970s. Instead, ministers now fight for space on the air waves; if the Opposition have a spokesman interviewed on *The World at One*, why is there not a minister replying to him? As Betteridge observes, political debate is now conducted in the home, through broadcasting, on an intimate personal level.

What of political accountability in all this? If by accountability we mean 'answerable', then politicians have undoubtedly become accountable for their actions in a way scarcely contemplated even 30 years ago. Not only is media scrutiny intense and unrelenting, it is also immediate: technological advance means that politicians will be required to respond to an incident in another part of the country within minutes of its occurrence, often before they have had the opportunity to check the facts for themselves. This tendency, in attenuated fashion, has spread down to sub-national level as well. On the other hand, if by accountable we mean 'liable to lose their heads if things go wrong', recent decades have seen a growing criticism of the unwillingness of ministers to accept the final responsibility when something goes wrong. But that pass was sold years ago: if we go back to the classical instance of ministerial responsibility in 1954, the Crichel Down case, we find that this episode actually ended in the propagation in the famous 'Maxwell–Fyfe' rules of a much narrower definition of ministerial responsibility: the politician was no longer responsible for every envelope licked in the department he ran, but only for acts of which he knew or which flowed from his explicit decisions.

Yet there is an undoubted groundswell of feeling that accountability is inadequate – a sense which, as I argue in my chapter, is
the main impulse behind the judiciary's development of judicial
review as a control parallel and supplementary to parliamentary
control over the executive. The answer is probably not that accountability has declined, but that expectations have risen; with the
decline of deferential electoral attitudes and the growth of more
sceptical journalistic scrutiny, and increasing public cynicism about
politicians' motives – given point by the 'sleaze' crisis of the mid-
1990s – the world expects blood more often. This has probably been
fuelled by new consumerist attitudes towards the delivery of public
services. These ideas, essentially commercial in origin – the phrase
'customer care' has been done to death, but encapsulates a radically
different attitude towards service delivery – used the new mechanisms of contract specifications and service level agreements to require
newer, better (or more accurately, more sensitive) standards of service
to the public. This never came to supplant the concept of political
accountability, although some theologians of the free market were
prepared to argue seriously that what mattered was not whether
services were delivered by a democratically accountable body, but
simply whether the services were of good quality. These two types
of accountability were not easily separated in the public mind, and
raising expectations of one type of accountability inevitably raised
expectations about the other sort.

If this is the rather confusing emergent pattern of the polity of the
'current era', what does this mean for the methodology of the historians who will analyse it? Firstly, the whole picture will become far
more complex. In particular, the objects of study will be more diverse.
'Government' has become a more complex mosaic; beyond the traditional agents subjected to scrutiny, we will have also to study a
whole new, shifting cast of private sector contractors, interest groups,
voluntary service providers, and players in the new landscape of
Europe; the new apparatus of regulation, both external to the state
– regulation of the private sector – and internal, by inspectors and
auditors of sub-national government; and new actors on the scene,
like the institutions of Europe. In this kaleidoscope, the roles of existing players will change: some, like the judiciary, the media and the
voluntary sector, will play wider roles; others, like local government,
narrower ones; and the roles of some, like the central executive, will

be altered radically. And, as the field of study becomes more fragmented, so the concepts under study, like accountability, control of the executive, democratic pluralism and individual rights, will become more complex too.

Secondly, sources will become more complicated and elusive. One of the advantages of studying postwar British politics so far has been that it has been possible for scholars to rely heavily on a small number of reliable sources – parliament, official publications, Whitehall records, party archives – to generate the core of their material. Under the new dispensation, not only are those records going to be far more widely dispersed, but a certain proportion of bodies, especially those in the penumbra of the state structure, like private contractors and voluntary bodies, will not have the civil service's tradition of meticulous record-keeping, nor any incentive to develop it, nor to preserve in the long term such records as they generate. And, as the European dimension deepens and overseas firms win contracts to run domestic services, some of those archives will be overseas and in foreign languages. Historical records of this era could develop some of the confusion and serendipity of the archives of the seventeenth and eighteenth centuries.

Thirdly, the sources will take different forms. The implications of electronic communication are a problem to which many historians have already tumbled: the Public Records Office, for example, is working on the implications of e-mail. But the problem will run wider, and the record of contemporary historians in adapting their techniques to address a plurality of types of sources is patchy. One fault is common to all the essays in this book: the almost exclusive reliance on written sources. Over-dependence on archival research is a profound weakness in contemporary British historical scholarship: a very high percentage of references in the chapters that follow are to written archives, and the same would undoubtedly be true of an analysis of the papers delivered at the conference, or footnotes in the ICBH's journal, *Contemporary British History*. Amongst these written archives, the Public Records Office bulks largest in the repertoire of contemporary historians – understandably, given its size, scope, coverage and relative ease of access. Beyond that there is an exceptionally heavy reliance on the written archives of institutions and individuals, and on written biography. Perhaps the one area of source material into which contemporary historians have most successfully diversified their efforts in the past 15 years has been newspapers, access to which has been greatly improved by the production of indexes by quality newspapers other than the sadly diminished *The Times*, and more recently by the possibility of searching newspapers on CD-ROM.

Two other types of source are neglected. One is the paltry use of interviews. Admittedly, they are time-consuming to conduct; tapes are costly to transcribe; and interview material can be frustratingly unreliable. But these difficulties are surmountable, and the effort invested yields a richer, more realistic history. The biggest barrier is, rather, the abiding and pernicious prejudice against interview evidence amongst many historians: not necessarily contemporary historians, but those who fund their research or supervise their theses. The audio archives generated by Anthony Seldon's elite interviewing project at the LSE are scarcely ever used. Yet this material offers valuable additional information on the subtleties, secrets or tensions which do not make their way into contemporary documents. Its neglect is a loss.

Another glaring omission is the shortage of broadcast material. Even in the two articles devoted to broadcasting, most of the references are to written sources, occasionally supplemented by interviews. In the other articles in this book – and for that matter in virtually all contemporary history – television and radio sources are either omitted or used as a garnish to the stolid fare of written archives. Admittedly, the difficulties standing in the way of access to even quite recent broadcast material are formidable: obsolete technology, copyright difficulties, the increasing pressure on broadcasters to cover their costs and – all too often – the indifference of broadcasters to the historical importance of the material they generate. Yet the sluggishness of historians to exploit even current television and radio programmes to inform their research programmes does not inspire confidence: and even if this barrier is overcome, the willingness of research funders and supervisors to take it seriously is a speculative commodity. In short, the ability of contemporary history to exploit contemporary research forms is distinctly and disquietingly limited.

So the scholarship of contemporary history will have to start changing its scope and style. We can expect the question 'what is contemporary history?' to open up in earnest now that we have passed the psychological milestone of the millennium. The danger is that scholars will invest more energy in debating this intriguing question than in grappling with the problem of fragmentation, both of social and governmental structures, and of historical sources. But if the problem of sources is not addressed soon, the real risk is that large swathes of evidence – non-governmental, overseas, electronic and oral – will be lost, while the coverage and utility of written sources shrinks. Let us hope that, if a conference is held in the year 2020 to mark 75 years since the end of the Second World War, it will not conclude that contemporary historical scholarship has fallen into decay.

Note

1. 'Periodisation in British History', *Contemporary Record*, vol. 6, no. 2 (Autumn 1992), pp. 326–40.

2

The Rise and Fall of Party Government in Britain and the United States, 1945–96: the Americanisation of British Politics?

Samuel H. Beer

A word about the subtitle. That is not just a hypothesis of my concoction. Not long ago, while Margaret Thatcher was in office, she herself said that it would be a great achievement if, when she stepped down, she could leave British politics looking like American politics, the Conservatives as a kind of Republican party alongside Labour as the Democrats. It would not be fair to put the blame for such a development on any one person. Today Tony Blair's purge of socialism from the Labour Party nicely complements Lady Thatcher's demotion of Tory paternalism among Conservatives. Intentionally or not, for better or worse, these changes do seem to indicate a trend towards Americanisation.

My point, however, is not so much to show imitation, as rather to use comparison and contrast to bring out the nature of what has been going on. In Britain and the USA, as in all modern nations, a welfare state has come into existence intended to correct and supplement the operations of the free market. These remedies for market failure, however, often mean government failure. Where the government is democratic, there is a strong tendency towards self-destructive pluralism, which, taking the form of gridlock or incoherence, constitutes one of the more common and noxious of these failures. Party government on the British model has sometimes been seen as a way of avoiding this disorder of the modern democratic state. I propose to make a comparison of the fortunes of that model in Britain and the United States to see if we can shed any light on this urgent problem of Big Government.

Party government and the consensus, 1945–70

In the early postwar years, when I first took up the study of British politics, many Americans – and this included politicians as well as professors – looked to Britain as the exemplar of how democracy could cope with the problems of modern capitalism. From the end of the war until the late 1960s the Westminster model compiled a record of solid social, economic and political success. Building on prewar foundations, successive governments created a welfare state and managed economy which provided proximate solutions to some of the worst problems of industrial society. Although marred by miscalculation and misfortune, the overall economic record was, in the words of Professor James E. Meade, 'an outstanding success story for a quarter of a century'.[1]

The political success was that this radical programme of the Attlee government, although initially enacted by a partisan majority, was soon accepted by the Opposition, signifying that it had won the general assent of the British nation. Majoritarianism had been converted into consensus. A more accurate term for what happened is convergence. The political parties did not surrender their opposing principles, but moderated the application of those principles as the parties competed for votes and adjusted action to economic realities. There was still significant disagreement and both sides held their basic commitments in reserve for deployment when the opportunity or necessity arose – as happened in later years.

The postwar settlement also included foreign and imperial policy. I am mainly concerned with domestic matters, so I will merely note that in these spheres of policy also, as in domestic affairs, the two parties, despite internal ructions, moved towards agreement, as Labour came to accept the realities of the cold war and the Conservatives the loss of empire.

In admiring American eyes, the key to this political success was party government: that is, a stable, competitive two-party system based on mass party memberships, which, by providing governments

with cohesive legislative majorities supporting distinctive programmes, gave voters an effective choice. In this system the prime
minister and his cabinet enjoyed that combination of executive and
legislative power which had been passed on to them from the old
monarchy as it gave way to popular government. Thanks to this
constitutional fusion of powers the British legislature could decide
who governs, but could not itself govern, since if it turned out one
monopolist of executive and legislative power, the option was only to
put in another. Policy would presumably be changed but the ministerial monopoly of power would not. A few American reformers did
propose the adoption of features of Britain's constitutional system,
such as allowing heads of departments to be members of Congress, or
giving the President the power of dissolution. Most advocates of
party government in the USA, however, thought that changes in
party organisation, requiring no constitutional amendment, could
sufficiently bridge the separation of power established by the Constitution to approximate the British fusion.

In 1950 in a celebrated report, entitled *Toward a More Responsible
Two-Party System* and sponsored by the American Political Science
Association, a committee of eminent authorities showed how such
a concentration of political power could be achieved by reforms of
party organisation in the legislature and in the country.[2] Among
political scientists and generally among people who took a professional interest in the study of American politics, this idea of a more
responsible party system was soon widely accepted.

Indeed, the course of political development seemed already to be
moving in this direction. Thanks to the realignment of parties in
1932, the Democrats under the leadership of President Franklin Roosevelt were enjoying a long period of dominance, informed by a fairly
coherent social and economic outlook. To this public philosophy
Roosevelt gave the name liberalism, a term which until then had
not been much used in American politics and which Roosevelt had
adopted in an echo of the interventionism advocated by the British
Liberal Party earlier in the century.[3] In this period of New Deal liberalism, Congress and President were usually commanded by the same
party. A similar pattern of unified government had prevailed under
the Republicans during most of the preceding generation. It was
therefore not unreasonable to expect that party organisation, if prop-
erly designed, could deliver the full power of governing, as in the

British model, to one party or the other as the pendulum of politics continued to swing back and forth from one realignment to another.

This American attraction to party government had a considerable history, going back at least to Woodrow Wilson's *Congressional Government* in 1885. Inspired by contrast with the glowing portrait of the British system in Walter Bagehot's *English Constitution* (1867), Wilson gave a depressing report of the disorderly regime of a weak presidency and a fragmented Congress, which he saw in the years after the Civil War. In the 1940s the same logic informed the impassioned pleas of the leading advocate of party government and the principal author of the Report of 1950, Professor E. E. Schattschneider of Wesleyan University. Starting from his study of the self- destructive political process that brought the Smoot–Hawley Tariff into existence in 1930, Schattschneider enlarged his analysis to demonstrate the need for more orderly and responsible government which emerged from the growing interventionism of government in the years of the Great Depression.[4]

The history that gave urgency to the topic in the 1940s spoke to these weightier concerns. As the Great Depression devastated the capitalist economies of the Western world, their governments often found themselves distracted to the point of paralysis by the chaos of conflicting interests and pressures. Their consequent inability to muster the central power to control events weakened their hold on their citizenry and heightened the appeal of dictatorship. The most compelling illustration was the bitter group conflict in German politics, which opened the way for Hitler and the fall of the Weimar Republic.

This wider relevance gave rise to the topic of stable democracy, a bland denomination for a deep affliction of modern politics. The 1950 report was fully aware of this context, as one can see from its sober concluding passages. They echoed the ancient wisdom of the West, from Plato to St Thomas Aquinas to Machiavelli and Montesqieu, warning against the self-destructive pluralism of popular government. In my generation's quest for 'the secrets of stable democracy', as Richard Rose observed in 1965, students of politics looked to Britain.[5] My own assessment was no less admiring when in the same year I concluded *British Politics in the Collectivist Age* by saying: 'Happy the country in which consensus and conflict are ordered in a dialectic that makes of the political arena at once a market of interests and a forum for debate of fundamental moral concerns.'[6]

Understanding the British phenomenon, however, required more than a study of organisational design and constitutional principle. Underlying these was the 'civic culture'. This term comes from the title of that magisterial work by Almond and Verba published in 1963, in which they sought by comparative analysis to get at the basic attitudes and values that best support a regime of both governmental order and democratic responsiveness.[7] Britain and the United States led the field, but Britain clearly had the edge, thanks to its unique integration of traditional and modern values, which provided the cultural foundation for what the book called its 'strong and effective government' and 'efficient and independent administration'.

On the one hand, there was Toryism, a tradition which still managed to show recognisable traces of *noblesse oblige* and deference dating from a premodern sense of hierarchy. The Conservative Party made no bones about its adherence to this tradition, unabashedly emphasising in its publications the need for such distinctions between leaders and followers in politics and government. On the other hand, there was the solidarity among Socialists which drew on the values of an older organic community. In both Tory and Socialist conceptions, class, that premodern graft onto modern capitalism, was an essential force for integration, for the Tory acting vertically and for the Socialist acting horizontally. A third tradition, weaker than the other two and entertained by Britain's centre party, the Liberals, embraced the values of radical democracy, more egalitarian than the Tory and more individualist than the Socialist. As all readers of Louis Hartz will know, American politics is dominated by this liberal tradition to the virtual exclusion of Toryism and Socialism.[8]

British political culture had its admirers not only in the USA. On the continent, where similar premodern survivals had often embittered conflict, fuelling the passions of reaction and revolution, observers had long admired Britain's fusion of old and new in her political outlook. One thinks of de Tocqueville, Taine, Halévy, Mosca, Schumpeter, de Jouvenel. Across the Channel, as well as across the Atlantic, therefore, it appeared during the first postwar years that

Britain was once again leading the way through the trials of modernisation. In Britain itself, as the 1960s dawned, the mood was euphoric. In 1959 Macmillan won re-election on slogans that have not inaccurately been summarised as 'You've never had it so good!', and the cheerful data for the civic culture study were gathered, showing British trust in their government and politics at a peak in comparison with other nations. In these same years the USA discovered its affluence, reported its high pride in its government and, despite the menace of the cold war and the trauma of Kennedy's assassination, acclaimed the reforms of Johnson's Great Society. 'For,' as our foremost journalistic authority on the presidency, Theodore White, proclaimed in 1965, 'Americans live today on the threshold of the greatest hope in the whole history of the human race.'[9] Was it only incidental that, as one political scientist revealed, during the period 1948–64, the voting of Democrats in Congress – setting aside the Southern dissidents – had moved 'quite closely to the model of responsible party government'?[10]

Government failures and cultural upheaval

In both countries this happy continuum was disrupted by a series of government failures which, beginning in the 1960s, stretched on into the following decades. Their essence was a loss of control: a loss of control of governments over the economy, displayed in soaring inflation, and a loss of control of governments over themselves, displayed in an explosion of public spending. Nor were these afflictions confined to these two countries. They were so common that Richard Rose could ask of Western countries in general, 'Can governments go bankrupt?'[11] About the same time, displaying a similar change of mood, I published a book in which, analysing 'the political contradictions of collectivism', I asserted: 'In an ironic sense, Britain is maintaining its leadership. As it once showed the way toward democratic success, today it blazes a trail toward democratic failure.'[12]

What I have to say in the next few pages is a summary of that analysis. Students of the period generally agree that governments in the two countries suffered such a loss of control at this time. As for explanations, some claim that in the British case the cause was at bottom economic, specifically the long-run decline in the British economy. But this view does not fit the facts. As Peter Jenkins, who favours this hypothesis, himself grants: how speak of economic decline when output is growing and standards of living are rising?[13] Although in comparison with other countries Britain was falling behind, in comparison with her own past, Britain was growing faster in the postwar years than ever before. As for her one-time economic leadership, we must recognise that Britain had never been a fast-growing economy; it simply got started on capitalism and industrialisation before the others.

My explanation of the loss of control is more political. I find the background of causation in an upheaval in culture that transformed the political process and the character of the party system. This cultural revolution attacked authority and order in every sphere: in dress, music, manners, education, sex, marriage, work, religion, race relations and perhaps most harshly in politics and government. The counter-culture struck not only Britain and America. It raged through all Western nations. Nor was the Roman Catholic church spared: recall Vatican II and the rise of liberation theology. And similarly the secular church of Marxism lost its old discipline, succumbing to the romantic anarchism of student protest in American, British and other Western universities.

Each country and sphere of activity has produced its own special explanation. So in the United States it is often all blamed on the Vietnam war. But the upheaval was more than political and affected countries that had nothing to do with that war. Moreover, the 1960s sentiments of alienation have persisted, prevailing to such an extent that today the main themes have been absorbed into the emotional and normative fabric of everyday life. Consider how widely in Britain and the USA, for better or for worse, the general public accepts and approves: cohabitation, abortion, homosexuality, pornography, protests of all sorts, women doing jobs formerly done by men, blacks doing jobs formerly reserved for whites, incivility in the media for all persons and causes, and, above all, pervasive distrust of and cynical dissatisfaction with politics and government.

Opinion surveys continually and abundantly confirm that finding for both countries. They show that in the United States trust in government has fallen steadily, with only brief recoveries under President Reagan and during the Gulf war. Confidence that government will do what is right all or most of the time declined from 76 per cent in 1964 to 19 per cent in 1994. Those believing that government is run by a few big interests for themselves rather than the benefit of all rose from 29 per cent in 1964 to 80 per cent in 1992.[14] In Britain likewise the decline of the civic culture has continued steadily. From the high level of the 1959 data, which reported that 83 per cent of respondents said they expected to get equal treatment in dealings with government officials, trust in government had fallen off sharply by the early 1970s, well before the economic deprivations of that decade had set in. A study published in 1977 reported that for none of four measures did a majority of respondents express a 'trusting' response, only 39 per cent, for example, believing that the government would do what was right most or all of the time. In the whole period, according to MORI polls, trust in government fell from 60 per cent in 1970 to 40 per cent in 1980 and to 22 per cent in 1995.[15]

It helps to understand the causes and effects of this upheaval in political culture to look at it as another stage in modernisation. Its rationale was 'the will to equality' which Nietzsche identified as the very root of modernity. A major force guiding the development of the modern state, this norm had been embodied in reforms extending the various rights of citizenship, legal, political and social, to ever wider circles of the polity. This politics of civic inclusion, one must note, also had the negative effect of dissolving old bonds of subjection and obligation. The resulting erosion of community has haunted Western thought since the eighteenth century.

In the United States and Britain during the 1960s and 1970s, this pressure for equalisation was expressed in a demand for greater participation, such that participatory democracy became a catchword in agitation and a principle of reform. Closely related to the demand for greater equalisation in the political process was the demand for greater equalisation in its results, often formulated as a claim on new legal rights and new government benefits. The attitudes supporting these demands are not to be confused with the nihilistic negations of postmodernism. The distrust they inspired was not anomie. They were not normless, but stood for something, fragile as the chance of their hopes being fully realised might be. Yet the conflict of these new attitudes with the reigning civic culture was so severe as substantially to weaken the capacity of the political system for stable and coherent government. The impact on political parties and the political system was one aspect of this deterioration.

Keeping in mind the comparison we will look at the impact of the new egalitarianism on political parties in the United States and then at its impact in Britain.

Party decline in the United States

Given the relative absence of feudal and communal targets in this country, the effect on us in America was less radical. Since we had long before experienced Jacksonian democracy, the renewed assertion of participatory values was simply more of the same. But it did make a difference as forms of direct democracy were imposed on established structures of representative democracy. In the name of 'community input', much Great Society legislation (such as Medicare and federal aid to education) attempted to give power at the level of immediate impact to people affected by government policy. Reforms of congressional procedure reduced the power of leaders and widened access to committee deliberations, inviting public scrutiny, criticism and pressure.[16] The most consequential change was the disintegration of the process of presidential nomination. In my recollection it is also the most vivid, since I attended and took part in nearly all Democratic conventions from the 1950s to the 1970s.

One measure of the change was the substitution in many states of the direct primary for the caucus convention system in the choice of delegates to the nominating convention. In 1932 11 states had primaries. By 1968 the number had risen to 17. Then came a sudden increase, doubling the number to 34. The important fact, however, was not the change in formal organisation, but the use made of the structure, whether based on primary or caucus. Judging by my experience in Massachusetts, even if a state had a primary system, as Massachusetts did, the active partisan became a delegate thanks to the influence of a party leader who put him on an official slate, which would then be elected in a modest turnout of registered party members. Emerging from this system, the 1952 and 1956 conventions were in the old style, in effect closed arenas where leaders and delegates talked about and bargained over the choice of the nominee and the stand on sensitive issues. Their deliberations, even when controversial and broadcast on television, excited no great response among the general public. It was as if the ordinary viewer, although enjoying the entertainment, felt that the conventions, being the business of politicians, did not involve him personally as the subsequent contest between the two nominees would do.[17]

The changing function of the convention was already beginning to show at the 1960 meeting, when Kennedy's use of television and primaries pretty well clinched the nomination before the delegates assembled in Los Angeles. The turning point was the tumultuous meeting in Chicago in 1968. That was the last occasion when party leaders did make the choice. Thereafter, in both parties participation in the election of delegates, which also often explicitly involved an expression of presidential preference, increased enormously, rising from 11 million in 1968 to 30 million in 1976. In each party the convention became a body which ratified the outcome of an intense and vastly expensive competition in the state-by-state contests and which otherwise served as a public relations event to launch the nominee's election campaign.

As experience with the direct primary in other elections to legislative and executive office had shown, such mass participation in the nominating process tended to shift the focus of the general election towards the candidate and away from the party. Organised interest groups gained leverage as aspirants pieced together support in the intraparty contest. Carried over into the general election, this focus on the candidates brought its benefits and burdens to the winner when he entered the White House. Groups acquired a connection with the President quite apart from any relation as fellow partisans. That connection meant that the President could count on them for support in achieving their legislative goals. It did not extend to other goals of his party.

The party bond was further weakened and the power of groups increased by reforms in delegate selection introduced by the McGovern–Fraser Commission of 1969–72, of which I happen to have been a member. In an attempt to offset the very real discrimination against blacks, especially in the South, the Commission mandated reforms in delegate selection so general in their formulation that other groups could call on them to legitimate their demands for similar advantages.[18] As a result, in many contests quotas were recognised, in effect extending proportional representation to women, homosexuals, the elderly and in due course various ethnic groups. At the same time, there was a falling off of partisanship among voters and legislators. The proportion of voters identifying with a party, especially the

strong identifiers, declined and the proportion of self-declared inde-
pendents rose. Ticket splitting increased as more and more voters
broke from their habit of supporting the candidates of the same
party for President and Congress.[19] Some observers thought these
changes heralded a party realignment, comparable to the shifts in
voter preference from Republicans to Democrats in the 1930s and
from Democrats to Republicans in the 1890s. Conceivably such a
party realignment could bring into power a new public philosophy
expressing a conservative break from liberalism and so a renewed
promise of coherence and direction in policy.

That realignment failed to appear, as the long period of unified
government, whether Republican or Democratic, came to an end and
American politics reverted to an earlier pattern of divided government with the presidency going to one party, usually the Republicans, while Congress remained on balance Democratic. In these
circumstances the President came, even more than in the past, to
depend for congressional support not on party majorities – always far
rarer in American than in British politics – but on bipartisan majorities changing ad hoc from issue to issue. The outcome of these shifts
toward a candidate-centred, group-empowered, non-partisan
politics was to weaken the President as a party leader and to cause
him to rely more on his constitutional powers and his personal
political skills. The promise of party government was giving way to
the strong bias of the American system towards presidential leadership.

The new group politics

The pluralism of American politics was enhanced not only by the
decline of parties, but also by the rise of a new group politics, which,
ironically, had been brought into existence thanks in no small degree
to party government. Pressure groups are active in all democratic
polities. The programmes of the New Deal had been a response to
the grievances of farmers, workers, homeowners, bankers, depositors,
businessmen and other groups suffering from the effects of the
Depression. In the governmental response spending was important.
It was, however, regarded as an emergency measure and in fact as
prosperity returned, it did taper off, except in some programmes such
as social security. The other great permanent programmes of New

Deal liberalism depended on the exercise of the regulatory powers of the federal government, especially the power to regulate commerce.

The civil rights reforms of the Great Society widened the politics of inclusion of the New Deal. Moreover, the legal rights established by these measures, primarily intended to remedy discrimination against blacks, were also claimed by other groups suffering similar disabilities. Often related to the same groups, the main Great Society programmes, however, originating from the public, not the private sector and involving massive public expenditure, gave a new meaning to liberalism.[20] The War on Poverty, for instance, did not result from pressure by the poor, but from initiatives of people in and around the federal government who had professional knowledge of urban poverty. Thus equipped, they designed specialised services requiring substantial spending to cope with the problem. Once identified and activated by such government initiatives, the beneficiary groups took care to maintain and possibly to expand the programmes. Politically, instead of the lobby creating the programme, the programme had created the lobby. In a private conversation a former Secretary of HEW (Department of Health, Education and Welfare) made the connection quite clear. When asked why the programmes were often narrowly defined, he replied: 'A narrow definition of the programme will create an homogeneous and intense constituency which will carefully monitor the administrative and legislative fortunes of the programme and quickly bring to the attention of its sponsors in the executive and legislative branches a failure of fulfillment or a need for further extension.' Programmes characterised by professional inspiration and substantial expenditure were not confined to the social sphere. In defence, the 'military–industrial complex', against whose political power President Eisenhower had cautioned, was composed of similar elements linking highly skilled scientific and technical personnel, whole new branches of industry spawned by their programmes and the relevant subunits of the Pentagon and the Congress.

Economic science also seemed to have progressed to the point where fine tuning of fiscal and monetary policy could produce both stability and growth. Brought into existence during a period of marked party vitality among the Democrats, the new group politics led the way in an enormous expansion of the public sector. While spending was not the only medium of government action, it provides the handiest measure of this outcome of the new liberalism. In the decade 1954–64, leaving out defence and looking only at domestic expenditure, the ratio of government expenditure at all levels – federal, state and local – to national income, rose from 12.9 per cent to 17.5 per cent. In the decade of 1964–74, after the advent of the Great Society, the PE/GNP (Public expenditure/gross national product) ratio reached 25.4 per cent, almost twice the rate of increase per year. It was not Vietnam but the Great Society that inaugurated the sharp surge in public expenditure in the mid-1960s. Moreover, while the new programmes came from the federal government, the increase in expenditure was also driven by the states. During the years 1965–70 the state tax effort – the amount of tax per $100 of personal income – rose more rapidly than the federal tax effort.[21]

Reflecting the continuing power of the new group politics, the rising PE/GNP ratio was not reversed by the conservative shift of opinion which ushered in the period of divided government in the 1970s and 1980s. Far from producing gridlock, this political change led to an even more incoherent process of 'growth without purpose'. While President Nixon sought to decentralise the burgeoning welfare state, he also encouraged more spending by both federal and state governments. What happened in Washington could also happen in the states. In Massachusetts, for example, Republican governors happily fathered rising expenditure in harmony with an agreeable Democratic legislature, much as a Republican President was doing in co-operation with a Democratic Congress. In 1981 Ronald Reagan took office pledged to reduce big government, especially at the federal level. With no inconsiderable help from Democrats, he sent the deficit into orbit. The government's loss of control of itself was reflected in its loss of control of the economy as inflation, likewise dating from the late 1960s, soared.

Britain matches American failure

Such profligacy was no doubt what one would expect from the easygoing, populistic Americans with their fragmented political and constitutional system. The surprise for admirers of the Westminster model was that Britain's centralised, top-down system produced the same results in its reaction to the collapse of the civic culture.

Deprived of the guidance of that invisible hand, party government faltered and failed. As surveys of opinion and the darkening mood of political discourse show, the 1960s was the period when the attitudes constituting the civic culture began to fade. This was also the hinge of time on which door swung shut on the successful politics of the postwar era and opened on the self-defeating pluralism of the 1970s and later years.[22]

In Britain, the very success of party government contributed to its failure, as the pluralism engendered by the welfare state and the managed economy rose up and defeated the agent of their creation. In a sense party government suffered from the weakness of its strength. Like parties in any democratic system, British parties bid against one another in their campaign promises. The distinction of the British system was that, thanks to the constitutional and organisational strength of a victorious party, it could actually deliver on its promises. Thus situated and motivated, the two evenly matched parties in their competition for the votes of the beneficiaries of the new social programmes raised public expenditure to inflationary heights. At the same time, efforts to manage the economy failed, as groups of producers in business and labour frustrated government attempts to make them serve the ends of public policy. Strategies of co-ordination and control that had worked in the heyday of the civic culture failed in the context of the self-defeating pluralism of the new group politics.

Reflecting the culture change, class decomposition weakened the class/party tie that had sustained party government in its days of strength. For two decades after the war, manual workers, unskilled and skilled, had voted overwhelmingly for Labour while the supervisory and managerial middle class gave a similar steady allegiance to the Conservatives. Squeezing the Liberals towards what seemed certain extinction, the two big parties divided the electorate into two evenly matched forces whose support, according to opinion surveys, varied by differences no greater than the statistical margin of error.

From the late 1960s the class/party tie began to weaken, as skilled workers moved towards the Conservatives, while higher occupational groups suffered losses to Labour. This growing convergence in the social foundations of the parties coincided with a decline in strong party identification, expressed in a pronounced fall in the two-party vote. Having persisted at about 90 per cent from 1945 to 1970, the vote for the two parties as a percentage of the total vote cast in a general election dropped sharply in 1974 to 75 per cent, remaining roughly at this level through the next five general elections from 1974 to 1992. By the 1980s, surveys showed that partisan dealignment had gone so far as to make half the electorate 'floating voters', thereby undermining the dualism required by the Westminster model. Class decomposition therefore weakened governments by the decline in not only the solidarity, but also the relative size of their electoral support. The same processes of decline in class solidarity and party identification led to a huge decline in the mass memberships and the corresponding organisational strength of the two parties.

In parliament a similar break from the norms of party government appeared, fairly suddenly in the late 1960s. Over the next decade back-benchers on both sides rebelled more frequently, in larger numbers and over more important issues than at any time since the latter part of the nineteenth century. In due course they also began to give more attention to service for their constituents and to enhancing their personal vote.[23] Lending institutional recognition to the less deferential and more participant attitudes of back-benchers, a system of select committees was established, dealing with special fields and exercising wide powers of review and criticism of policy, although still without authority in law-making.

In this weakened condition in the electorate and in parliament, party government was confronted in Britain, as in the United States, by the rising strength of a new group politics.

It had been party government itself which in its prime had brought forth this new pluralism. In this development, Labour – like the Democrats in the USA – had played the leading role. When it came to power in 1945, Labour was still, as it had been at its inception, a coalition of pressure groups. The members of these groups were, however, also a body of partisans who in their millions were united in varying degrees by faith in the socialist commonwealth. This was a commitment to fundamental change: to a substitution of common ownership for private property, government planning for the free market, co-operation for competition and, above all, the substitution, as the governing value and motivation, of fellowship for self-interest. This commitment gave momentum and direction to the furious whirl of legislation and reform generated by the Attlee government. By the time it left office in 1951, Labour had created a welfare state and managed economy which were socially, economically and politically a remarkable success, but which, however, flourished within what was still a distinctly capitalist order.

The failure of the old orthodoxies of nationalisation and planning in the midst of this success caused a severe crisis in the early 1950s, especially among the intellectual elite of the party. The solution was a radical and rapid transformation of the meaning of socialism, set forth pre-eminently in the writing of Tony Crosland and exemplified politically in the leadership of Hugh Gaitskell.[24] In this new conception, the traditional socialist goal of equality of condition would be achieved not by the old methodology, but by the redistributive spending of the welfare state and the corporatism of the managed economy in a capitalist system now admittedly moved by self-interest. Although much more radical than the ideas of the Kennedy/Johnson liberals, the new methodology of government action brought the British much closer to the American Left – also unintentionally inviting similar difficulties in the future.

Rejecting the egalitarianism of Labour for the paternalism of One Nation Toryism, the Conservatives, inspired by Rab Butler and led by Harold Macmillan, adopted, however, a similar methodology when making their contribution to the developing convergence on policy. As programme and method converged, the party battle subsided into intense bidding for the support of interest groups. As in the United States, new programmes created new lobbies. From the late 1950s a spectacular increase in the number of pressure groups accompanied an unprecedented surge in social spending which contributed substantially to the price inflation that plagued the British economy for the next 20 years.

How far party government was failing, however, appeared only in the 1970s when Conservative and Labour party leaders successively sought to break with the consensus in order to impose a sharply partisan alternative which would restore fiscal discipline and economic control. First Heath's move towards a free market economy, and then Wilson's effort in the opposite direction towards more state control, was defeated by the pressures of the new group politics, each government being forced in turn to execute a painful U-turn back to the consensus.

The decline of the parties shifted power towards the groups. But a mere collection of interest groups cannot impose upon its members the constraints necessary for coherent collective action. Even if the individual group recognises its long-run interest in compliance, it will be strongly tempted to choose the short-run benefit, in the absence of bonds of mutual trust and solidarity, such as those that arise from strong party identification, which assure it that the other groups will also accept these constraints. A party reduced to nothing more than a coalition of interest groups is self-defeating. Its pluralism, admirable as an expression of responsiveness, becomes a source of incoherence and disorder.[25]

Labour's self-destruction

For the sake of more concrete illustration of this analysis, I will follow the fortunes of the Labour Party. It had taken the initiative in the postwar reforms, and the failure of its attempts to cope with the problems of the 1960s revealed the failure of the collectivist polity that it had fathered. The crux was the inability of the Wilson government to persuade the trade unions to accept a wage policy in 1968. The immediate background of that crucial non-decision was the spending explosion which Macmillan had ignited by his generous social policies and which Wilson more than matched, even though, contrary to his promise, no white-hot technological revolution had produced the growth in the economy necessary to finance the expenditure. A central exhibit of that well-intentioned loss of control is Wilson's hour-long address at the Labour conference of 1967, claiming credit for provision for the old, the sick, the disabled, the young; for health and welfare services, housing and slum clearance, education, scientific and technological research, with each heading being matched with beneficiary groups, sometimes personalised as 'an old age pensioner' or 'a newly bereaved widow'.

While Roy Jenkins's austerity at the Treasury after some delay coped with the fiscal excesses, it did not re-establish control over the economy. Rather it displaced the lack of control from the clamant consumer groups of the spending explosion to the resistant producer groups of the wage/price explosion. Specifically, if the fruits of Jenkins's regime were to be gathered, wage demands had to be moderated. For this purpose the government offered the unions a fabulous deal. The government paper entitled *In Place of Strife* would have given the unions real power in making policy, if they had in return agreed not to resist government sanctions against unofficial strikes. The unions refused – and thereby, as Tommy Balogh said in despair, 'smashed the most hopeful social experiment of our time'.[26] The ensuing wage scramble which set off the wage/price explosion of the late 1960s continued to foil government efforts to control inflation. The bogus social contracts of the 1970s arranged by Labour and the unions culminated in the 'winter of discontent' of 1978–79, which put Thatcher in power.

Various conditions contributed to the failure of 1968: for instance, the maintenance of full employment by all governments, Conservative as well as Labour, which enormously strengthened the bargaining power of individual groups of workers and local leaders; the loose structure of British trade unions in contrast, with say, German or Swedish centralisation. Yet these conditions were not new, but had prevailed for a quarter of a century, indeed, since the recovery brought on by war production. In the early postwar period, labour relations in Britain had been remarkably peaceful. We may recall that President Truman, facing a turbulent labour front in the USA, had sent a committee to inquire into the secret of industrial peace in Britain. In 1948–50, moreover, the unions had accepted and carried out a successful policy of wage restraint and had continued their co-operation under the Monckton regime of succeeding Conservative governments. Nor will it do to say that the British working man was too ignorant or indifferent to realise the need for a wages policy. Surveys showed that by the mid-1960s the union rank and file, like British voters generally, understood the connection between wages and prices and in principle approved of a policy of wage restraint.[27]

The novel force was the new situation, the increasing fragmentation of the labour movement. The old sense of working-class identification was in sharp decline, eroding the class basis of the Labour Party and weakening the solidarity of trade unions and their deference toward their leaders. What has been called the 'new unionism' of the 1960s had sharpened inter-union and inter-occupational rivalry. The growing independence of local groups and the greater sectional competition among categories of workers fomented these 'self-destructive bonanzas', to use Robert Taylor's apt characterisation, of unfettered wage bargaining in the following years.[28] In these displays the collapse of the civic culture showed its connection with the failures of policy. The long-run political effect of the inability of British governments to negotiate an effective wages policy can hardly be exaggerated. For any fully employed economy, socialist or capitalist or in between, some such instrument of wage restraint is indispensable. Students of the problem had expected that trade unions under a favourable government would be able to deliver this essential outcome. When such a government proved unable to do so, because union leaders, even when themselves willing, found that they could not mobilise support among their members for wage restraint (neither in 1968 nor under the bogus social contracts arranged by later Labour governments and the unions), the unions became useless to the Labour Party and indeed a burden as partners of a party which aspired to become a government.

It made eminently good sense in 1981, therefore, for the Gang of Four to secede from the Party and, as the Social Democratic Party, (SDP) to try to lead the British left to a new posture, breaking with the unions and shedding socialism. Quite apart from other things, the failure of the unions had shown the impossibility of democratic socialism in Britain. Such good sense did the SDP make that ultimately the Labour Party itself, the lessons being driven home by repeated defeats, gradually came to the same conclusion under the leadership successively of Neil Kinnock, John Smith and above all Tony Blair. The good sense of the SDP, however, was premature. Speaking of their secession, Denis Healey has commented: 'Its most important effect was to delay the Labour Party's recovery by 10 years and to guarantee Mrs. Thatcher two more terms in office.' Some differ, arguing that the new party took votes equally from Conservatives and Labour, so that if *ex hypothesi* there had been no split, the Conservatives would still have enjoyed overwhelming dominance in the 1980s. Healey's judgement is confirmed, however, by opinion surveys showing that supporters of the new third party issuing from the split strongly favoured Labour over Conservative positions.[29] For whichever reason, the prolonged unpopularity of Labour struck a deep and damaging blow to party government by removing that crucial balancing force of the two- party Westminster model, the credible Opposition, and thereby opened the way for a full-scale assault by Thatcher upon the postwar settlement.

A credible Opposition is an essential of not only party government but also the British constitution. It is often argued that, although Britain lacks a legally binding Bill of Rights, an equivalent protection against the concentrated authority of a British government is provided by the pressure of an Opposition which has a reasonable chance of ousting the government at the next general election. As an element in party government, the credible Opposition had demonstrated its power, for better or for worse, by the convergence of the postwar consensus and then by the increase in spending that resulted from party competition. During that earlier period, when the parties were evenly matched, as Anthony King has observed, 'Governments, knowing they could be defeated, always had to run scared.'[30] The fate of the Heath government of 1970–74 illustrates this function and power. Although today, in contrast with Thatcher, Heath looks like a One Nation Tory, he actually sought to follow a not dissimilar neo-conservative policy, explicitly rejecting the paternalistic interventionism of Butler–Macmillan Conservatism. To be sure, one reason for his U-turn was that the miners were a far more formidable economic power then than they were later when Thatcher fought out her momentous battle with Scargill. The main cause, however, was political – the still vital presence of a credible Opposition. With unemployment rising very much higher than Heath had expected, he faced an Opposition that he had defeated by only the narrowest margin in 1970. In those circumstances, he felt obliged to switch to a policy of expansion, swinging back to the consensus. In Thatcher's case, by contrast, after Labour had been diminished by the split and its own leftward swing, she could carry on with her deflationary policy, despite unemployment figures reaching heights unheard of since prewar days, and yet win convincingly in 1983 and 1987. In the light of those results and the unexpected victory of 1992, it was no exaggeration for Anthony King to see the arrival of 'one Party Government'.[31]

Thatcher's dubious achievement

What did Thatcher make of the exceptional opportunity presented by this breakdown of party government? Her intentions, no less radical than the programme actually carried out by the Attlee government, included the reversal of its achievements as well as the later extensions of the welfare state and managed economy. As a party the Conservatives suffered from the partisan dealignment and the other forms of political deterioration of recent years, their electoral strength remaining well below what Labour had enjoyed under Attlee and what the Conservatives themselves had enjoyed under Macmillan. Thatcher's personal appeal did nothing to strengthen the standing of the party with the voters, the Gallup poll showing her to be the second least popular prime minister since the war, surpassed in that negative respect only slightly by Edward Heath. Yet the formidable constitutional authority of the British executive was still available, now being driven by the ideological single-mindedness of the Prime Minister. The ideology was important, undeniably doing much to dissipate the cloud of disapproval which had hung over the commercial ethic during a generation of triumphant social democracy. Less was accomplished, however, than the rhetorical display suggests.

Thatcher scored her most striking success in her demolition of that pillar of the managed economy, nationalisation. Her adventure with monetarism, on the other hand, was such a failure as to inspire a corrosively critical report from a Select Committee chaired by a prominent member of her own party.[32] Thereafter Conservative chancellors of the exchequer were obliged to revert to the usual stratagems of taxing and spending and, under Major, even to devaluation in their attempts to 'steer' the economy.

The attack on corporatism was a complicated but instructive mixture of success and failure. As the use of private bodies to carry out public services, corporatism in this broad sense has been widely adopted by governments of developed countries. It makes sense to reduce the burdens of officials and ministers by utilising the energy and skills of private organisations and individuals to carry out public programmes. In Britain war production was organised and directed in great part by such government–industry combinations, consisting of representatives of business, labour and government. After the war these arrangements were used not only by Labour but also by Conservative governments, as in Macmillan's grandiose scheme for tripartite planning on the French model. At its peak the scheme brought together representatives of the government, the Confederation of British Industry (CBI) and the Trades Union Congress (TUC) in the National Economic Development Council (NEDC) at the head of a score or so of little 'Neddies'. In the 1960s and 1970s a vast array of such representative bodies arose, administering a massive programme of subsidies intended to boost investment and to heighten productivity. The self-defeating scramble among the multitude of firms represented on these bodies frustrated their efforts to discriminate rationally among the claims for assistance. Looking back over some 20 years of public assistance to industry, one economic historian concluded: 'Industrial policy in the United Kingdom since the 1960s can only be characterized as incoherent.'[33]

Needless to say, these bodies, which had been jokingly christened 'quangos', short for 'quasi-autonomous non-governmental organisations', were immediately attacked by Thatcher.[34] She abolished the system of subsidies for industry and set about dismantling the structure of public/private co-operation by which they had been administered. Alongside these bodies, however, was another set of quangos that were concerned not primarily with managing the economy, but rather with dispensing the benefits in money and services of the welfare state, mainly under the aegis of the departments of education, employment, environment and health. Despite Thatcher's pledge to reduce the size and cost of government, these quangos actually increased in number and in expenditure. By 1993 their number at the national, regional and local levels had risen to 5521. Between 1978 and 1993, their expenditure (in constant prices) increased from £35.2 billion to £46.7 billion, the latter figure amounting to about one-third of total central government spending. While many quangos could trace their origins to agencies of tripartite corporatism, their form and function had been greatly altered. They were no longer to be representative, but managerial. Representatives of labour, environmental and consumer interests being largely excluded, members were almost entirely businessmen chosen for their managerial ability gained from private enterprise in the relevant fields. As administrative bodies, these quangos were to have no voice in policy, which was to be determined solely by the department to which they were attached. At one time, for example, employment training in England and Wales was carried out under the Manpower Services Commission, a central tripartite body including representatives of the CBI and the TUC and utilising local bodies with members from local education authorities, trade unions and employers. Under Thatcher its functions were devolved to 82 Training and Enterprise Councils operating at the regional level. Charged with carrying out policy laid down by the Department of Employment, these were not classed as public bodies, but were private companies, consisting almost entirely of employers, yet spending in 1992–93 some £2.2 billion of public money.

Quangos have been much criticised in recent years. Patronage is one charge, since many of their members have substantial ties with the Conservative Party. The new structure has also been criticised as one-sided, in effect a 'selective corporatism', in which the businessmen who predominate in their membership cannot help being biased in favour of the interests of employers. The most serious fault has been a loss of control, made depressingly evident in the enormous increase, unintended and indeed contrary to declared policy, in the number and expenditure of the quangos. Although Thatcher's reforms sharply centralised formal authority by eliminating the functional representation of interests and transferring many responsibilities from elected local governments to appointed bodies, the actual exercise of power has been dispersed throughout a huge labyrinth of decision-making. Echoing the familiar lesson that policy and administration cannot really be separated, the critics find that the attempt to do so has, as usual, led to action which escapes control at a grave cost both to democratic accountability and to government effectiveness. The lack of co-ordination that defeated the earlier attempt to carry out an industrial policy through a system of subsidies has not been remedied. As a recent study of public policy in Britain has concluded, the dispersion of administrative power has been accompanied by a diminution of both party and parliamentary government.[35]

From the financial point of view, the welfare state in Britain has survived more than a decade of Conservative dominance virtually intact.[36] The privatisation of council housing was popular and successful, adding to revenue and reducing subsidies. Pension reform also brought some budgetary savings, although the government was obliged to retreat from more radical proposals. Repeatedly, it also backed off from fundamental reforms of the health service and by the end of the decade was continually assuring voters that the NHS is 'safe with us'. As a whole, apart from housing and pensions, social spending remained almost unchanged. As a percentage of gross domestic product, total outlays on social programmes for merit goods and income transfers, which stood at 27.5 per cent in 1979, remained at 27.4 per cent in 1990. Total government spending, including defence, likewise was stable, falling slightly from 44.9 per cent to 43.2 per cent.

For the sake of comparison we can look at the American figures. While the totals are smaller they show the same relative stability. For the decade 1979–89 US social spending rose slightly from 20 per cent to 21.4 per cent of GDP, and total government outlays from 33.2 per cent to 36.9 per cent. In both countries the size of the bureaucracy has been reduced hardly at all. In Britain from 1980 to 1990 government employment as a percentage of total employment fell from 21.1 per cent to 19.2 per cent. In the United States for the same period the figures went from 15.4 per cent to 14.4 per cent. In both countries, as elsewhere in the West, over the past two decades of acclaimed austerity, Big Government has not been reduced, but consolidated. The political forces that sustained the British welfare state were not those that brought it into existence. The Labour Party, which had been the prime initiating and driving force in the early postwar years, could not even as a credible Opposition make a contribution to its maintenance. When one looks for explanations, it appears that the new group politics had struck again. Elicited by the programmes of the welfare state and the managed economy, these offspring of collectivism had assisted at the convergence of party policies in the 1960s and had turned back the ideological attempts to escape from the consensus in the 1970s. Now through the 1980s and into the 1990s, in the teeth of the Thatcherite revolution, they had successfully defended the great bulk of social spending.

The failure of the Conservative attack, despite its exceptional political opportunities, is an especially vivid illustration of the power of pluralism in the modern democratic state. In his study 'The New Politics of the Welfare State', Paul Pierson has shown how similar forces have beaten back similar efforts of retrenchment not only in Britain and the United States, but also in Germany and Sweden. Much along the lines of the present analysis, he finds that 'maturing social programs produce new organised interests, the consumers and providers of social services'. Concentrating specific and substantial benefits on certain sets of people, these programmes strongly motivate them to organise for and participate in politics, in order to maintain and extend their benefits. Thanks to this 'new politics', despite a generation of attempted retrenchment, he finds nothing like 'a dismantling of the welfare state'.[37] Big Government has come to stay. Co-ordination of this massive and complex force is no less needed today than it was half a century ago, when party government was most promising.

Tony Blair's dilemma

By requiring that the two parties offer 'distinctive programmes' giving voters an 'effective choice', the model of party government implies that in its electoral appeal each party will not only assemble the preferences of a set of private interests, but will also assimilate them to some overall view of the common good. Voters respond to both sorts of appeal, reflecting not only their self-interest, but also their concern for the common good, expressed as a public philosophy or in what is currently called 'vision'. Not much of the Tory paternalism which traditionally lent this sort of coherence to British conservatism has survived Thatcher. As she has said, she likes to think of herself as a 'liberal' in the sense that Gladstone was a 'liberal'. Accordingly, the rationale which orders most of her policies has been to move social choice from public choice to market choice. Nor does she hold this preference merely as a principle of political economy. She rightly sees it as informed by Victorian values of thrift, enterprise and self-reliance.

As put into effect by Thatcher and her successor, John Major, however, that public philosophy has had such disastrous effects upon British society that, at the time of this writing, support for the Conservatives has fallen precipitously to the lowest point since the war. Under the spellbinding leadership of Tony Blair, Labour, on the other hand, has become so credible an Opposition that many see it as certainly forming the next government. Do these developments signify a revival of party government? Specifically, has Blair given Labour a conception of the common good sufficiently coherent and relevant to control and guide the welfare state of the future?

Blair's ferocious attack on Thatcherism at the 1994 party conference was superb as oratory and as criticism. His attempt to accentuate the positive has been less successful. He has clearly broken not only with the Webbian socialism of fellowship and planning but also with the Gaitskellite socialism of what he has called the 'tax and benefit regime'. Marking a third and perhaps final phase in the emaciation of the concept, he confessed to the party conference of 1995: 'Socialism for me was never about nationalisation or the power of the state. It means,' he continued, 'I am my brother's keeper. I will not walk by on the other side. We aren't simply people set in isolation from one another, face to face with eternity, but members of the same family, the same community, the same human race.' Giving expression to this sincere sentiment of his Christian socialism, Blair has picked up the One Nation rhetoric which the Thatcherites had so ostentatiously discarded. Recognising the legitimacy of this slogan of New Labour, Alan Howarth, a former Conservative minister, has recently justified his switch to Labour, saying: 'I'm a one-nation man, not a class warrior. Tony's values in politics are very much mine....The world...recognizes that unrestrained market forces will destroy all relationships. You need to sustain the cohesion of society.'[38]

Historically, nationalism has been a powerful force offsetting the fragmenting effects of modernisation. The communitarian pledge to restore social cohesion – 'to bring us together' – can stir the heart. But if it is to satisfy the mind, it must be embodied in programmes that convincingly promise movement towards that goal. So judged, Blair's substantive proposals are cautious and miscellaneous. He is for a market economy, including most of Thatcher's reforms, but also for 'social provision'. As promised at the 1995 conference, a Blair government would return the railways to public ownership. The now privatised utilities would be taxed and regulated. The government would stand for law and order, fighting against crime and for the family. Its main concern would be education. There is no pledge of full employment. When Blair, however, turns from substance to procedure, from social and economic reform to constitutional and institutional reforms, he presents a wide array of weighty and specific proposals, informed by a coherent outlook and backed by a powerful movement. Rising out of the explosion of distrust of the 1960s, the movement for constitutional reform expressed the demands of radical democracy for the restoration of trust. Since that time it has consolidated its organisation, elaborated its demands, increased its following, and won wide acceptance among the political elite and the general public. Consider, for instance, the massive public support for a series of radical institutional reforms reported by a MORI survey of May 1995. A few of the items are: a written constitution, a bill of rights, devolution for Scotland and Wales, an elected second chamber, proportional representation and a fixed term for parliament.[39]

Blair has not accepted every item. But he has repeatedly come out for 'constitutional change'. In a major address of February 1996 he called it 'an essential of new Britain', promising major steps towards decentralisation and devolution, a bill of rights, freedom of information, reform of the Lords and consideration of Proportional representation (PR).[40] Intentionally or unintentionally, the thrust of this programme of institutional reform is to weaken that formidable monopoly of power of a British government which has enabled it to carry out radical economic and social reforms. As a whole, their effect would be to reduce British government to the weakness and instability that have commonly afflicted parliamentary systems in other countries. Indeed, if the British were seriously to go through with such an Americanisation of their institutions, they would be obliged to take that final step in this direction by providing for a popularly elected President.

So deep, therefore, is the threat of constitutional reform to British government as we know it. Moreover, to take note of more immediate, but less dire consequences, constitutional reform is a time-consuming business, as the long, futile struggle under the first Wilson government to reform the Lords demonstrated. If a Blair government were to attempt the reforms of procedure that he has proposed, it would have little time or energy for substantive programmes. It would be ironic, indeed, for Tony Blair, who has done so much to strengthen leadership in his party, to champion such enfeeblement of its power to govern. Yet in the minds of its advocates, constitutional reform promises to restore trust, that gift of the old civic culture and an even more fundamental condition of effective government than constitutional authority or party organisation. Blair himself regards constitutional reform as the remedy for that 'disaffection with politics', which he finds 'intense' and which he says citizens feel under 'the most centralized government of any large state in the Western world'.[41]

The special relationship revisited

Can anything helpful be learned from American experience? Comparisons are never close enough to yield laws of political behaviour which answer such questions with certainty. A look at our condition, however, cries out with the lesson that the American system has all the institutions (except PR) proposed by constitutional reformers in Britain. Yet distrust of our politics and dissatisfaction with our government run as deeply here as there. A *New York Times*/CBS poll of August 1995, to cite only one of many such gloomy reports, presented evidence of disenchantment so powerful as to justify the summary that 'frustrations run deep, perhaps deeper than at any other time in modern American history'.[42]

One can see, however, clear signs of party revival. In the Congressional elections of 1994, the Republicans took over not only the Senate, but also, for the first time in 50 years, the House of Representatives. For a year and more thereafter, the new Speaker, Newt Gingrich, in a performance as theatrical and unfamiliar as his name, launched a massive legislative programme, mandated by an election manifesto, titled *Contract with America*, and supported by a firmly united party in the legislature. Through months of furious battle with President Clinton and the Democrats, Gingrich, despite intense and continual strains of group pressure, held his majority together and prevented the breaches of party unity usual in American legislative behaviour.

A unifying vision, much the same in essentials as the anti-government passage of Reagan and Thatcher, made the Republicans more than a mere coalition. As of this writing, however, the original promise of triumph had given birth to only a modest victory and in bringing about that outcome pluralism played no small part. A leading example was the fate of the Republican attempt to make cuts – actually not terribly radical – in the prospective benefits of Medicare. Enjoying support among older people comparable to the attachment of the British public to their National Health Service, Medicare is defended by The American Association of Retired Persons, an organisation which had increased its dues-paying membership from 400,000 four years before the enactment of the programme to 28 million in the late 1980s, by which time it had assembled a head-quarters staff of 1300 and a legislative staff of about a hundred.[43] Reflected in the opinion polls continually being taken during the legislative struggle, the bipartisan strength of this exemplar of the new group politics was crucial in curbing the Republican assault. In mustering support for the 1996 presidential campaign, the Clinton/

Gore headquarters in a February circular advised partisans that 'Medicare far outweighs any other issue on the agenda nationwide among those polled'.[44]

On the Democratic side, President Clinton, in attempting to find a rhetoric of defence, like Blair appealed to a new nationalism, although that word itself is too politically incorrect for use in current political advocacy. He did, however, in his 1996 State of the Union message, for instance, call on his listeners to 'come together' as 'One Nation, One People' and, when asking a divine blessing on the United States of America, he emphasised with gusto the word 'United'.

But how should he give body to this appeal of national communitarianism in specific proposals of government action? Unlike Blair Clinton has eschewed constitutional reform. That has been left to the Republicans. Their efforts by constitutional amendment to limit the length of congressional service and to require a balanced federal budget could not muster the necessary two-thirds majorities in the legislature. Their principal institutional initiative, however, to change the balance of the federal system by moving money and power to the states, has been more successful. Here the American conservatives differed from their centralising British colleagues, although their ultimate purpose was the same, namely, reductions of spending and taxation weighted heavily in favour of business and the well-to-do.

Clinton's emphasis has been on substance rather than procedure. Reminding one of Blair's fiscal caution, he has reined in the deficits resulting from the spending spree initiated by Reagan. His preoccupation, however, has been to manage a tactical retreat in defence of certain core programmes of the American welfare state: Medicare, Medicaid and basic measures relating to poverty, education and the environment. His moves are tactical in the military sense that they typically consist in taking a step which enables him to change to a more defensible stand or to avoid being pushed back in some other sector, but which serve the larger strategy of defending the front as a whole. Proclaiming an 'end to big government' Clinton has literally echoed Blair's call 'to take power back from big government', while at the same time like Blair setting forth a substantial list of proposals for further government action.

But can he change that strategy from defence to offence? The challenge is to give body to the new nationalism in specific programmes that are coherent with one another and relevant to the circumstances of the time. As a sympathetic observer, recalling my own experience with party reform, I would urge him first of all to avoid what Tony Blair disparagingly calls 'the tax and benefit regime', that major policy misadventure of both countries in the 1960s and 1970s. Such schemes of distributive politics dispense benefits to particular constituencies at the cost of dividing a coalition which must recognise its interdependence if it is to be effective. The premise of a programme should be not the presumed 'right' of the beneficiary, but rather the contribution which the programme enables the beneficiary to make to the common good. Benefits are provided, whether as money, services, tax relief or legal remedies, but they function as instrumentalities of a national purpose. In this way rights and responsibilities are reciprocal. Most important of all, this interdependence is not a static exchange, but a function of movement towards a goal. Parties, like nations, thrive on a sense of motion. Hence political leaders boast of 'growth' and 'progress' and promise 'to get this country moving again', in moments of hyperbole summoning their followers to a 'crusade' or proclaiming a 'revolution'. Liberal or conservative, they must promise 'change'. Rightly so, as order and coherence are properties of collective action.

Such are the not impossible prescriptions, if party government is to be revived and a civic culture of trust restored in Britain and in the United States. These similarities in the politics of the two countries have made their famed special relationship a new and different, but even closer bond. Brought together by foreign policy during the struggle against Hitler, they remained differentiated in their domestic politics by British exceptionalism, the Toryism of their conservatives and the socialism of their progressives. In recent years that gap also has been closed, as Margaret Thatcher's hope that British might become more like American parties has been realised. This special relationship in domestic politics, first personified by the mutual admiration of Thatcher and Reagan, has now been strengthened by the close personal contacts and community of views and problems of Blair and Clinton. Sharing a communitarian outlook that is liberal and national, each faces the challenge of forging the programmatic instruments which will control the unruly pluralism and direct the huge public sector of the modern democratic state. Their task, in short, is to fit Big Democracy to Big Government.

Notes

1. Wayland Kennet (ed.), *The Rebirth of Britain* (London: Weidenfeld and Nicolson, 1982), p. 172.
2. Supplement, *American Political Science Review*, XLIV (September 1950).
3. On the history of the term 'liberalism', see Samuel H. Beer, 'Liberalism and the National Idea', in Robert A. Goldwin (ed.), *Left, Right and Center: Essays on Liberalism and Conservatism in the United States* (Chicago: Rand McNally, 1965).
4. See especially his *Party Government* (New York: Rinehart, 1942).
5. Richard Rose, *Politics in England* (London: Faber & Faber, 1965).
6. Published in Britain under the title *Modern British Politics: A Study of Parties and Pressure Groups* (London: Faber and Faber, 1965).
7. Gabriel A. Almond and Sidney Verba, *The Civic Culture: Political Attitudes and Democracy in Five Nations* (Princeton, NJ: Princeton University Press, 1963).
8. Louis Hartz, *The Liberal Tradition in America* (New York: Harcourt Brace, 1955).
9. Theodore H. White, *The Making of the President, 1964* (New York: Atheneum, 1965), pp. 391–2.
10. Julius Turner, *Party and Constituency: Pressures on Congress*, rev. edn edited by Edward Schneier, Jr (Baltimore, MD: Johns Hopkins Press, 1970), p. 245.
11. Richard Rose and Guy Peters, *Can Government Go Bankrupt?* (New York: Basic Books, 1978).
12. Samuel H. Beer, *Britain Against Itself: The Political Contradictions of Collectivism* (New York and London: Faber and Faber, 1982), p. xv.
13. Peter Jenkins, *Mrs Thatcher's Revolution: The Ending of the Socialist Era* (Cambridge, MA: Harvard University Press, 1988), p. 48.
14. From a survey by the University of Michigan Research Center, reported in Seymour Martin Lipset, 'Malaise and Resiliency in America', *Journal of Democracy*, vol. 6, no. 3 (1955), p. 5.
15. Alan Marsh, *Protest and Political Consciousness* (Beverly Hills and London: Sage, 1977), Table 5.5, p. 118. Gallup poll cited in Trevor Smith, 'Postmodern Politics and the Case for Constitutional Reform', *Political Quarterly*, vol. 6 no. 2 (April–June 1994), p. 134.
16. I have looked at the impact of the idea of participatory democracy on reforms of the Great Society period under President Johnson in 'In Search of a New Public Philosophy', in Anthony King (ed.), *The New American Political System* (Washington, DC: American Enterprise Institute for Public Policy Research, 1978), pp. 27–8.
17. In some personal recollections I have given an account of such an episode at the Democratic Convention of 1956. The point of it is that the party establishment – and there really was one in those days – being determined not to allow a roll call vote on a minority report on civil rights, prevailed when the chairman of the convention, Speaker Sam Rayburn, put the report to a voice vote, declared it defeated and promptly adjourned the convention. This was despite an array of protesting delegates in front of

the podium waving banners and repeatedly chanting 'Mr Chairman', the whole encounter going out on television, but causing no great public reaction, as it certainly would have in later years. 'Memoirs of a Political Junkie: The Ups and Downs of American Liberalism from Roosevelt to Reagan', *Harvard Magazine*, vol. 87, no. 1 (September–October 1984), p. 69.

18. At the meeting of the Commission on 3 October 1969, after a discussion of the need for black delegates from the South, a rule was proposed which would require state delegations to include members of 'minority groups' in numbers 'bearing a reasonable relationship to the group's presence in the population of the state'. This rule, which in my pencilled marginalia I termed 'the fatal amendment' and 'the bomb', was then also applied to women and young people, over my strenuous objections. Troubled by the generality of this rule and its restriction of the voters' power to choose, I expressed my fear to chairman McGovern, during the lunch hour, that we had mandated quotas. Surprised by that reading, but sharing my concern, McGovern with the Commission's approval added a footnote to the rules that categorically rejected 'the mandatory imposition of quotas'. In the later battles over quotas, however, this footnote fell by the wayside.

19. I will not attempt even to sample the immense literature on the subject of party decline. A good, brief, general account with copious references to other works is the enlarged and updated edition of Martin P. Watternberg, *The Decline of American Political Parties, 1952–1994* (Cambridge, MA: Harvard University Press, 1994).

20. I have discussed this change in programme structure in 'In Search of a New Public Philosophy', op. cit., pp. 20–2.

21. See 'Political Overload and Federalism', *Polity*, vol. x, no. 1 (Fall 1977), pp. 6–7.

22. My *Britain Against Itself* elaborates this analysis, which is summarised in the introductory chapter.

23. On this increased concern for 'constituency service', traditionally so important for the American politician, see Pippa Norris, 'The Puzzle of Constituency Service', paper prepared for the annual meeting of the American Political Science Association, Chicago, 1995.

24. The confusion and distress arising from the failure of the old Webbian socialism is expressed in *The New Fabian Essays*, ed. R. H. S. Crossman (London: Turnstile Press, 1952), the new approach is set out in C. A. R. Crosland, *The Future of Socialism* (London: Jonathan Cape, 1956).

25. In game theory terms, the situation could be described as 'a multi-group prisoner's dilemma'. See *Britain Against Itself*, p. 26, note 7.

26. *New Statesman and Nation*, 11 December 1970, pp. 789–90.

27. James E. Alt, *The Politics of Economic Decline: Economic Management and Political Behaviour in Britain since 1964* (Cambridge: Cambridge University Press, 1974), pp. 59, 205, 270.

28. Robert Taylor, *The Fifth Estate: Britain's Unions in the Seventies* (London: Routledge and Kegan Paul, 1978), pp. 337–8, 353.

29. Denis Healey, *The Time of My Life* (London: Michael Joseph, 1989), p. 480. For a contrary view, see Ivor Crewe and Anthony King, *SDP: The Birth, Life and Death of the Social Democratic Party* (Oxford: Oxford University Press, 1995), pp. 467–8. For the opinions of Alliance voters (Social Democrats plus Liberals) see Table 16.7 of Appendix 5 in Crewe and King, *SDP*.
30. Anthony King et al., *Britain at the Polls, 1992* (Chatham, NJ: Chatham House, 1993), p. 225.
31. King, ibid., Chapter 7.
32. Treasury and Civil Service Committee, Session 1980–1, Third Report, Monetary Policy, Chapters 8 and 9. Edward duCann (Con., Taunton) was chairman.
33. Geoffrey Denton, 'Financial Assistance to British Industry', in W. M. Corden and Gerhard Fels (eds), *Public Assistance to Industry: Protection and Subsidies in Britain and Germany* (London: Macmillan, 1976), p. 161.
34. Stuart Weir and Wendy Hall (eds), *EGO Trip: Extra-Governmental Organisations in the United Kingdom and their Accountability* (London: The Democratic Audit of the United Kingdom, 1994), p. 6. This work is the principal source for the following discussion of quangos.
35. Stephen P. Savage, Rob Atkinson and Lynton Robbins (eds), *Public Policy in Britain* (New York: Macmillan, 1994).
36. The principal sources of the following discussion of the financial aspects of the welfare state in Britain and the USA are Paul Pierson, *Dismantling the Welfare State? Reagan, Thatcher and the Politics of Retrenchment* (Cambridge: Cambridge University Press, 1994) and Pierson, 'The New Politics of the Welfare State', in *World Politics*, vol. 48 (January 1996), pp. 143–79.
37. Pierson, 'The New Politics', pp. 173, 175.
38. Quoted by Sidney Blumenthal, 'The Next Prime Minister', *The New Yorker*, 5 February 1996.
39. Market and Organisation Research Institute Ltd, *State of the Nation, 1995*, survey for the Rowntree Reform Trust (London: Rowntree Reform Trust, 1995).
40. John Smith memorial lecture, given at the Queen Elizabeth II Conference Centre, London, 7 February 1996.
41. Ibid.
42. Poll conducted 5–9 August 1995 with 1478 adults throughout the USA.
43. Pierson, 'The New Politics', pp. 146–7.
44. *Memorandum*, Clinton/Gore Campaign Headquarters, Washington, DC.

3
Social Class, Affluence and Electoral Politics, 1951–64

Kevin Jefferys

Introduction

'I am always hearing about the Middle Classes', Harold Macmillan wrote to the head of the Conservative Research Department, Michael Fraser, shortly after becoming prime minister in January 1957. 'What is it that they really want? Can you put it down on a sheet of notepaper, and I will see whether we can give it to them.'[1] The reply Macmillan received from Fraser was not encouraging. The main wish of the middle classes, he began, was something that no government could reasonably provide – a return to prewar standards, which had fallen 'both absolutely and/or in relation to the rapidly rising living standards of the manual workers'. They also felt that 'Conservative Governments, who should understand their problem, have not shown them much sympathy'. Income tax reductions introduced since the Tories came to power in 1951, Fraser noted, had been largely nullified by inflation. It was true that those in the highest income brackets might be helped by further reductions in direct taxation. But for the majority of the middle classes, those with incomes below £1000 per year, tax cuts would only be beneficial if the government succeeded in restraining price rises. What they really want, concluded Fraser, is to 'bash the other fellow': to restrict the growing power of trade unions in securing higher wage claims for industrial workers, and to reform the welfare state 'so as to make it more and more a matter of helping people to help themselves'. Strictly speaking, though, the problems of the middle classes were insoluble 'since we could not restore their position relative to other classes'.[2] In short, the government faced a 'middle class revolt'.

Middle-class anxieties have not, however, figured prominently in studies of British electoral politics during the 1950s and early 1960s. A detailed assessment of middle-class voting patterns in the immediate postwar years was published in 1954 by John Bonham.[3] But for those concerned with the years of Conservative rule between 1951 and 1964, middle-class concerns appear to pale in significance beside the influence of the 'affluent worker'. The affluent worker debate has generated an extensive literature, as much among social scientists as historians. Successive Tory election victories in 1951, 1955 and 1959, it has been claimed, owed much to rising living standards, which led to many manual workers adopting middle-class values and voting habits. The assumption of a levelling process within British society coloured the Nuffield election studies pioneered by political scientists. Social change, it was said, had weakened traditional working-class loyalties and made discussions of British politics in terms of class divisions less meaningful. From the realm of sociology Ferdinand Zweig wrote of a 'deep transformation of values', such that working-class life 'finds itself on the move towards new middle-class values and middle-class existence'.[4] This theory of 'embourgeoisment' has itself come under critical scrutiny. Working-class voters, some countered, remained deeply attached to Labour politics: a claim apparently borne out by the election triumphs of Harold Wilson in 1964 and 1966.[5] The affluent worker nevertheless remains a potent symbol. According to popular histories of the 1950s, changing consumption patterns, dress styles and voting patterns were all part of the 'middle classation' of British society. Throughout the length and breadth of the land, wrote Harry Hopkins, 'on council estates as in Acacia Avenue, Sunday morning was devoted to the ritual laving of the car'.[6]

The aims of this article are to revisit the affluent worker debate and to turn the spotlight on to the neglected issue of middle-class voting patterns. The role of the affluent worker, it will be suggested, was much exaggerated by contemporary observers; affluence was not as widespread as many assumed, and its impact varied according to time and place. Nor should shifts in working-class voting patterns obscure other movements of opinion, notably a drift of white-collar workers away from the Tories that slowly undermined the foundations of two-party domination. It will be shown that, as Michael Fraser made clear in 1957, middle-class support could not be taken for granted by the Conservatives. In spite of the apparent ease of Tory success at the polls, the loyalty of traditional supporters was in doubt for much of the 1955 parliament, and some abandoned the party in 1959. After the 1959 election, middle-class voters began to turn against the government in larger numbers, sufficient not only to prompt talk of a Liberal revival but also to assist in the return of Labour to power in 1964. The nature of middle-class protest, with its emphasis on 'bashing the other fellow', points to the vital place of the trade union question in linking high and low politics, and also indicates the need for caution in assuming that class conflict was becoming less influential in determining electoral behaviour. Far from withering away, as we shall see, class divisions remained at the heart of popular politics.

Social class and social change

Any discussion of affluence and popular politics must first consider the nature and extent of social progress in the 1950s. On all sides it was agreed that prosperity had outwardly transformed living standards. In the words of Mark Abrams, one of the pioneers of survey research:

> Much more money is now being spent on household goods. The proportion of families with a vacuum cleaner has doubled, ownership of refrigerators has trebled, owners of washing machines have increased tenfold; we have stocked our homes with vastly more furniture, radiograms, carpets, space heaters, water heaters, armchairs, light fittings, lawn mowers, television sets...and film projectors.... And all this means that for the first time in modern British history the working-class home, as well as the middle-class home, has become a place that is...pleasant to live in.[7]

But three qualifications must immediately be added. In the first place, it would be wrong to exaggerate the speed at which consumption standards were changing. While a majority possessed television sets, in 1960 only one in five working-class families owned a car; one-third had washing machines and only 13 per cent refrigerators.[8] Secondly, there were important regional variations. Much of the discussion about affluence centred on prosperous industries or new estates and satellite towns, often in southern England. Visitors to, say, Tyneside were struck by a very different picture: of 'the musty taint of poverty', for the north-east has 'more places in it which look as if they are wasting away than anywhere else in the country'.[9] Related to regional variations was a third qualification. The 1950s affluence had little impact on the poorest groups in society, for example the growing number of coloured immigrants struggling in run-down inner-city accommodation. London had a homeless population of over 5000 in the early 1960s. Figures collected by the Ministry of Labour suggested that those living below the poverty line were increasing not decreasing, owing to longer life spans and larger family sizes. Scraping a living was an everyday reality for three million members of families whose head was in work, two and a half million pensioners, one and a half million families of unemployed fathers and over a million families whose head was either deceased or chronically ill.[10]

Nor should it be assumed that rising living standards easily eroded class identities and voting preferences. Nancy Mitford's attempt in 1955 to define differences between 'U' and 'non-U' speech (the upper classes would always use a napkin not a serviette) pointed to the survival of an aristocracy that retained political influence and 'social position through the Queen'.[11] In a survey of 6000 people carried out during the mid-1950s, less than one per cent of those questioned refused to place themselves in an identifiable social bracket. 'Unquestionably', wrote Mark Abrams, the author of the survey, 'we are divided into groups with distinctive ways of life; people are aware of these divisions and they do rank some as carrying more prestige than others.'[12] Abrams, like most contemporaries, categorised voters according to their occupational ranking within the class system. For the growing band of polling organisations, the British electorate could be divided into two: middle-class professionals and white-collar workers (social groups A, B and C1), making up one-third of voters; and the working classes, ranging from skilled artisans to the poor (groups C2, D and E), comprising about two-thirds of the total electorate. This categorisation was far from ideal, taking little account of the voting preferences of women, for example, or different age groups within the electorate.[13] It did nevertheless point to the strongest determinant of voting behaviour. Both major parties, in order to secure a parliamentary majority, had to appeal across class boundaries. But at every election since the war, certainly through to 1959, a broad pattern had been evident: whereas some three-quarters of middle-class voters supported the Conservatives, nearly two-thirds of the working classes backed Labour.

Underpinning such allegiances were class barriers that remained more stubborn than many have recognised. In spite of a 10 per cent improvement in living standards per head of the population between 1938 and 1958, the relative income of middle and working classes as a whole remained almost unchanged.[14] What had occurred was the reduction of earlier gross inequalities. Differences in income nevertheless remained, and were reinforced by contrasts in hours and conditions of work. Segregation at the workplace was still commonplace: 'the cotton millhand does not yet sip martinis from his lunchbox'.[15] Aside from consumer spending and a more home-centred lifestyle, there was little evidence of manual workers adopting middle-class modes of behaviour, such as formal entertainment or involvement in community work. Drew Middleton found that workers' deep-rooted attachment to collective action was reflected in the absence of any desire to establish their own small businesses.[16] Other local studies suggested that as equalisation occurred in terms of consumption, so the middle classes became more liable to pull themselves apart by exaggerating cultural differences – in speech, social manners and patterns of leisure activity. In the London suburb of Woodford, most working-class inhabitants lived in particular enclaves. Those who lived in mixed areas found integration difficult. 'Those people from the East End are good-hearted folk, but you couldn't make friends of them', commented one resident. 'Sounds a bit snobbish . . . but we've got nothing in common with them.' This was reciprocated by incomers to the district, such as the docker from Poplar who complained that the stand-offishness of neighbours made it impossible to make friends. 'Inside people's minds . . . the boundaries of class are still closely drawn', concluded the authors. 'There were still two Woodfords in 1959, and few meeting points between them.'[17]

It was the case that a sizeable minority of skilled workers, when asked, were describing themselves as middle class. This reflected a blurring of the most obvious distinctions between affluent workers and the lower middle class. Income, though, was only one of the

economic aspects of class: job security and prospects for advancement still pointed up the differences between the teacher and the
engineer.[18] Similarly changes were taking place which promised
greater social mobility. Unlike the prewar period, a steadily increasing
number of children from working-class families were gaining access
to state-funded grammar schools. But progress was painfully slow.
There was widespread disdain among working-class parents for a boy
'stuffing 'is head with a lot of nonsense 'e'll never use' by staying on
at school.[19] Children from middle-class families still made up nearly
90 per cent of those attending grammar schools or continuing in full-
time education beyond the age of 19.[20] Instead of a drive towards the
'endless middle', the 1950s primarily witnessed new ways – in changing circumstances – of being working class. Workers might be enjoying more leisure, but holiday camps were far removed from 'private'
holidays for the middle classes; pop music appeared to have a uni-
versal appeal, but on closer inspection showed strong class pattern-
ing.[21]

There were, of course, major differences *within* working-class communities. 'Roughs' and 'respectables' were often found to have little
in common, and the new towns around London were a world away
from the industrial heartlands of northern England and Scotland,
where miners, dockers and shipyard workers continued to live in
densely populated areas of terraced housing: 'a world of tough,
hard-drinking men, clearly demarcated conjugal roles and a class
imagery which sharply divided the world into "them" and "us"'.[22]
Yet it was not difficult to find evidence from all parts of the country
to indicate that – whatever new opportunities were arising in education, employment or housing – class consciousness remained acute.
The Dean of Balliol College, Oxford, was scornful of 'inky fingered
grammar school boys' and maintained that only those with independent means should be entitled to higher education. In the same city
middle-class residents erected a wall in the 1950s to prevent council
tenants from walking past their houses on the way to the shops. In
the early 1960s one London commuter complained that he paid 'God
knows how much in income tax and . . . I go home from the station
past a council housing estate full of TV aerials with Consuls outside
the doors . . . yet I have to subsidise their rents'.[23] British people on
the whole were less impressed by social change than historians have
been, looking back with the benefit of hindsight. A majority of those

questioned by Gallup thought living standards had not improved but rather 'stayed the same' in the 1950s, and shortly before the 1964 election more voters agreed than disagreed with the view that 'there is a class struggle in this country'.[24]

Working-class voting patterns

At the beginning of the period it was not therefore surprising to find a close alignment between social class and party preference. Labour took comfort from the 1951 election as a 'victory in votes but defeat in terms of seats'. The highest-ever vote polled by a party in British politics (nearly 14 million) derived from Labour piling up huge majorities in working-class industrial strongholds. Churchill's slim majority was primarily the result of reduced Liberal intervention compared with 1950; the Conservatives won support among erstwhile middle-class Liberals especially, winning seats such as Buckingham, King's Lynn and Yarmouth.[25] Although there had been a small but uniform swing across the country, the Nuffield election study calculated that on balance only 'a handful of former Labour supporters' switched allegiance between 1950 and 1951.[26] Pioneering sample surveys of individual constituencies confirmed that 'social class ... is the chief determinant of political behaviour'.[27] In Bristol North-East Labour supporters were found to be mainly male, working-class and young; Tory backing was concentrated among women, the middle classes and older voters.[28] It was true that the minority of workers supporting Churchill was much greater than the minority of middle-class Labour voters. Yet there was no suggestion that the former were guided primarily by material considerations. In areas of relatively weak support for Labour among industrial workers, such as the High Peak town of Glossop, working-class Toryism was associated with the Anglican church.[29] In Banbury, where only a fraction of Labour's support earned more than £500 a year, nearly 30 per cent of manual workers backed the Conservatives on the basis of 'traditionalism', identifying with the town's native community against incomers over recent decades.[30]

Eden's election victory in 1955, though based upon a prosperity ticket, produced surprisingly little evidence of a shift in working-class voting patterns. Shortly before polling day one newspaper reported that 'it is strangely difficult to discover candidates or agents who claim to have unearthed any appreciable number of voters who have changed their allegiance since the election of 1951'.[31] This was borne out when a steep fall in the Labour vote was not matched by a corresponding Tory increase. Labour leaders agreed with newspaper commentators that apathy was the prime cause of an increased Tory majority. Labour had polled well in close fights, but elsewhere large numbers of former supporters had stayed at home. As Morgan Phillips observed, some voters may have changed sides, but more important was 'comparative "prosperity" which has lulled many of our supporters into inactivity'.[32] In Bristol North-East over eight out of ten people voted the same way as in 1951. The main source of a small swing in Bristol was confirmed to be Labour abstentionism; economic stability had eroded the party's association with full employment.[33] Tory strategists developed the same theme, questioning why the government had not managed to win more votes in such favourable circumstances. Many within the lower social groupings, it was conceded – while disillusioned with Labour – still harboured a prejudice against voting Conservative.[34] According to one of the party's candidates, 'they weren't listening because emotionally they are incapable of giving the Tories a fair hearing. This is not just the old class war game. Rather it is an underlying suspicion of Conservative intentions as being interested in successful and established interests.' The task for the parliament ahead was to win not just the approval of such voters but also their hearts and consciences.[35]

This was exactly what Central Office sought to do in the years that followed. Before 1955 neither party had systematically engaged in market research. But in 1956–57 the Tory chairman Oliver Poole, looking for ways to counter government unpopularity, gave the go-ahead for an advertising agency to undertake survey research into voter attitudes. This and findings from opinion pollsters appeared to highlight an important social development. Younger manual workers and their wives, it was found, those earning reasonably high wages and buying their own homes, were keen to dissociate themselves from outdated notions of working-class life. Hence skilled workers and white-collar clerical staff were made the target of concerted Tory propaganda in the run-up to the 1959 election. By contrast, apart from minor experimental surveys, Labour relied on no polling evidence other than what could be gleaned from newspapers.[36] Within Labour ranks there was much residual hostility both to new marketing techniques and to outright pandering to material interests. As one MP put it: 'What man eating cornflakes wanted to be in danger of swallowing a toy submarine?'[37] There was similar ambivalence towards home ownership, which many activists saw as a solely middle-class aspiration and a distraction from the preferred policy of producing more municipal housing for rent.[38]

Macmillan's 'never had it so good' triumph in 1959 thus had an element of self-fulfilling prophecy. Conservative rhetoric was said to be more in tune with the wishes of the young and upwardly mobile; a larger proportion of skilled manual workers voted Tory than at any election since 1935. *Tribune*, meanwhile, was left to lament that Macmillan had received a mandate for 'the unjust society, the casino society, the ugly society'.[39]

Inquests by both main parties appeared to confirm the arrival of the 'affluent worker' as a potent electoral force, at least in the southern half of England. The Conservative Research Department believed there was more evidence than in 1955 that removal of working-class voters from city centres to new towns and housing estates 'tends in some cases to change their political allegiance from Socialist to Conservative'.[40] Labour's National Executive Committee was told that for the first time since the war there had been a significant movement of voters away from the party. Young married couples in their twenties, especially if both were in employment, were said to be particularly reluctant to vote Labour. Workers living on newly established housing estates were deemed to be immune from older forms of collective loyalty, choosing instead more privatised and home-based lifestyles which revolved around the garden and the television set. One candidate defeated in a London suburb said that in his home 'the Red Flag, the Co-op, the trade union, are things that get an answer in the tingling of my blood. They get no answer in tingling blood in the suburbs of London.'[41] In the new towns Labour hoped that the movement of workers out of London would push up its level of support. But in Horsham, Hemel Hempstead, Epping, Basildon and Hitchin – all with electorates expanded by over 10,000 – Tory majorities were increased. A post-election survey in Stevenage new town (part of the Hitchin seat) revealed considerable support for the Conservatives among working-class incomers in the electronics and aerospace industries, several of whom expressed the view that 'I voted for them this time because the standard of living of the working classes has gone up.'[42]

In the months following Macmillan's triumph, the affluent worker became an object of fascination. Polling companies commissioned research which found that whereas manual workers supported Labour by two to one, the Tories held a narrow lead among non-manual workers in the C2D class. 'It is no exaggeration to say that the Conservatives govern by permission of the working class and in particular of the lower paid non-manual worker.'[43] In the spring of 1960, Mark Abrams carried out a survey of 500 working-class voters which found that Labour was suffering among groups of voters most susceptible to the appeals of affluence, especially women and the young.[44] This study also reinforced the idea that those workers who labelled themselves middle class were more likely to vote Tory (see Figure 3.1).

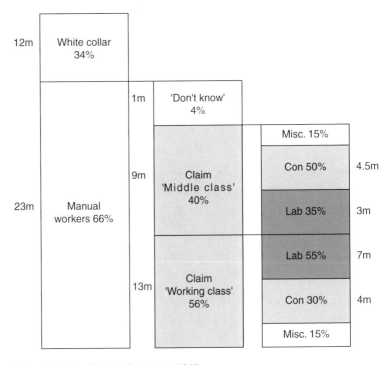

Figure 3.1   The British electorate, 1960
Source: M. Abrams, 'Social Class and British Politics', *Public Opinion Quarterly*, xxv, 3 (1961), p. 343.

At the time, though, there was as much scepticism as support for the affluent worker thesis. Although bitterly disappointed, Gaitskell was right to question the scale of his election reversal: only three voters in every 200 had switched sides. Nor was the changing allegiance of skilled workers the only electoral movement of note in 1959. Gallup polls indicated that equally significant was Labour's loss of middle-class backing since 1955. At the same time, promises to pensioners had produced stronger support among the elderly and the poor, sufficient to deny the Conservatives many more seats. This was offset by a modest swing from Labour, mainly to the Liberals and non-voting, in the lower middle/working classes. The movement here was slight, but because these voters made up the great majority of the adult population, it was 'sufficient to tip the scales'. A new group set up by Tory leaders to monitor public opinion after the election reported that disgruntled Labour supporters still tended to abstain or vote Liberal rather than change to Conservative at once. The group also denied any simple link between affluence and voting patterns, noting that:

> It is among those moving from manual to non-manual work that we are making headway, but the frequent assumption that this is connected with middle-class consumption patterns and the ownership of durable consumer goods seems very doubtful. House ownership is apparently much more important in changing voting habits, particularly among working-class electors who have bought houses since the war, or are currently in the process of buying them.[45]

More detailed studies into working-class Conservatism went further in challenging economic determinism. One post-election study carried out in a new town and a more traditional working-class area of London found that in both cases the 'deference voter' was just as important as in the past. Respect for a natural ruling class was summed up by one respondent: 'The Conservative Party is the gentleman's party... I always vote for them. I'm only a working man and they're my guv'nors.'[46] A larger survey undertaken in the early 1960s also found that personal income was not the key to voting behaviour: the proportion of those workers voting Tory was the same in a range of income groups. The importance of middle-class identification was reaffirmed, as was 'deference', though an equally large number were guided by 'secular objectives': the Conservatives were regarded as best at maximising personal well-being, especially in relation to the economy, whereas many Labour sympathisers defined their vote largely in terms of satisfying class interests.[47] Central to studies of this type was the finding that workers could be swayed by their sense of satisfaction or dissatisfaction with the government of the day. 'Floating' voters could not be relied upon by either main party.[48]

It follows that the Conservatives, in spite of a large majority in 1959, would be at the mercy of unfolding events. The authors of *Must Labour Lose?* concluded that the question could not be answered with certainty in 1960 because 'politics is continually in a state of flux'. Although loyalty to Labour had been weakening, Tory popularity could easily be dented if the economy slumped or if expectations of prosperity – fed by 1959–style rhetoric – proved impossible to fulfil.[49] This prophecy was rapidly borne out; indeed the major shortcoming of the affluent worker theory was its failure to pass the test of time. Labour's recovery from 1961 onwards, at local and by-elections as well as in opinion polls, cast doubt on the notion that aspiring workers were being irretrievably led to Conservatism. Hard empirical evidence was also provided by a survey of several hundred factory workers in Luton, carried out in 1963. The survey revealed a consistently high level of support for Labour among manual workers in the car, chemical and ball-bearing industries, with no evidence of a long-term shift towards the Conservatives. The small number of Tory supporters among the sample were characterised not by higher standards of living, but by larger numbers of white-collar workers among their kin. On this basis, it was concluded that what distinguished 'new' from 'traditional' working-class communities was that the former were more volatile and 'instrumental' in their support for Labour. Home-centred lifestyles in Luton were a far cry from the collective solidarity of the coal-mining districts. As a result, affluent workers supported the party less through instinct than through the calculation that Labour could best serve their economic interests.[50]

This debunking of the affluent worker thesis, published in full by a team of sociologists in the late 1960s, was itself later challenged. The Luton sample did not, for example, allow comparisons to be made between small- and large-scale enterprises.[51] Other social scientists, such as Ivor Crewe, pointed out that the Luton study was carried out at a single point in time when Labour was riding high, and yet there was no evidence of *increased* support, as might be expected. There was little solid basis, other than guesswork, for the alternative theory of 'instrumentalism'; nor was there any analysis of 'traditional' workers or of other 'affluent' constituencies. Ivor Crewe's own wider examination of 15 seats, carried out in 1970, showed modest backing for the idea of embourgeoisement but none for instrumentalism as a guide to voting patterns.[52] Yet as far as the early 1960s were concerned, it was clear old habits died hard. By the time Harold Macmillan resigned, Conservatives were sensing that the 'prosperity ticket' had backfired, especially among those who had reached the shores of affluence in 1959 and had passed on to a stage of disillusionment. Any change in working-class voting behaviour was therefore a protracted and uneven process. Harold Wilson was able to command the loyalty of working-class voters in all regions and occupations, whether 'traditional' or 'new'. A majority of the Luton sample questioned in 1963 explained their allegiance to Labour in terms more readily associated with a past age or with workers in heavy industry. Labour, said one respondent, 'are always inclined to do that bit more for the working man. My opinion of Tory government is that they're for the capitalists'.[53]

The middle-class vote

What then of middle-class voters? As this report from one of the polling companies shows, white-collar workers – like the working classes – varied considerably in terms of income and lifestyle:

Group A: Upper Middle Class
Professional workers, Company Directors, Professors, Doctors, Dentists, Headmasters of large schools, Editors, High Local Officials such as Town Clerks, High Civil Servants, High ranking Army or Police Officers, Farmers of large farms. ... Nearly all people in this class will probably have a telephone and a car, employ servants and live in large detached houses or expensive flats.
Probable income: Over £1750.

Group B: Middle Class
Junior Executives, Managers of middle sized shops, workers in Insurance or Banks...with responsibility for department, Head Librarians, Lecturers, medium ranking Army or Police officers...

Headmasters of smaller sized schools. ... Many of these people will have telephones and cars and many employ part-time domestic help. Their houses will not be as luxurious or as large as Group A but will still be pleasant, probably semi-detached houses in the suburbs ...
Probable income: £950–£1,750.

Group C1:   Lower Middle Class
Primary or Secondary School Teachers, Nurses, Bank Clerks, Junior Lecturers, Junior Civil Servants, Managers of small shops, Shop Assistants with high responsibilities or training. Typists, Laboratory Assistants, Junior Army Officers, Police Sergeants ...
Probable income: £950.[54]

This list was by no means exhaustive. Several groups might be added: those, for example, with private incomes, wives and dependants, and pensioners who before retirement were engaged in business or white-collar employment. The ranks of the middle class were also being swelled in the 1950s by newly emerging professionals, such as television producers and market research consultants. Nor was a definition of middle-class voters based on occupation alone without complication. A minority of those engaged in manual employment insisted on defining themselves when asked as middle class – a reflection of how rising living standards were blurring the most obvious differences in lifestyle and income between skilled workers and the lower middle class. In 1949 there were 1.9 million workers with an income of *c.* £750 per annum; by 1954 this had trebled to £5.8 million. Nevertheless the middle classes remained broadly recognisable. They were, according to *The Times*, all those people who 'do not clock in and out'.[55] Middle-class voters were also relatively stable in terms of political allegiance. Between the wars they helped to bolster the Conservative-National governments of Baldwin and Chamberlain. A central feature of 'safety first' Conservatism was its opposition to higher taxation – the antithesis in middle-class eyes of individual initiative and business risk-taking. This tradition of anti-socialism was interrupted briefly in 1945, when Labour captured the likes of Chislehurst, Wimbledon and Winchester as part of its election landslide. But flirtation with the left proved short-lived. Dalton's maintenance of high wartime taxes and the privations associated with Crippsian austerity soon hardened attitudes. Echoing events just after the First World War, a Middle Class Union was formed and tales abounded of 'bishops' wives scrubbing floors'.[56] This provided the backcloth for a Conservative revival that served to reinforce the class basis of party alignment.

In 1945, middle-class voters were estimated to have backed the Tories by 2:1. In 1950 this ratio was 3:1 and by 1951, when Churchill defeated Attlee to secure a narrow majority, it had risen to 3.5:1. Whereas Labour secured a higher total vote by polling heavily in its working-class heartlands, the Conservatives relied for more seats on capturing middle-class constituencies such as Buckingham, King's Lynn and Yarmouth. The narrow margin of victory posed an electoral dilemma for the new government. On the one hand, Labour had been defeated in part by raising the expectations of middle-class voters: Churchill's pledge was to 'set Britain free' by attacking bureau-cracy, controls and high taxes. On the other hand, the Tories could ill afford to alienate working-class support. In the circumstances bequeathed by the out-going administration – of progressive taxation helping to finance an extensive welfare system – any return to 1930s-style minimalist government geared to middle-class concerns was out of the question. Yet by a mixture of skill and good fortune Churchill succeeded in facing both ways. Expanding world trade helped to ensure the maintenance of full employment and the welfare state, and moves to free up the economy – through denationalisation, the ending of controls and rationing, and reduced income tax – all won plaudits among business and middle-class interests. In the spring of 1955 the Chancellor, Rab Butler, decided to cut income tax further from 9s to 8s 6d in the pound. A month later the government comfortably secured re-election, its cross-class appeal remaining undiminished. In addition to a sizeable minority of lower-middle and working-class support, 66 per cent of middle-class voters were estimated by Gallup to have backed the Tories, compared with only 18 per cent for Labour. In the months that followed, however, during the troubled premiership of Anthony Eden, the alliance between the government and its middle-class supporters came under intense strain. Indeed as early as 1956 there was to be talk of a middle-class 'revolt'.

The primary cause of discontent was the prolonged economic downturn that followed the 1955 election. As memories of the early-1950s boom receded, middle-class grievances became a prime concern for press editorials. *The Times* underlined how far inflation had eroded favourable prewar conditions: it estimated that someone earning £400 a year in 1935 might now receive £1000 per annum, but would be over 10 per cent worse off in terms of income tax. For the upper middle class the position was worse still. A top civil servant would find his income 'worth only 44 per cent of what it was then'.[57] Newspaper columns began to fill up with case studies of those who complained about life as 'hardly interrupted drudgery' on £2,600 a year. One lamented that instead of two living-in staff, he could only afford 'a part-time daily woman', with the result that an 'increasing burden of cooking, cleaning and mending has been assumed by my wife'. Another complained that his family had 'not had an hotel holiday for six years; . . . [we have] no TV and we think twice about going to the theatre or buying a bottle of sherry'.[58] Central to much middle-class disaffection, as portrayed by the press, was the language of class rivalry. While newly emerging professional workers might not hark back to a prewar golden age, they often shared anxieties about social status. While the thrifty suffered, it was alleged, ministers spent too much time 'coddling the workers', either by giving in to high wage demands or through welfare handouts. According to the *Sunday Times*, the middle classes were the Cinderellas of the economic system. 'They have no trade unions to keep them, like a skilled surf-rider, on the foamy crest of the inflationary wave, but have been doused and buffeted in its trough.'[59] What was worse, tax rises imposed in the emergency budget of 1955 looked like 'Socialist egalitarianism under a Conservative administration', and were said to have left a feeling of hopelessness among the middle classes. If relief from 'monstrously' high tax rates 'is not given by a Conservative Government, will it ever be given?'[60]

Disquiet amounted to more than individual complaints taken up in sympathetic newspapers. Other manifestations of middle-class revolt were evident more broadly in popular politics. The first was voter disenchantment with Eden's government. After the Tories came close to losing the Tonbridge by-election in June 1956, one angry supporter, Mrs Beryl Platts, wrote to *The Times* to say that the government must act upon middle class grievances or face the consequences:

The Conservative agents who describe the result as due to apathy delude themselves. It is a wonderfully encouraging gesture from a class which . . . refuses to be exterminated. For – and let the Conservative headquarters be under no misapprehension about this – if we refuse to vote and thereby admit the Socialists to power, we allow a period of Socialist legislation which can later be revoked. If we permit the Conservatives to frame Socialist measures in their ill-considered bid for left-wing support, we are saddled with such measures for ever. Which is the greater evil?[61]

A second example of discontent was the emergence of new pressure groups on the fringes of mainstream politics, notably the People's League for the Defence of Freedom (PLDF) and the Middle Class Alliance. The fears of Tory leaders about these nascent groups should not be exaggerated. Neither was taken very seriously by the national press, and no attempt was made to co-ordinate protest action against the government. Both groups lost momentum when the Suez crisis became a test of national loyalty. But if new fringe movements caused concern rather than alarm, the underlying causes of middle-class disquiet had yet to be addressed. Inflation continued to rise and those attracted by the People's League were dismayed to see that Eden shied away from any legislative reform of trade unionism. The abrupt resignation of Eden in January 1957 left the Tories facing an unresolved electoral dilemma: how to maintain the balance between 13 million who voted Conservative and the vocal middle-class groups who included 'so many of the Party's zealots'.[62]

Between 1957 and 1959 the tide of middle-class disquiet slowly receded. Indeed the Middle Class Alliance was quickly wound up altogether, the victim of internal wrangling. It would, though, be wrong to assume that tension disappeared overnight. In his first year as prime minister, Eden's successor Harold Macmillan was forced to tighten the deflationary belt further and faced the resignation of his entire Treasury team. In these circumstances further Liberal advances, for example at the Ipswich by-election, were seen by local Tories as 'further evidence that the middle classes, by abstaining or supporting the third party, are still registering a vote of censure on the Government, in particular over its failure to check the ever-rising cost of living'.[63] The first signs of a turn-around came with the London bus strike in May 1958, which at last saw the government taking an anti-union line that satisfied middle-class sentiment. Macleod, the Minister of Labour, told colleagues that legislation on the closed shop or sympathetic strike action 'would be extremely popular within the Party and attract the Liberal vote more than almost anything else'. But such change, he added, might 'frighten the trade union world more than it would bring in the Liberal vote'.[64] Macleod recognised that the best way of securing cross-class support was to ensure a flourishing economy that bene-fited all sections of the community. The year 1958, as we have seen, also brought a change of fortune for the government on this front. The combination of an improving economy and a triumph over the unions had a discernible impact on middle-class voters. By-elections in June 1958 witnessed a recovery attributed by commentators to the reputation of union leaders as bully boys in the eyes of the middle classes.[65]

By the time of the general election in October 1959 the govern-ment had behind it the advantage of a budget that gave full rein to Macmillan's expansionary instincts. Supermac's triumph swept out of sight mid-term blues. Aside from a strong showing among skilled workers, the Conservatives had maintained a strong lead over Labour in all sections of the middle class. Among the upper middle class (socioeconomic group A), this was by as much as 85.5 to 5.7 per cent. Within the middle and lower middle class (groups B and C1) the lead was an impressive 66.3 to 17.4 per cent.[66] But the Tories had not entirely won back their traditional supporters. Labour had lost ground among the middle classes since 1955 but so too, according to Gallup, had the Tories, with a movement among the upper middle classes especially towards the Liberals (and to abstentionism) in 1959. As senior Conservatives recognised, the Liberals had stopped the inexorable decline evident earlier in the decade by doubling their vote to one and a half million, and had done so primarily at the expense of Tory candidates.[67] The party's bond with the middle classes had been growing stronger at every election since 1945; this trend, if not reversed, had been checked in 1959. Middle-class doubt-ers who had returned to the fold were won over ultimately by an expansionary economic policy that on past experience would be difficult to sustain. Neither could it be taken for granted that the Labour Opposition would forever be shackled by its image as a party for the working classes. Loyalty among the middle classes, in other words, was becoming conditional – just as it was for affluent workers – on the government 'delivering the goods'.

Indeed the drift of the middle-class vote away from the Conservatives accelerated during the early 1960s when Macmillan again ran into economic difficulties. The Liberals once more benefited. In September 1959 there were just 475 local Liberal councillors; by May 1962 this figure had more than trebled. Success was mainly evident in suburbia and 'resort' towns such as Bath, Harrogate and Eastbourne.[68] Growing support for the Liberals in by-elections culminated in the resounding triumph at Orpington in 1962, explained by Macmillan in his diary as a 'conjunction of a spiritual vacuum and a vague feeling in the middle classes that all they had striven for was turning to dead sea fruit'.[69] As long as the Liberals were the main beneficiaries of protest voting, the prime minister could hope that the pattern of 1956–58 might be repeated. But the differences from the previous parliament were as striking as the similarities. After 11 years in power, Macmillan conceded, voters 'really are tired of us', and the 'second middle class revolt' was different from its predecessor in nature and scope. Many of the 'new' middle class were young couples migrating from areas of heavy industry to rapidly expanding suburbs, especially around London. For these families, high mortgage costs and commuter charges were major grievances. 'This', claimed *The Economist*, 'rather than the retired brigadiers and fixed-income widows, is the pressured middle class that Mr Macleod has to deal with now.' It followed that this new class was more uncertain of its political identity: while the Liberals had been quickest off the mark in recruiting supporters, the new middle class contained the largest available 'pool of floating voters'.[70]

What made matters worse for Macmillan was the growing appeal of Labour among such voters. By the time Liberal popularity peaked in the summer of 1962, Labour had re-emerged as a credible alternative government, maintaining a clear poll lead and securing three by-election gains from the Tories. The first of these, at Middlesborough West in June 1962, was described as 'Labour's revenge for Orpington', showing that the party was beating back 'the Liberal effort to sweep up Labour's share of the white-collar, suburbanite vote'.[71] This transformation resulted partly from government failures and partly from determined efforts to reshape Labour's image. Party leaders were firmly told after 1959 that an attempt had to be made to appeal to the rapidly expanding sector of administrative, technical and clerical workers, who had grown from 16.5 per cent of the workforce in 1950 to 21 per cent in 1960. The pay pause was regarded as a prime opportunity to win over those who had previously been hostile or indifferent.[72] With this in mind, Labour for the first time used new advertising techniques to underline its support for the material ambitions of the aspiring classes. This process was enhanced – rather than initiated – by the arrival of Harold Wilson as Opposition leader after the unexpected death of Gaitskell in January 1963. His emphasis on technology was designed not only to contrast his own Kennedy-style vision of a 'new Britain' with Macmillan's allegedly outdated appeal. It also aimed – via its promise to liberate the talents of the ambitious – at reducing middle-class fear about the prospect of a Labour government. 'I am', claimed Wilson, 'making myself acceptable to the suburbs.'[73] His claim was soon to be put to the test.

Conclusion

The impact of white-collar disaffection on voting patterns in the 1951–64 period must be kept in perspective. Middle-class voters made up only one-third of the total electorate, and as the evidence presented here demonstrates, class divisions survived the arrival of postwar affluence to a greater extent than has often been realised. The link between class and party preference remained powerful. At every election between 1945 and 1964 more than 60 per cent of middle-class voters backed the Conservatives, just as over half of the working-class electorate supported Labour. Both major parties, in attracting the great majority of votes cast, relied on traditional sources of support. In one Bristol constituency the archetypal Conservative voter was found to be a retired middle-class teacher, a lay reader in the Church of England who had always supported the Tories because they stood for the 'general well-being of the people'. By contrast, the working-class lorry driver was a trade union member and regular Labour voter: he was unswerving in his support because Labour stood for 'the average man' and not 'the capitalist class'.[74] But neither party could depend exclusively on a natural constituency of voters. The class-party axis had never been complete. and electoral success was contingent upon appealing across the class divide, as senior Tory strategists noted in 1960:

It is a striking fact that though the divisions between the classes have narrowed, people are voting more by class than before the war. The rise in the number of white-collar workers and the fall in the number of manual workers has favoured us.... Nevertheless, it must be remembered that the tendency towards a more middle-class society has a long way to go yet, and it is still from the working-class two thirds that we get more than half our votes – and have to if we are to win an Election.[75]

Conservative governments thus had to strike a balance between satisfying bedrock middle-class interests, especially through tax cuts, and attracting a critical minority of working-class voters. This necessity not only explained the drive to cultivate the 'affluent worker', but also coloured the whole approach of successive administrations towards domestic politics. With Labour commanding well over 40 per cent of the vote, even at its 1959 low point, risk-taking with popular elements of the postwar settlement was out of the question. In addition, preoccupation with the 'working class two thirds' explains why – in later years – subtle shifts in middle-class voting patterns went unnoticed. Yet the white-collar sector was expanding rapidly and had the potential to make and unmake governments, as had been shown in 1945 and 1951. In the early 1950s an expanding economy made the task of maintaining a broad electoral coalition relatively straightforward. But the reconciliation of class interests became more difficult after the economic downturn of the mid-1950s. The first middle-class revolt was primarily a protest against inflation, which hit those on fixed incomes and caused resentment among professionals who were frequently denied the opportunity of overtime or outside work to supplement their salaries. Hence the strident element of class antagonism in the complaints of middle-class Tories who resented 'the burden of taxation required to provide lavish ... welfare services for a section of the community whose incomes are steadily advanced by Trade Union pressure'.[76] The danger this posed for the government was more limited than it might have been. Since 1951 Labour had forgotten that it too needed cross-class support to win elections; it gave every indication – to paraphrase Manny Shinwell – that it gave not 'a tinker's cuss' for the middle classes. In addition, Macmillan engineered a consumer boom that persuaded all but the poorest voters that they had 'never had it so good'. Many of the Tonbridge-style protesters returned to the fold at the 1959 election.

But not all did so. The Tories, as well as Labour, lost ground among the middle classes to a revitalised Liberal Party.

This movement of opinion continued in the early 1960s, though it was overlaid by growing receptivity to Labour as a more credible alternative government. The second middle-class revolt had more to do with deflation than rising prices. As consumer purchasing power dwindled and unemployment rose to its highest level since 1947, confidence in Conservative economic competence was severely dented, both among affluent workers promised ever-rising living standards and among professionals suffering from high mortgages and commuter fares. Middle-class discontent was again frequently couched in terms that made premature Macmillan's claim that the class war was obsolete. But if for many, even within the 'new middle class', anti-socialism remained an article of faith, others were less settled in their outlook and shared the view that after 13 years of Conservative rule, it was time for a change. At the 1964 election the alignment between class and party looked less secure than at any time in the past decade. Orpington gave the Liberals enhanced respectability, and the party's targeting of young professionals helped to attract over three million voters. The loss of ground by the Tories among the middle classes between 1955 and 1964 was almost exactly the same as that made up by the Liberals, posing a long-term threat to two-party hegemony. More damaging still, in the short term, was the progress made by Labour, which recorded a higher level of middle-class backing than at any election since 1945.[77] The bark of 'disgusted of Tonbridge' may have been worse than the bite. But the bite of disgusted of Buckingham, King's Lynn and Watford was real enough. All three were among the Labour gains that propelled Harold Wilson into Downing Street in 1964.

Notes

1. Macmillan to Fraser, 17 February 1957, cited in Alastair Horne, *Macmillan*, volume II of the official biography (London: Macmillan, 1989), p. 62.
2. Fraser to Macmillan, 20 February 1957, cited in Horne, *Macmillan*, p. 62; Conservative Policy Studies Group minutes, 1 April 1957: Conservative Party Archive hereafter (CPA), Bodleian Library, Oxford; Conservative Research Department, hereafter (CRD) 2/53/24.
3. John Bonham, *The Middle Class Vote* (London: Faber and Faber, 1954).

4. David Butler and Richard Rose, *The British General Election of 1959* (Basingstoke: Macmillan, 1960), p. 15; F. Zweig, *The Worker in an Affluent Society: Family Life and Industry* (London: Heinemann, 1961) p. ix.

5. For a review of the origins and development of the affluent worker debate, see Nick Tiratsoo, *Reconstruction, Affluence and Labour Politics: Coventry, 1945–60* (London: Routledge, 1990), pp. 2–4.

6. H. Hopkins, *The New Look: A Social History of the Forties and Fifties in Britain* (London: Secker & Warburg, 1963), pp. 161, 351.

7. M. Abrams, 'The Home-Centred Society', *The Listener*, 26 November 1959.

8. M. Abrams, writing in *The Observer*, 23 August 1960.

9. G. Moorhouse, *Britain in the Sixties: The Other England* (Harmondsworth: Penguin, 1964), pp. 164–5. Moorhouse rejected the idea of a simple division between north and south, noting for example the high unemployment rate in Cornwall. He did, however (pp. 18–19), endorse the notion of a 'Golden Circle', whose perimeter 'is approximately one hour's travel by fast peak-hour train from the main London termini'.

10. B. Abel-Smith and P. Townshend, *The Poor and the Poorest: A New Analysis of Ministry of Labour's Family Expenditure Surveys* (London: Bell, 1965), pp. 65–6.

11. N. Mitford, 'The English Aristocracy', *Encounter*, 24 September 1955, p. 5.

12. M. Abrams, 'Class Distinctions in Britain', in *The Future of the Welfare State* (London: Conservative Political Centre, 1958), pp. 61–3.

13. There were several variations on this system of voter classification: many social scientists, for example, used the Registrar-General's multi-occupational grading scheme. In this article the A–E social groupings will be used throughout. On the importance of the women's vote, see I. Zweiniger-Bargielowska, 'Explaining the Gender Gap: the Conservative Party and the Women's Vote, 1945–64', in M. Francis et al. (eds), *The Conservatives and British Society, 1880–1990* (Cardiff: University of Wales Press, 1996).

14. R. Titmuss, *Income Distribution and Social Change* (London: Allen and Unwin, 1962), p. 21.

15. Cited in J. Ryder and H. Silver, *Modern English Society: History and Structure, 1850–1970* (London: Methuen, 1970), p. 206.

16. D. Middleton, *The British* (London: Secker & Warburg, 1957), p. 123. Middleton, an American journalist, added that: 'The ideal seemed to be a community of equals protected from economic dangers by full employment and high wages. … Everyone earned about the same amount of money, spent it on the same things and appeared to think and talk alike.'

17. Peter Willmott and Michael Young, *Family and Class in a London Suburb* (London: Routledge and Kegan Paul, 1960), pp. 121–2. These findings were echoed in C. Rosser, *The Family and Social Change: A Study of Family and Kinship in a South Wales Town* (London: Routledge and Kegan Paul, 1965), pp. 113–14.

18. J. Goldthorpe and D. Lockwood, 'Affluence and the British Class Structure', *Sociological Review*, II (1963), pp. 133–56.

19. Middleton, op. cit., p. 122.

20. Abrams, 'Class Distinctions', p. 68.
21. Nick Tiratsoo, 'Popular Politics, Affluence and the Labour Party in the 1950s', in Anthony Gorst, Lewis Johnman and Scott Lucas (eds), *Contemporary British History, 1931–91* (London: Pinter, 1991), p. 50.
22. B. Williamson, *The Temper of the Times: British Society since World War II* (Oxford: Blackwell, 1990), p. 109.
23. John Bonham, 'The Middle Class Revolt', *Political Quarterly*, 33 (1962), p. 244.
24. George Gallup (ed.), *The Gallup International Public Opinion Polls*, vol. 1 (New York: Gallup, 1977), October 1959 and August 1964, pp. 544, 751.
25. 'General Election Campaign 1951', report by Morgan Phillips, 7 November 1951, Labour Party NEC Minutes.
26. David Butler, *The British General Election of 1951* (Basingstoke: Macmillan, 1952), p. 248.
27. M. Benney and P. Geiss, 'Social Class and Politics in Greenwich', *British Journal of Sociology* (December 1950), pp. 326–7; M. Benney, A. P. Gray and P. H. Pear, *How People Vote: A Study of Electoral Behaviour in Greenwich* (London: Routledge and Kegan Paul, 1956), pp. 114–20.
28. R. S. Milne and H. C. Mackenzie, *Straight Fight: A Study of Voting Behaviour in the Constituency of Bristol North-East at the General Election of 1951* (London: Hansard Society, 1954), pp. 36–50.
29. A. H. Birch, *Small Town Politics: A Study of Political Life in Glossop* (Oxford: Oxford University Press, 1959), pp. 100–12. The same point was made more tentatively in P. Campbell et al., 'Voting Behaviour in Droylesden in October 1951', *The Manchester School of Economic and Social Studies*, xx (1952), p. 62.
30. M. Stacey, *Tradition and Change: A Study of Banbury* (Oxford: Oxford University Press, 1960), pp. 41–56.
31. *Observer*, 22 May 1955.
32. 'The General Election 1955', report by Morgan Phillips, June 1955, NEC Minutes.
33. R. S. Milne and H. C. Mackenzie, *Marginal Seat: A Study of Voting Behaviour in the Constituency of Bristol North-East at the General Election of 1955* (London: Hansard Society, 1958), pp. 43, 91–2, 139 and 166.
34. 'Report on General Election 1955', CRD 2/48/54.
35. Ralph Harris, *Onward*, June 1955.
36. M. Abrams, 'Public Opinion Polls and Political Parties', *Public Opinion Quarterly*, xxvii (Spring 1963), pp. 10–18.
37. Cited in Tiratsoo, 'Popular Politics', p. 54.
38. M. Pawley, *Home Ownership* (London: Architectural Press, 1978), pp. 700–2.
39. *Tribune*, 16 October 1959.
40. 'Report on General Election 1959', CRD 2/48/71.
41. Cited in Steven Fielding, 'White Heat and White Collars: the Evolution of Wilsonism', in Richard Coopey, Steven Fielding and Nick Tiratsoo (eds), *The Wilson Governments, 1964–70* (London: Pinter, 1993), pp. 34–7. See also

NEC Minutes, 28 October 1959; *Labour Organiser*, October/November 1959, pp. 183–4.

42. R. Samuel, 'The Deference Voter', *New Left Review*, 1 (1960), p. 10.
43. 'The General Election of 1959', report by National Opinion Polls (NOP), CPA, Conservative Central Office (hereafter CCO), 4/8/104.
44. M. Abrams and R. Rose, *Must Labour Lose?* (Harmondsworth: Penguin, 1960), p. 58.
45. Material in this paragraph is taken from Conservative Party Public Opinion Group, 'First Report to the Chairman of the Conservative Party Organisation' (Autumn 1960), CPA, CRD 2/21/6.
46. Samuel, op. cit., p. 9.
47. R. McKenzie and A. Silver, *Angels in Marble: Working-Class Conservatives in Urban England* (London: Heinemann, 1968), pp. 83–4 and 246–7.
48. E. Nordlinger, *The Working-Class Conservatives (Authority, Deference and Stable Democracy* (London: MacGibbon and Kee, 1967), p. 175.
49. Abrams and Rose, op. cit., pp. 97–8.
50. J. Goldthorpe, D. Lockwood, F. Bechhofer and J. Platt, *The Affluent Worker: Political Attitudes and Behaviour* (Cambridge: Cambridge University University Press, 1968), esp. pp. 73–82.
51. G. Mackenzie, 'The "Affluent Worker" Study: an Evaluation and Critique', in F. Parkin (ed.), *The Social Analysis of Class Structure* (London: Tavistock Publications, 1974), pp. 237–52.
52. I. Crewe, 'The Politics of "Affluent" and "Traditional" Workers in Britain: an Aggregate Data Analysis', *British Journal of Political Science*, 3:1 (1973), pp. 29–52.
53. Cited in Goldthorpe et al., op. cit., p. 17.
54. 'General Election of 1959', Report by NOP, CCO 4/8/104.
55. *The Times*, 27 February 1956.
56. Bonham, *The Middle-Class Vote*, pp. 10–19.
57. *The Times*, 27 February 1956.
58. *The Economist*, 28 April 1956.
59. *Sunday Times*, 10 June 1956.
60. *The Times*, 13 and 27 February 1956.
61. *The Times*, 12 June 1956.
62. Michael Fraser to R. A. Butler, 10 October 1956: R. A. Butler papers, Trinity College, Cambridge, H36, ff. 120–1. Butler's papers also contain a copy of the Tory party's internal report on new middle-class groups.
63. 'Monthly summary of reports [from party workers] on public opinion' (November 1957), CPA, CCO 4/7/375.
64. Minutes of Conservative Steering Committee (23 July 1958), CPA, CRD 2/53/31.
65. *The Economist*, 19 April, 24 May and 21 June 1958.
66. 'General Election of 1959', Report by NOP, CCO 4/8/104.
67. Memorandum by James Douglas, n.d. (1960), Psephology Group papers, CPA, CRD 2/21/6; 'Report on General Election 1959', CRD 2.48/72.
68. R. H. Pear, 'The Liberal Vote', *Political Quarterly*, 33 (1962), p. 247.

69. Diary entries 24–5 March 1962, cited in Harold Macmillan, *Memoirs: At the End of the Day, 1961–63* (London: Macmillan, 1973), pp. 58–60.
70. *The Economist*, 14 April 1962.
71. Ibid., 9 June 1962.
72. 'Non-Manual Workers and the Labour Party', report by the Home Policy Committee, NEC Minutes, January 1960.
73. Fielding, op. cit., p. 39.
74. Milne and Mackenzie, *Marginal Seat*, pp. 169–72.
75. Public Opinion Group, 'First Report' (Autumn 1960), CPA, CRD 2/21/6.
76. 'Monthly summary of reports [from party workers]' (November 1957), CPA, CCO 4/7/375.
77. See K. Jefferys, 'British Politics and the Road to 1964', *Contemporary Record*, 9: 1 (1995), pp. 120–46.

4

The Lasting Impact of Margaret Thatcher

Peter Riddell

'Asked what he thought was the significance of the French Revolution, the Chinese Premier Zhou En-lai is reported to have answered, "It's too soon to tell".'[1] This is even more true of Margaret Thatcher, even over a decade after her forced departure from office. Like her hero Sir Winston Churchill, she herself sought to become one of the main interpreters of her record in office, through her own two volumes of memoirs and through regular speeches and interviews. Moreover, she remained a participant in current politics, occasionally descending from Concorde, rather than the hills, to deliver a broadside at her successors. Her evident frustration at her loss of office, and consequent unwanted image as a bitter exiled monarch critical of the current regime, in itself led to a decline in her reputation. Much of the history of the Conservative Party after November 1990 was a debate, at times a battle, about the meaning of the Thatcher legacy. The Conservative leadership contest of June/July 1995 was in part a revolt by discontented Thatcherites against what they saw as her unworthy successor – one who in turn had spent much of his premiership trying, unsuccessfully, to escape her shadow. It was in many ways appropriate that the leadership challenger in 1994, John Redwood, was a former head of the Downing Street Policy Unit at the high point of the Thatcher era in the mid-1980s.

There is a vast academic and journalistic literature on the meaning of Thatcherism,[2] to which I contributed at various stages of her premiership. Much of it is concerned with the question of 'Thatcherite exceptionalism' – the extent to which the Thatcher governments reflected continuities with past Conservative administrations or marked a distinctively radical new departure. In retrospect, much of this debate appears beside the point. Merely by being in office for so long the Thatcher governments were bound to be very different from their more short-lived predecessors. Longevity ensured exceptionalism. The policies of her governments certainly had roots before the late 1970s and, more importantly, developed and altered during her eleven and a half years in office. The more pertinent question is whether she, and her administrations, made a difference to the longer-run history of British politics and public policy. How far did her achievements match up to her often repeated claim to have 'changed everything'?

This claim is absurd if taken literally. Even by the end of her period in office, much of what the government did reflected decisions taken long before she entered Downing Street.[3] Moreover, as Marsh and Rhodes have argued,[4] the Thatcher governments often faced big difficulties translating their radical aspirations and legislation into changes on the ground. In many areas, there were problems of implementation. But there is a definite sense in which she, and it was primarily her, changed the political landscape. The overall, widely held, impression matters as much as the detailed analysis of the lasting impact of particular policies. Her first election victory in May 1979 marked one of the key turning points in twentieth-century British politics – comparable with the Liberal election victory in 1906 or the Labour landslide of 1945. In both these cases, there were ideological and policy roots in what had happened before they took office. But in James Callaghan's memorable phrase towards the end of the 1979 election campaign: 'There are times, perhaps once every thirty years, when there is a sea-change in politics. It then does not matter what you say or what you do. There is a shift in what the public wants and what it approves of. I suspect there is now such a sea change – and it is for Mrs Thatcher.'[5] Following the earlier sea changes, the reforming Liberal and Labour governments introduced wide-ranging reforms which not only changed the state's role but also forced far-reaching reappraisals by the main Opposition party which, often gradually and painfully, came to accept what the governments had enacted. The Thatcher governments were in this mould both by their attempts to roll back some, though not all, of the postwar settlement and by forcing the Labour Party to alter its own approach and to accept many of the post-1979 reforms.

In the epilogue to her memoirs, Lady Thatcher herself attempted what she admitted was an unusual exercise in introspection. After a reference to the transience of all human achievement, she wrote that

> as Prime Minister, the most I could aspire to was to hand on to my successor a better country than the one I had inherited in 1979's Winter of Discontent. I worked hard to do so and, along with some disappointments, I can claim many successes. By 1990, the British people were freer, more prosperous, less torn by civil strife, and enjoying better prospects for world peace than at any time since the First World War. But there are no final victories in politics. Will these gains prove permanent? Will they be reversed? Will they be overwhelmed by new issues or clouds which now are no bigger than a man's hand?[6]

Lady Thatcher went on to argue that at least future conflicts would take place on a battleground permanently altered by earlier victories. In particular, she suggested that a future Labour government 'is unlikely to nationalise the industries privatised in the 1980s, nor restore the 98 per cent top tax rates of 1979, nor reverse all the trade union reforms, let alone implement the proposals contained in the Labour election manifesto of 1983'. In a revealing passage, she drew a comparison with the regaining of freedom in Eastern Europe after 1989 and the defeat of communism. While people in Britain lived in a free society before 1979, she claimed that after her government was elected,

> they enjoyed a self-fulfilment that the rolling-back of socialism and the expansion of freedom made possible. Some were no longer prevented by union power from doing the best work of which they were capable; some were able for the first time to buy a home, or a private pension, or shares in a privatised company – a nest egg to leave their children, some found that a good private school or a private hospital bed was no longer a privilege of the rich – they could buy it too; some exercised their new prosperity by sharing it with others in the upsurge of charitable giving in the 1980s; and

all enjoyed the greater freedom and control over their own lives
which cuts in income tax extended.

These reflections, contentious and self-justifying though they
inevitably are, illuminate one of the most telling features of her
lasting impact. Unlike all other postwar British prime ministers, she
became an icon. The Thatcher myth became embedded in the minds
of politicians and the public as much as the reality of the Thatcher
years. Hers was a heroic era to her followers and admirers, a time of
freedom and of reduced state power, to which they looked back with
fondness and yearning. Lord Blake, the dean of Conservative historians, wrote in *The Times* just after she resigned that, 'Margaret
Thatcher's place in history is assured, the first woman to be Prime
Minister, the first since Palmerston to win three successive general
elections, the longest continuous holder of the office since Lord
Liverpool...She was on the British political scene a giant among
pygmies.'[7]

The Thatcher myth – the sense of what she was and said as much as
what she did – altered the terms of the political debate. No matter
that much of the detailed policy work on the central aspects of what
has become known as Thatcherism was done by others – Keith
Joseph, Geoffrey Howe, Nigel Lawson, Nicholas Ridley. No matter
that many of the key policies of the 1980s – the rejection of Key-
nesian demand management and the acceptance of limits to the size
of public spending and the tax burden – originated in the struggles of
the Wilson and Callaghan governments of the 1970s to get to grips
with soaring inflation and an apparently ever-expanding public sector. No matter that there was a big gap between what she claimed and
what was achieved. Lady Thatcher epitomised the spirit of the 1980s
just as Ronald Reagan did in the United States. Robert Skidelsky has
argued that, 'Ronald Reagan and Margaret Thatcher provided the
ideological drive and personal leadership which made anti-
collectivism a cause'.[8] In that sense, the Thatcher myth was the
reality. But that still does not establish whether she had a lasting
impact. The footprints of giants can quickly blow away.

In her case, however, the existence of the myth has by itself
ensured that her impact has been lasting. Consequently, Andrew
Gamble is taking too short-term a view in arguing that: 'The Conservative Party never became a Thatcherite party. It remained the

Conservative Party led by Mrs Thatcher.'⁹ Many Tory members, and MPs, were never ideological and were loyal to the leader of the day – first Heath, then Thatcher and then Major. But her impact on her party was as great after she left office as during her nearly 16 years as Conservative leader – because of the gradual pace of generational change. By her example, she helped to make the Tory party more political – even, for some, more ideological. By defining the political debate in such stark terms, she encouraged a generation of young people to enter politics as Thatcherites, preaching what they saw as her gospel of nationalist, free market, anti-union and anti-public sector policies – even though she personally had little interest in party organisation and Tory membership declined sharply during her period in office. The recruitment of at least a cadre of political zealots was reflected in the takeover, first, of the Conservative students and, then, of the Young Conservatives by the committed right, passionately devoted to her beliefs. But since the rate of turnover of MPs is only gradual, there were few Thatcher's children in the House of Commons during her time in office. The grandchildren came after she left Downing Street. Many of her fellow MPs, and ministers, remained fair-weather Thatcherites. They backed her when the going was good but they were never avid readers of the Centre for Policy Studies' pamphlets. There were enthusiasts for privatisation and the introduction of market disciplines into health and education in the No Turning Back group, founded from the 1983 new entrants, but they were a minority within the parliamentary party. When the crunch came in November 1990, she was forced out by her own cabinet, by traditional One Nation Tories like Kenneth Clarke, Malcolm Rifkind and Chris Patten, whom she had herself promoted. She also failed to ensure that the succession went to one of her committed allies. Favoured ones such as Cecil Parkinson, John Moore, Norman Tebbit, Nigel Lawson and Geoffrey Howe, had all either fallen by the wayside or fallen out with her. Her anointment of John Major was partly self-delusion since he had never presented himself as a Thatcherite, but he was not Michael Heseltine, or Douglas Hurd.

Her influence on the party became more apparent after her departure, notably following the 1992 and 1997 elections when many of the new Tory MPs were people who had first become interested in active politics under her influence and lead. The main outlet for their views was Europe. Many of these younger MPs were sceptics, signing the 'Fresh Start' early day motion tabled in June 1992 after the first Danish referendum on the Maastricht Treaty on the European Union. Although few of the 1992 intake became out-and-out Maastricht rebels, many were sympathetic. Her anti-Brussels rhetoric, notably in her Bruges speech of September 1988, encouraged the growth of a substantial anti-Brussels group within the Tory party. The stand she took in the last two years of her premiership, and which triggered her downfall, helped push the Tory party in a more Euro-sceptic direction, particularly after the 1997 election of William Hague as Conservative leader. Some shift might have happened anyway in reaction to the centralist ambitions of Jacques Delors as president of the European Commission. But she made such views more respectable and helped make the Tories a more nationalist party. This was underlined by the selection of many more Euro-sceptic candidates.

Many of the most distinctive aspects of the Thatcher years were ephemeral in the sense that they were to do with her style as much as with the substance of her policies, which were often more qualified and less clearcut than her rhetoric. Therefore, many familiar features of the Thatcher years disappeared with her. Talk of a presidential style of government, reducing the role of the cabinet and flouting the conventions of Whitehall, disappeared almost the moment she made her tearful farewell from Downing Street. Her alleged personal authoritarianism was more stubbornness and intolerance for disagreement than a permanent change in the powers of the prime minister – though there were lasting changes in the relations between central government and local authorities and other parts of the public sector. If Lady Thatcher often ignored the constitutional textbooks, John Major played by the traditional rules – indeed made many of them public for the first time by publishing 'Questions of Procedure for Ministers' and the details of cabinet committees. John Wakeham, who served both Lady Thatcher and John Major closely as a business manager, noted in 1993 that, after 1990, the move towards the use of ad hoc groups of ministers to settle difficult issues appeared to have been halted, except where it was necessary for the speedy resolution of problems between two ministers. 'Indeed my impression is that the balance has shifted back towards greater reliance on standing (cabinet) committees.'[10] Lady Thatcher was no innovator in her relations with parliament. Indeed, many important changes, such as the expansion of the select committee system in the Commons in 1979 and the televising of the Commons in 1989, occurred either with her reluctant acquiesence or against her express views. As I argued in my chapter in Dennis Kavanagh and Anthony Seldon's *The Thatcher Effect* in 1989, the Thatcher impact on both cabinet and parliament was 'primarily personal rather than institutional. She has been dominant through her use of the existing levers of power rather than by creating new ones.'[11]

The Thatcher impact on government – central government at any rate – was less than is commonly alleged. She abolished the Central Policy Review Staff and merged the departments of Trade and Industry (returning to the Heath plan of 1970). But, otherwise, she left the organisation of Whitehall remarkably unchanged. It was only under John Major that the big changes in government's relations with industry and the unions were recognised in the abolition of a separate Department of Energy in 1992 and of the Department of Employment in 1995, and the creation of the new Department of National Heritage after the 1992 election. Admittedly, the challenge to the unified Whitehall structure of the civil service began at the end of her years with the creation of the Next Steps executive agencies and the start of the market testing and contracting-out programmes. But, again, these programmes developed momentum under John Major, as did the reorganisation of the health service and the school system with the creation of hospital trusts and grant-maintained schools.

A common charge is that Lady Thatcher politicised Whitehall: that loyal civil servants were promoted and others ignored. But there is no evidence of political favouritism. What did happen was that her conviction style of politics challenged traditional Whitehall ideas of the balanced examination of alternative policy options and the provision of independent, and often unwelcome, advice. These tensions were reflected in the criticisms made of ministers and civil servants by Lord Justice Scott's inquiry into exports of defence equipment to Iraq, which covered events in the late 1980s. Rather, her approach put a premium on the more aggressive type of civil servant, seen as being able to implement the Thatcher agenda. More important was the sheer length of time the Conservatives had been in office. By the end of her premiership, there were few civil servants aged under 35 who had any real experience of working for anything other than Conservative ministers. That might have happened whichever party was in power. All these changes, and particularly the introduction of techniques of commercial management into Whitehall, raised questions about how far the traditional values of public service had been eroded. The Commons Public Accounts Committee highlighted these worries in a number of reports. Fears about the blurring of lines and the growth in ministerial patronage in appointments to the new quangos were among the reasons for the establishment in October 1994 of the Nolan inquiry into standards in public life as a standing body.

Her impact was much greater, if less satisfactory, on local government. Through well over a hundred separate pieces of legislation and strict Treasury controls over spending, her administrations emasculated local government, restricting both its powers and its ability to raise revenue. Both she and key allies such as Nicholas Ridley had essentially centralist instincts and little interest in local government. These measures were partly in order to force though changes in policy such as reducing subsidies on rented housing and encouraging the sale of council houses to their tenants, as well, later, to implement the contracting-out of services and compulsory competitive tendering. The continual battles to establish a balance between curbs on excess spending and local democracy and accountability reached their disastrous end in the community charge, or 'poll tax'. This contributed heavily to her unpopularity at the end of her premiership and was seen as vividly illustrating the flaws in her style of government. One of the earliest acts of the Major government was to bring forward proposals to replace the poll tax with a new hybrid council tax. This established a new record of introducing and abandoning a major new tax all within the lifetime of a single parliament. The overall result was to leave a messy structure of local government and its financing which provided neither adequate accountability nor fiscal responsibility. The shortcomings and contradictions of the Conservative approach continued under the Major government, with its confused attempt to reorganise the tiers of local government. Taken together, as I wrote in my *The Thatcher Era and its Legacy*, her premiership also posed questions about 'the role of the state. As she decried the power of government over economic decisions, she centralised power over local government and other bodies which had stood between Whitehall and the individual.'[12]

One of the main contradictions of the Thatcher years was between its rhetoric of individualism and its practice of strengthening the power of central government over wide areas of national life – from local government, through the health service, the funding of much of secondary and further education to a multitude of other White-hall-appointed quangos. Simon Jenkins concluded that: 'Like so many leaders before her, Thatcher found that the magnetism of power overwhelmed any ideological disposition to repel it. She shared with Lord Hailsham a familiar syndrome among British politicians: an aversion to "elective dictatorship" when out of office and a sudden conversion to its glorious subleties when in power.'[13] Her legacy of central control proved lasting and was taken further by the Major government, for instance, in its attempt to undermine the role of locally elected education authorities by encouraging opting-out by grant-maintained schools. This left an imbalance between the centre and the local which fuelled attacks on an unelected state and stimulated demands for a strengthening of local democracy. The Thatcher and Major governments argued that individuals were being given new rights as parents, patients and consumers of public services, but the framework and priorities were set in Whitehall.

The central test of Lady Thatcher's lasting influence is, however, whether she helped to stem Britain's decline, economically and politically. That is the yardstick which she consciously set herself. Her administrations broke the inflationary trends of the 1970s, for a time, but at an enormous cost in lost output and higher unemployment. Talk of an economic miracle, in which even the normally cautious John Major indulged when Chief Secretary to the Treasury at the height of the boom in spring 1988, was soon shown to be hubris, as shown by the severity of the recession of the early 1990s. The government's macroeconomic policies were often confused and changed several times during the 11 years, with the early focus on money supply targets being replaced by a more diverse, and often contradictory, approach. Far from the alleged certainties of monetarism, there was no consensus on macroeconomic policy at the end of the Thatcher era. The policy disagreements between Lady Thatcher and Nigel Lawson in the late 1980s about how far to pursue a fixed exchange rate target were merely a prelude to more intense battles within the Conservative Party during the 1990s over the European exchange rate mechanism (ERM) and the European single currency. The economic legacy of the Thatcher years left problems of high inflation and rising public spending and borrowing which it took the Major government several years to reverse. But low inflation was regained by the mid-1990s, a return to the intentions, if not necessarily the actions or the record, of the Thatcher era.

Moreover, if the Thatcher administration failed to achieve a significant reduction in the relative size of the public sector – and spending on social security continued to grow rapidly – it did succeed in checking the previous rate of growth in public spending. The lid was more or less kept on, even though there were usually lapses before elections which had to be paid for later. The end result of these mixed efforts to control spending and public borrowing was, however, to leave the tax burden broadly unchanged – though cuts in income tax, especially for the better-off, were financed by increases in indirect taxes and national insurance contributions.

If Lady Thatcher failed to find the Holy Grail of macroeconomic stability, she had more success with microeconomic changes. The British economy may have been battered when she left office but large parts were more efficient and competitive than before. The Thatcher governments slew some the dragons of the 1970s. The seemingly inexorable power of the trade unions, which had helped to bring down two governments in the 1970s, was checked and then broken. This was achieved through a combination of the manufacturing recession of the early 1980s, a succession of legislative measures limiting what unions could do and, most symbolically, the defeat of the miners' strike in 1984–85. This shift in the balance of power against the unions was sustained after she left office, and was reflected both in a continuing fall in trade union membership and in a drop in the number and impact of strikes. The far-reaching changes in the legislative framework – such as requiring ballots before strike action and for the election of union officers – were eventually accepted by Labour. Trade unions only really retained influence, and occasional power to disrupt, in monopoly public services. These changes were linked with attempts to stimulate productivity and competitiveness in industry. This was partly inadvertent through a very high exchange rate in the early 1980s which put intense competitive pressures on industry, and partly deliberate through a mixture of big tax cuts and deregulation. Management was given more authority and self-confidence and there was a revival of enterprise. There remains controversy as to how far the gains were limited to a small number of internationally competitive organisations and whether the long-standing bias in favour of finance rather than industry remained. But much of industry was in a stronger position at the end of the Thatcher era than at the start, even though the cost of substantial productivity gains was a high level of redundancies and higher long-term unemployment. The structure of the Labour market also changed, with a shift away from full-time jobs for men to part-time and casual employment, often more for women.

The government also shifted most of the state-owned industries and utilities and services into the private sector. The privatisation programme – covering telecommunications, British Steel, British Airways, Jaguar, Rover Group, the ports, gas, electricity, water and coal, as well as a host of smaller enterprises – transformed the landscape of industry. The management of these industries was able to become more commercial and less bureaucratic and there were gains to consumers in greater choice and, in some cases, lower relative prices. There was, and remains, controversy over those utilities which, though privatised, were still mainly monopolies, particularly water, electricity and gas, both over the behaviour of their directors in raising their own salaries and over their pricing policies. The regulators set up to monitor their behaviour were left by the original privatisation legislation in an anomalous position, neither fully independent, nor clearly accountable to anyone. The overall impact of privatisation has, nonetheless, both been substantial and lasting – as reflected in its imitation throughout the world, not least in the former communist regimes of central and eastern Europe. The Major government continued the programme in some of the trickiest areas such as the coal and railway industries, though it was deterred by the threat of a back-bench revolt from privatising the mail services of the Post Office.

Some of these economic changes might have happened anyway. In many other countries, ruled by centre-left as well as right-wing governments, there were pressures to hold down public spending and to cut taxes after the increases of the 1970s. There was also an awareness in many countries of the need to reduce the burden of regulations and to open competition. But in many respects the Thatcher governments were first in pioneering these changes. Moreover, without Lady Thatcher's personal drive, it is questionable whether any government would have been so single-minded in its confrontations with the unions and in pushing through these changes. At moments of decision, her determination to press ahead was often critical.

But did she, as she claimed in her memoirs, help create a less collectivist and more entrepreneurial society? In some economic ways, she did. There was a growth of enterprise and self-employment. Capital ownership was also spread, both via a sharp rise in owner-occupation from 53 per cent to more than 66 per cent of all households during her period in power, and via a trebling to more than a fifth in the number of adults with shares, largely as a result of the privatisation programme. The rise in share ownership looked impressive but was often quite shallow in quantity. The total percentage of shares held by individuals as opposed to financial institutions continued to decline. The proportion of people's assets held directly in shares was usually only a fraction of the value of their houses. The really significant build-up of financial capital was the growth of occupational and personal pensions and of various personal savings schemes such as PEPs and TESSAs. This was reflected in the large number of pages devoted to personal finance in the weekend newspapers. These helped to achieve Lady Thatcher's aim of expanding the group who had a stake in capital rather than just relying on wages. However, most probably regarded themselves as savers rather than as investors who followed the fate of individual companies closely. Moreover, the gains from home ownership looked more double-edged to some after the housing downturn of the early 1990s left many with negative equity.

The British public remained attached to the welfare state. It was, after all, Margaret Thatcher, at the height of her powers in October 1982, who said that the National Health Service was safe in her hands. This was in response to a leak of a quickly ditched official study looking into other ways of financing health provision, such as private insurance. Repeated opinion polls showed that the public was attached – indeed more attached as the 1980s went on – to the extension of state social and welfare services, even if it meant higher taxes. In practice the public remained hostile to tax increases when they happened. Free-market radicals made little progress in moving away from state provision of education and health and an extensive system of social security benefits. The changes in education and health were mainly in organisation to replicate market disciplines in the creation of more independent providers, rather than in making parents and patients financially responsible as individuals for buying these services. In social security, people were encouraged to reduce their reliance on state pensions and to take up personal and occupational pensions, as noted above. But, overall, the large rise in unemployment and the social dislocation of the 1980s, such as the sharp rise in the number of single mothers, meant that many more people were dependent on the state for social benefits than before 1979. The dependency culture had become more, rather than less, ingrained. Welfare reform remained the big unanswered political question and the Major government was in many ways more radical than the Thatcher administrations in its willingness to consider measures to limit entitlements. The price of encouraging a more competitive private sector was a more unequal and troubled society, not only via a partly associated rise in crime and social disorder but also through increased insecurity about employment and personal prospects. Many people, middle-class as well as working-class, were frightened by global competition.

The lasting impact of Lady Thatcher may have been least in the area where she enjoyed the most fame and highest repute, foreign affairs. She was the best known British prime minister in the rest of the world since Harold Macmillan, and probably since Winston Churchill, particularly following the determination and courage she displayed in leading Britain during the Falklands conflict of April to June 1982. That established her international, as well as domestic, reputation, but in retrospect it looks more like a sideshow, important for her and for national morale and pride but largely irrelevant for British foreign policy. Sir Edward Heath, her predecessor as Conservative leader, was responsible for the really decisive shift in post colonial foreign policy by presiding over Britain's entry into the European Community in 1973. By contrast, Lady Thatcher increasingly uneasily managed the relationship with both the rest of Europe and the United States. Her natural instincts were Atlanticist and her relations with other European leaders were often tense as she fought them on securing a better budget deal for Britain (what she called 'our money') and, later, over proposals for closer integration. But she signed up to the legislation creating a single European market, which involved a sizable extension of qualified majority voting on the council of ministers and increases in the powers of the European Parliament, however much she later claimed to have been misled by the Foreign Office.

Lady Thatcher succeeded in securing considerable personal influence in Washington as a result of her close personal relationship with

Ronald Reagan during the 1980s. But, despite the undoubted close working links on defence and intelligence matters between London and Washington, Lady Thatcher's personal friendship with President Reagan may have created illusions about a special relationship with the USA as an alternative to closer relations with the European Community. But after Ronald Reagan was succeeded as President by George Bush in January 1989, the relationship changed and the American administration – and particularly James Baker, the ultra-realist Secretary of State – viewed Britain as one among a number of important European powers. Lady Thatcher resented what she saw as a greater American emphasis on relations with Bonn. This surfaced in tensions over nuclear arms policy and, following the collapse of the Berlin Wall in November 1989, over the speed of the unification of Germany. Lady Thatcher was seen by many as dragging her feet, if not her handbag, over unification, isolating herself from her closest allies. This coincided with her increasing resentment over what she saw as the drive towards the creation of a European superstate, involving both monetary and political union, as proposed by Jacques Delors, then President of the European Commission, first signalled in her Bruges speech of September 1988. Differences over European policy contributed to the departures from her cabinet of both Nigel Lawson and Geoffrey Howe, which weakened her and then precipitated her downfall. She left a party increasingly divided over Europe, as was seen in the debilitating battles over the Maastricht agreement following the 1992 general election. After her party's defeat in 1997, she seemed to regard Europe as the main failure of her administration. Her international stature was not matched by her foreign policy legacy. She left more problems than permanent achievements in foreign policy.

Overall, Lady Thatcher may not have altered Britain's position in the world, changed British attitudes towards the welfare state, or reversed economic decline. No one could have done that. But she did help shake up British society, and particularly business. The time was ripe in the late 1970s for a shift in the balance of power between management and unions and for at least a brake to the growth of the public sector. She not only exploited favourable conditions but provided a focus and a lead at critical moments, as during the miners' strike. Her achievements on the ground may have been patchy and not matched her grand rhetoric. But her main policies were maintained and developed by her successors and she had a lasting impact on the terms of the political debate. Perhaps this was most striking in its influence not on her own party but on Labour. Tony Blair's crusade to create a 'new' Labour Party was partly a tribute to what her governments had done. His acceptance of privatisation, his refusal to reverse the trade union laws of the 1980s and his embrace of the free market did not mean he had become a Thatcherite, even though he startled some of his own supporters by his admiration for her direct style of leadership and her achievements. Rather, it reflected his belief that Labour, if it was to succeed, must move beyond the Thatcher agenda by recognising that many of the changes of the 1980s were irreversible and that Labour must try to improve upon them. In seeking to develop a post-Thatcherite agenda when Labour won power in 1997, Mr Blair revealed the lasting impact of Margaret Thatcher.

Notes

1. Simon Schama, *Citizens* (New York and London: Alfred A. Knopf, 1989), p. xiii.
2. Among recent discussions of the meaning of Thatcherism, there are useful summaries of the state of the debate in Steve Ludlam and Martin J. Smith (eds), *Contemporary British Conservatism* (Basingstoke: Macmillan, 1996) and, in a more jargon-prone way, in Brendan Evans and Andrew Taylor, *From Salisbury to Major: Continuity and Change in Conservative Politics* (Manchester: Manchester University Press, 1996).
3. Richard Rose and Philip Davies, *Inheritance in Public Policy: Change without Choice in Britain* (New Haven, Conn., and London: Yale University Press, 1994).
4. David Marsh and R. A. W. Rhodes (eds), *Implementing Thatcherite Policies: Audit of an Era* (Buckingham: Open University Press, 1992), pp. 186–7.
5. Bernard Donoughue, *Prime Minister: The Conduct of Policy under Harold Wilson and James Callaghan* (London: Jonathan Cape, 1987), p. 191.
6. Margaret Thatcher, *The Path to Power* (London: HarperCollins, 1995), pp. 604–6.
7. *The Times*, 30 November 1990, p. 14.
8. Robert Skidelsky, *The World after Communism* (Basingstoke: Macmillan, 1995), p. 128.
9. Andrew Gamble, *The Free Economy and the Strong State: The Politics of Thatcherism*, 2nd edn (Basingstoke: Macmillan, 1994), p. 213.

10. John Wakeham, 'Cabinet Government', in *Contemporary Record*, vol. 8, no. 3 (Winter 1994), p. 482.
11. Peter Riddell, in Dennis Kavanagh and Anthony Seldon (eds), *The Thatcher Effect* (Oxford: Oxford University Press, 1989), p. 113.
12. Peter Riddell, *The Thatcher Era and its Legacy* (Oxford: Blackwell, 1991), p. 245.
13. Simon Jenkins, *Accountable to None: The Tory Nationalisation of Britain* (London: Hamish Hamilton, 1995), p. 267.

5
The Prime Minister's Role in Foreign Affairs and Economic Policy: Creeping Bilateralism in Action?

John Barnes

One casualty of the debate over prime ministerial power has been detailed consideration of what the prime minister does and does not do. In this context Richard Rose observed that where the prime minister was 'most involved, British government is now inevitably weak: this is true of the management of the economy as well as foreign affairs'.[1] Since the economy's performance is central to the government's performance and chances of re-election, no prime minister can afford to neglect it. Involvement in foreign policy looks more a matter of choice, and a temptation to become involved which few postwar prime ministers have resisted. Although it yields photo opportunities and affords politicians the chance to appear in a non-partisan context, psephologists are agreed that foreign policy issues are not of great moment to the electorate.

Not surprisingly, therefore, Harold Wilson's political secretary regarded his involvement in the conduct of diplomacy as a distraction.[2] Her Conservative successor writes that in December 1973, a

> rush of other events prevented senior ministers from giving the coal crisis that attention which it needed. On Sunday 8 December, for example, the Prime Minister entertained the Italian Prime Minister...to dinner at Chequers. The meal was hardly over when Mr Heath flew to Sunningdale by helicopter to preside over the last stages of the conference on the future of Northern

Ireland. Three days later it was time for the State Visit of President Mobutu of Zaire. Two days after that the European summit began in Copenhagen. These were four major events, two of them (Sunningdale and Copenhagen) of outstanding importance. They were all the kind of diplomatic event which in normal times Mr Heath would much enjoy and at which he would perform very well. They all involved talks, travel, long meals, extensive briefing beforehand; yet none of them had anything to do with the crisis which was swallowing us up.[3]

To imply choice is to ignore the extent to which these two areas of policy, increasingly linked through Britain's membership of the European Union, necessarily swallow up prime ministerial time and energy, precluding the sustained involvement in other policy areas which alone can lead to results.[4] In his second term Wilson consciously left more to his foreign secretary, but in a 242-page account of his *Final Term* eight pages are devoted to the European Council at Paris (December 1974), ten to that at Dublin (March 1975) and four to the abortive Rome summit (December 1975).[5] Study of decision-making in these key areas shows that it depends increasingly on bilateral relationships between No. 10 and the ministers principally concerned. While formal obeisance is paid to collective responsibility, genuine collegiality is at a discount. The involvement of cabinet committees and the full cabinet is limited even in crisis situations, but recently there has been a disposition for the prime minister to look to an inner cabinet, to ensure perhaps that potential successors cannot distance themselves from his actions.

'The round of international summits makes a Prime Minister's life nowadays very different from what it was', Mrs Thatcher writes.[6] In fact her cabinet secretary estimated that, during the early years of her premiership, about a third of her time had been 'taken up not just with meetings to discuss foreign policy, but conducting diplomacy'[7] and a glance at Mrs Thatcher's diary from May to December 1983 amply justifies this estimate. The earlier part of the year had been largely concerned with election preparations, although she found time for talks in February with Vice-President Bush about the deployment of Cruise missiles and to urge a new initiative in the INF talks. Although she cancelled pre-summit talks with the President in May, she attended the G7 meeting in Williamsburg even though – some would say because – she was campaigning for re-election at the time. Subsequently she attended the Stuttgart Council in June, met with the Dutch Prime Minister and the German Chancellor in September, visited Canada and the United States at the end of September (during that visit she also held an emergency meeting in the Washington embassy on the Hong Kong currency crisis which the chancellor and Governor of the Bank of England attended), had a second bilateral discussion about Northern Ireland with Garret Fitzgerald and one of her regular summits with Chancellor Kohl in November, and attended the Athens Council in December.

Sir Anthony Parsons, who became her adviser on foreign policy in 1982, doubts if there was any qualitative change in the formulation of foreign policy under her, although he acknowledges that many would differ. He believes that the Argentinian invasion of the Falklands

> may well have convinced the Prime Minister that she must take a closer interest in foreign policy questions, particularly those which contained the seeds of sudden crisis, in order to avoid the government being taken by surprise in the future. Accordingly she strengthened her personal staff in No 10 in 1982, but not to the extent of creating an alternative source of foreign policy formulation on the lines of the National Security Council in Washington.

However, he suggests that basically 'the system has continued to function as before, with the Prime Minister playing a greater supervisory role over important areas of policy', and doubts 'whether this change of emphasis is much greater than was the case under previous prime ministers who have developed, or come into office with, predilections for foreign affairs.'[8] Parsons is right: the two big changes came much earlier. The first was in part due to summitry, as both Macmillan and Wilson suggest, but was largely the result of Britain's position as a nuclear power. The second is clearly linked to British membership of the European Community. The timing of the change is significant. Wilson noted that in the 68 months of his first term of office, he met the President of the United States nine times and in the 25 months between 1974 and 1976 six times. The 'trend of world affairs in the mid-seventies and its close connection with overriding world economic problems, together with a noticeable trend to meet-ings between heads of government on overseas affairs, has meant that prime ministers were drawn more and more into the higher reaches of diplomacy', he wrote in *The Governance of Britain*. 'Both bilaterally and in NATO and the EEC, the Prime Minister was more and more involved.'[9]

A more independent and central role for the prime minister first appeared in the area of nuclear interdependence. From the moment that Churchill on his own authority agreed to the American decision to drop the atomic bomb on Japan, to Wilson's rejection in December 1965 of suggestions that he should commit Polaris irrevocably to NATO for the duration of the North Atlantic Treaty, prime ministers often took the initiative in nuclear matters and frequently acted without consulting more than a handful of ministers. Thus it was Macmillan who made the first moves in 1957 which led to his Washington visit, agreement on the Declaration of Common Pur-pose, and eventual amendment of the McMahon legislation. The Defence Minister was clearly consulted and the move approved, so Macmillan tells us, by the foreign secretary and chancellor. The cabinet were told of the purpose of the visit after it had been arranged.[10] The decision to abandon Blue Streak in February 1960 was effectively taken by a small group, which met twice before Mac-millan himself put a recommendation to the Defence Committee, and it was Macmillan who secured the Skybolt agreement with Eisenhower in March 1960 which allowed the decision to be imple-mented.

Similarly the discussions which led to the British bid for Polaris at the Nassau Conference were prefaced by a meeting of the ministers and officials concerned with Skybolt, and the negotiations were con-ducted by the prime minister backed by his foreign secretary and defence secretary. Regular reports went to the cabinet in London. Although Macmillan claims to have incorporated the amendments they suggested to the agreement he reached with President Kennedy, in fact he ignored their largely cosmetic reformulation of the key phrase safeguarding British control, certain that he must stick to what had already been agreed.[11] The decision to retain the Nassau agreement and hence the nuclear deterrent, in contradiction of pledges to renegotiate it, was made by Wilson in consultation with his foreign and defence secretaries and conveyed to Washington by the foreign secretary personally. Subsequently it was 'endorsed' (Wilson's phrase) by the Defence Committee 'and later by the Cabinet'.[12] The decision to go ahead with the Chevaline project to modernise Polaris was taken by a small group so secret that it was not even given a cabinet committee designation and the same formula was employed by the Callaghan government a decade later when considering Polaris's replacement. The matter was regarded as 'too delicate to put before the Cabinet's Defence and Overseas Policy Committee'.[13]

Only the decision to build the H-bomb in 1954 was fully debated by cabinet. The Wilson government's decision to go ahead with Chevaline was reported to the cabinet in September 1974 in terms sufficiently anodyne as to marginalise the dissenters; and the Thatcher cabinet's endorsement of the decision to buy Trident came just hours before it was announced to Parliament in July 1980. As with Chevaline, the real decision on Trident was taken by a small body of senior ministers chaired by the prime minister. It was Attlee, despairing of the possibility of international control of nuclear weapons, who had set this pattern of decisions confined to ad hoc cabinet committees and even smaller bodies, but it was the increasingly close involvement with the Americans which meant that much was settled in high-level talks, frequently between prime minister and President.

But it is membership of the European Community that has most affected the prime minister's job, drawing him firmly into the conduct of international affairs and greatly increasing his influence to the point where a recent cabinet secretary could speak of the job developing 'to include the conduct of international relations'.[14] The prime minister now has a formidable programme of overseas work, which includes two European Councils each year, any specially called European Council or intergovernmental conference, an annual Economic Summit, a Commonwealth prime ministers' meeting every two years, and a whole series of bilateral meetings, many of them devoted to easing Britain's path in Europe. In addition, for a six-month period every six years (1977, 1981, 1986, 1992 and 1998) the prime minister takes on the rotating presidency of the European Council and Council of Ministers, an increasingly important and onerous task, although one which can be turned to domestic political advantage.

Although Heath delegated the detailed negotiation of Britain's entry into the EC, his summit with the French President in May 1971 was crucial to the outcome and was a precursor of what was to follow. He took an equally crucial decision when deciding that the handling of European business should not be left to the Foreign Office or given to a ministry for Europe. Instead it was to be co-ordinated by the newly created European unit in the Cabinet Office. In retrospect it is clear that even if the prime minister did not wish to be the principal actor in Britain's European relationships, the machinery makes it almost inevitable that he should play that role. Margaret Thatcher demonstrated what was necessary to obtain success in EC affairs, although her tactics were controversial and some observers felt that she did not always know when she had won. But whatever the role of Carrington, Howe and on occasion others (including the senior British Commissioner) in paving her way, only the prime minister could conduct business at the summit, whether it was to obtain a permanent settlement of Britain's budgetary problem, engineer revisions to the Common Agricultural Policy (CAP) or negotiate the Single European Act. Similarly the negotiation of the intergovernmental pillars to Maastricht and the securing of opt-outs on the Social Chapter and single currency depended on John Major's conduct of the final negotiations in the European Council. Table 5.1 illustrates the possible relationships between Prime Minister and Foreign Secretary.

From the mid-1950s the norm has been either prime ministerial dominance or a close partnership between the two. If the foreign

Table 5.1   Relationship between Prime Minister and Foreign Secretary

	PM dominant	Foreign Secretary dominant	Partners
Harmonious relations	Eden/Lloyd	Bevin/Attlee	Macmillan/Home
	Wilson/Stewart	Callaghan/Wilson	Heath/Home
	Thatcher/Major	Hurd/Major	Owen/Callaghan
			Carrington/ Thatcher
Difficult relations	Attlee/Morrison [PM feels able to sack, e.g., Thatcher/Pym]		**Relationship under strain:** Eden/Churchill Wilson/Brown

secretary dominates the scene or seems to be the senior partner, that is invariably because the prime minister chooses to handle matters in this way. As Henderson sapiently observes

> Because of the crucial nature of foreign policy decisions and the way the conduct of such policy is bound to attract the limelight, with inevitable domestic consequences, some degree of friction is inherent in the relationship...The first...that I was able to observe directly for any length of time was that between Attlee and Bevin...and it was evident to me, as it was to every witness, that the avoidance of strife then depended not upon any clear-cut constitutional division of authority, but upon the forbearance and unobtrusiveness of the Prime Minister. Coming now to the present day [Henderson confided to his diary in December 1979] it did not require any profound perception of character to realise that, self-effacement not being Mrs Thatcher's long suit, any more than disregard of his proper responsibilities was Carrington's, tensions must be expected.[15]

Nevertheless there was a rapport which enabled Carrington, in a series of private conversations, to persuade Mrs Thatcher to alter her approach to the internal settlement in Rhodesia and which enabled her, with the exception of one helpful intervention, to leave the handling of the Lancaster House conference to him. In part, no doubt, it was because she recognised that he was much more than a mouthpiece for Foreign Office views.[16] This rapport simply did not exist between Mrs Thatcher and Carrington's successor, Francis Pym. During the Falklands crisis, when in the United States (as he confessed to the British ambassador), he was not adept at reading the mood in London and he subsequently clashed with Mrs Thatcher about their approach to Britain's continuing problem over the European budget. But it was less the clashes than a total absence of any affinity that brought about his dismissal. 'There is nothing so difficult or delicate in the management of a government as the relations between the Prime Minister and the Foreign Secretary', Macmillan concluded. 'Both sides of Downing Street must work in complete harmony if confusion and something worse are to be avoided.' It was on the grounds that the foreign secretary must be within walking distance of No. 10 and that the two should meet frequently and quite informally 'almost every day' that he refused to agree to proposals to move the Foreign Office.[17] 'There was hardly a day when I was not in touch with him', Lloyd recalled. 'If I was overseas by telegram; if the House was in recess by telephone; more usually by seeing him at No 10.'[18] Home 'had an arrangement by which we met twice a week, for a quarter of an hour, twenty minutes. Privately, off-the-record so to speak, and without officials. We reviewed the scene every third day, and so we knew exactly how we were thinking on the issues of the time.'[19] Howe was later to write with feeling about the way in which his frequent absences abroad prevented him, although he saw Mrs Thatcher in cabinet and committees, from 'keep[ing] up even the weekly timetable that was our aim'.[20]

Parsons was wrong to think that there has been no change at all in the prime minister's role. Macmillan blamed

> this flying business...Nowadays there is no particular difficulty about having a meeting almost anywhere in the world at the drop of a hat. So you get pressures to have them. And of course, quite a number of countries – it isn't only Russia – choose to do the really important business at the summit. So the Prime Minister tends to get more and more caught up in meetings, in travelling and receiving visitors.[21]

Owen points to the inevitable consequence:

> In the olden days you could have a Foreign Secretary who had an independent power base from the Prime Minister and who held different views. But in the last 20 years that's become progressively harder to imagine...heads of government are more and more being sucked into international affairs, they meet more frequently, they are involved in more detail, you can't shut the Prime Minister out any more. So the Foreign Secretary and the Prime Minister have got to have very similar views if the foreign policy of this country is to be properly pursued.[22]

Since Attlee few prime ministers have sought to avoid involvement. Some, notably Eden, Macmillan and, at times, Wilson, have almost reduced their foreign secretaries to the role of loyal executant of policies decided elsewhere. In Eden's case, this was scarcely surprising since it was his own field and he brought to it the experience of more than a decade as foreign secretary. Macmillan had always fancied himself in the job and enjoyed his brief tenure in King Charles Street. 'Foreign affairs was his vocation, economics his hobby', Maudling said. Stewart, who twice served Wilson as foreign secretary, read Macmillan's memoirs and 'felt glad that I had not been required to work with a Prime Minister so firmly resolved to take foreign affairs into his own hands'. Nevertheless he thought it axiomatic that, while the foreign secretary conducted foreign policy and took the lead in cabinet discussion of it, he could not make it by himself. Much of his time was spent in discussion with the prime minister, the Minister of Defence (with whom he met weekly) and the Chancellor. Further, on 'the great issues of power, defence, and international dispute', only heads of government could deal with them, even though 'the "summit conferences" to which they give rise are unwelcome to Foreign Ministers, and still more unwelcome to diplomats'.[23] Where Stewart wished to take a line of his own, most notably to renew Britain's application to join the EEC, Wilson refused to back his criticisms of de Gaulle or to allow him to circulate a paper to the cabinet.[24]

There is, of course, much more going on in the field of foreign affairs than the prime minister can hope to master, hence the need for mutual trust of the kind that Wilson and Callaghan clearly, if somewhat surprisingly, established in 1974–6. One way of handling the load is to split it as Heath and Home did in 1970–4. In effect Heath took control of the European scene (with Rippon handling the detail under his broad supervision) while Home handled the rest of the world. There was no significant divergence of view between them (the war between Indian and Pakistan is a possible exception), although Home was always more sensitive to the needs of the Atlantic alliance and the Commonwealth than Heath, the most genuinely Eurocentric of all postwar prime ministers.[25] But, even on issues which the prime minister regards as central to his concerns, the work simply cannot be done without full use of the Foreign Office. Even when No. 10 was taking the lead in EC matters, Carrington spent some four-fifths of his time on them, while his deputy, Sir Ian Gilmour, has detailed the trips he made to all the European capitals as part of the build-up to the Luxembourg summit.

Callaghan was the last foreign secretary before Hurd to have the predominant role in the partnership. In part, this was because Wilson was ageing, ill and reluctant to interfere. While he chaired the cabinet committee supervising the renegotiation of Britain's terms of entry into the EC, the real work was done by a subcommittee under Callaghan, and Wilson's part in the negotiations was confined to EC summits.[26] In retrospect it is clear that Wilson skilfully held the line at home until certain that the terms obtained were sufficiently good to command a majority in the cabinet. He then relied upon 'an agreement to differ' during the referendum to hold government and party together. Roy Jenkins thought renegotiation a 'smoke screen under which both Wilson and Callaghan could make their second switch of position on Europe'.[27] However, as an observer of government he might have made a rather different point – the extent to which a foreign secretary has to rely on the prime minister to guard his back and see his policies through Cabinet. Working with Mrs Thatcher, Hurd was of necessity the junior partner in European matters, although in close alliance with Major, then Chancellor, he secured Britain's entry into the Exchange Rate Mechanism and came to operate 'on the basis that both sides of Downing Street had a veto: the Prime Minister could block a decision by the Foreign Secretary but equally if the Prime Minister wanted something done by the Foreign Secretary, he could say "no"'.[28] As her third foreign secretary in a matter of months, he knew that to a large extent he was fireproof. Mrs Thatcher also relied a good deal on his expertise in Middle Eastern affairs. Major's deference to Hurd in the earlier stages of his prime ministership evolved into something approximating partnership, not least when it came to the negotiations which led to the Maastricht Treaty. If Major left much to his foreign secretary, it did not preclude him from initiatives like the proffer of safe havens for the Kurds. Relationships do change and develop; varying over time and from issue to issue, they should never be seen as static. Even formerly close partners – Mrs Thatcher and Howe are an obvious example – can fall out. The relationship between Hurd and Major confirms that prime ministers, even if they define the parameters within which it takes place, cannot prevent themselves from being drawn in. From the start of the Gulf War relationships with the other states involved were necessarily handled in No. 10, as Charles Powell has made clear. The Kuwait crisis and Gulf War 'occupied [the Prime

Minister's] waking hours almost solidly from the day he walked into Number Ten in November [1990] until well into the following year'.[29]

Although the pattern is similar to that identified by Hill in the late 1930s, when under Chamberlain the initiative and much of the content of policy lay in the hands of a 'foreign policy executive' consisting of the prime minister and foreign secretary, which operated within a framework formally constituted by the cabinet and Foreign Policy Committee,[30] there are differences. After 1945 Attlee left Bevin to operate in a loose co-ordinating role in overseas matters and no foreign policy committee came into existence before 1963. The Defence Committee, meeting infrequently with military matters uppermost, was no surrogate. Macmillan usually involved the Defence Secretary in a troika of decision-makers, sometimes by exchange of minutes, sometimes in meetings, for example when discussing how the prime minister should respond to American suggestions for action in Syria in 1957 or in Laos at the time of the second Geneva Conference.[31] There are similarities with the way in which Wilson, during the 1967 Middle East crisis, 'was in the closest touch with the Foreign Secretary, the Defence Secretary, the Chiefs of Staff and all our advisers, meeting either in ad hoc meetings at any time of the day or night, or more formally in the Defence Committee.'[32] Given the absence before 1963 of any forum short of the cabinet 'where ideas, issues and strategies could be reviewed',[33] prime ministers often turned to small groups to act, or at least prepare the way for a cabinet decision. The decision to commit troops to the Western European Union (WEU) was effectively taken by a small group of ministers at an evening meeting during the London Conference in September 1954, for example, and later in the decade Macmillan showed himself adept at using small groups to prepare the way for subsequent cabinet discussion – 'rolling the pitch' as it was jocularly described. Few prime ministers were as ready to 'bounce' the cabinet as Churchill was in his search for *détente*. The cabinet crisis in July 1954 was caused by his efforts to secure a personal summit with the Soviet leadership in July 1954: threats of resignation on the part of two senior ministers, counterbalanced by thoughts that the prime minister might appeal to the country over the heads of his colleagues, indicates why they chose not to do so. Eden was scrupulous in involving the cabinet in all the major decisions taken during the Suez crisis (even if they were not perfectly informed about the extent to which collusion with the Israelis had gone). Fourteen key decisions can be identified, nine of them taken in full cabinet. Decisions confined to the Egypt Committee were purely military and only the timing of the decision to go to the Security Council was taken by the prime minister and foreign secretary acting alone.[34] However, the Egypt Committee was also used by Eden as a way of predigesting decisions which were going to cabinet and, informally, as the only body to which the details of collusion were reported.

The cabinet remained an important forum for foreign policy decisions well into the 1960s, although the initiative lay with a foreign policy executive of varying composition centring on the prime minister. What then of the Defence and Overseas Policy Committee (OPD)? Its creation had been announced publicly in 1963 as a corollary of Macmillan's integration of the service ministries into a Ministry of Defence and was certainly responsible for major questions of defence policy.[35] Wilson gave the impression to Crossman among others that it was the cabinet's 'inner club', but in practice its detailed consideration of particular items precluded broad discussion of issues like 'east of Suez'. Even when such a discussion did take place, for example on 'a new position paper' in June 1967, Crossman noted the appalling quality of the documents submitted as the basis for their discussion.[36] He also became aware that when he secured decisions from OPD which the Prime Minister did not like, the latter quietly engineered their reversal and that much was simply fixed by the prime minister and Defence Secretary. In retrospect it is clear, as Crossman and others suspected, that prior commitments had been given by Wilson and his foreign secretaries in Washington.

Although the Committee continued to meet under successive governments to take a number of detailed decisions (it agreed, for example, the negotiating position on the Falklands in 1977 and the deployment of forces later that year when it looked as if Argentina might resort to force, meeting three times in November 1977)[37] it was not allowed near nuclear decisions and issues like Rhodesia were handled elsewhere in the committee structure. There is no evidence to suggest that it was anything other than a purely reactive body, in general confirming the line already agreed by its senior members. By Howe's time it met only rarely.[38] While it met more often in the

1990s, at least on matters related to the development of the EC (now the European Union, EU), this is less the result of a change in prime ministerial style than a reflection of the increased impact of the Community on the domestic agenda. The detail is for the Cabinet Committee on European Questions (EQ). John Major left the chair of that committee to the foreign secretary, but he regarded European policy as domestic policy and it took up a sizeable part of his week.[39]

While it would be wrong to ignore the part played by EQ or the Prime Minister's need, on so disputatious an issue, to take issues to cabinet and go round the cabinet table – most notably on the British negotiating position at Maastricht and on the White Paper setting out Britain's approach to the 1996 intergovernmental conference – thus ensuring that collective responsibility will hold, the plain truth is that the more senior ministers and in particular the prime minister, foreign secretary and chancellor are taking the key decisions on 'trade-offs' and securing the endorsement of their colleagues. Under Major, however, an inner cabinet can be discerned in which Heseltine and Clarke were involved, whatever their formal posts, together with the chancellor and foreign secretary. Later on, Howard was added to the group. But no one doubts that on the European agenda, the prime minister's role is central. This suggests that the initiative in international affairs is no longer solely with the prime minister, foreign secretary and defence secretary, although that pattern, which obtained until the 1970s, can still be detected in the handling of the Bosnian crisis and in most British dealings with the United States. However, governments cannot ignore the extent to which the economy has become part of a global economy. The chancellor himself is an actor in the international field, consulting with and on occasion being stimulated by the prime minister.[40] With Britain's membership of the European Community, not least because she is a large-scale net contributor, a new troika was bound to emerge with the chancellor heavily involved. The *démarche* made by Howe and Lawson before the Madrid Council is usually recalled because they were trying to force the prime minister's hand on membership of the Exchange Rate Mechanism. More significant for this chapter is Howe's complaint that Mrs Thatcher, unusually, had failed to involve the two of them in the preparations for a European Council.

If prime ministers retained some choice about involvement in foreign affairs before summit diplomacy became commonplace, none could escape involvement in the work of the Treasury. Nor would they have been wise to try. Even before the chancellor was vested with responsibility for managing the economy, no one but the prime minister had 'such influence, or starting point for influence in the whole field of policy': the Treasury has, Lawson notes, 'a finger in pretty well every pie that the Government bakes.'[41] Uniquely powerful amongst the world's finance ministers, the chancellor need consult only the prime minister before taking action on tax and interest rates and the initiative in economic matters is almost invariably in his hands. Even the prime minister may find it difficult to control so powerful a figure. Economic success may make him 'unassailable'. However, chancellors have few friends and the economic switchback is such that 'few Chancellors of the Exchequer have left office with their reputations enhanced.'[42] They are conscious therefore of their need for prime ministerial backing. Together they are a match for almost any cabinet combination.

'It was not my intention when I became Prime Minister to over-involve myself in economic policy', Callaghan recalled, but alas for his intentions, 'I found, as I suppose other Prime Ministers have done, that economic problems obtruded at every street corner...'[43] No prime minister since the war has been able to escape considerable involvement in economic affairs. Even Home, who memorably confessed to his lack of economic expertise and left the chair of his Economic Policy Committee to his chancellor, talked with him regularly. His first act as prime minister was to ask him whether there was a case for an economic 'squeeze'.[44] Despite an evident lack of touch in economic matters, Attlee could not avoid taking the chair of the Economic Policy Committee when it was created in 1947. Nor did Churchill fail to see his chancellor daily, although, doubtful of his understanding of modern economics, he gave him an increasingly free rein. Despite a background confined to international affairs, Eden was more active than his immediate predecessors in proffering advice to his chancellors and became actively involved in the search for wage and price restraint in 1956. Macmillan, with more economic expertise, constantly chivvied his chancellors, as Richard Lamb records.[45]

During his first term, Wilson played his chancellor and first secretary against one another, successfully dividing and ruling. After devaluation he found himself forced to live with a man whom he knew to be after his job. Miraculously their relationship, although strained between April and November 1968, survived.[46] In his second term, more relaxed, Wilson gave Healey what amounted to a free hand and firm backing, although prompted otherwise on occasion by his Policy Unit and by the Chancellor of the Duchy, Harold Lever, whom he had lodged in No 10 because of his economic expertise. Healey recalls with satisfaction how Lever became 'something of a double agent, helping me as much as the Prime Minister.'[47] Callaghan was equally supportive of his chancellor, although more involved. To him goes the credit for the development in 1977 of the 'informal "Seminar" to discuss interest rates and exchange rates, on which prime ministers and chancellors so often disagree.'[48] It consisted of prime minister, chancellor, the Governor of the Bank of England, Lever in his personal capacity and a handful of officials. It was an innovation which Mrs Thatcher continued in a somewhat different guise, and it was at a meeting attended by the foreign secretary, the Trade Secretary, as well as the chancellor, Governor, Nigel Lawson and some key officials, that it was decided to abolish exchange controls.[49]

Perhaps the most dominant prime minister of all in economic matters was Edward Heath, a verdict which may surprise those who saw Mrs Thatcher at close quarters. But, as Heath's biographer notes, Barber 'was never able to stand up to Heath . . . Heath already had a poor opinion of the Treasury, which he suspected of a lack of enthusiasm for Europe . . . it was increasingly marginalised, as Heath sought more congenial economic advice elsewhere.'[50] The 1972 budget was 'not in reality the Chancellor's Budget, but the Prime Minister's', framed in opposition to the Treasury as a deliberately European policy and derived in large part from a small group comprising members of the cabinet office and the CPRS (Central Policy Review Staff) led by the Head of the Civil Service.[51]

Mrs Thatcher worked closely with both Howe and, initially, Lawson. 'My regular pattern of contact with the Prime Minister comprised a weekly "bilateral" (this was part of the bureaucratic routine for senior colleagues, with agenda items and sometimes papers flagged up in advance) and two or three brief informal chats a week,' Howe recalls, and he attended the Thursday 'breakfast group' also, which predigested the cabinet agenda. There would also be a Sunday evening chat and drink with the prime minister every two to three weeks.[52] Lawson notes the prime minister's fondness for seminars in the context of three on monetary policy held in the autumn of 1980, and he writes of her 'intense, if spasmodic, attention to Treasury detail' which he saw as advantageous to the Treasury.[53] Although less close than Howe, he saw the prime minister each week. Every alteration in interest rates also required a meeting with her, usually with the Governor of the Bank of England present as well. On two occasions in 1986 she prevented Lawson from raising the rate and on a further occasion in May 1989 insisted on a cut, but for the most part was content to welcome any cut in interest rates and to acquiesce grudgingly in decisions to raise them. Comparison of their memoirs suggests that Howe kept the prime minister more closely informed on the progress of budget-making than Lawson, although the latter invariably took her into his confidence about the broad shape of his thinking late in January each year and subsequently submitted two or three minutes detailing alterations to the Medium Term Financial Strategy, tax changes and reform proposals. It is evident also that the final draft of the budget speech was usually cleared with No. 10. There were also other meetings *à deux* or with small groups of ministers where decisions were reached, the most notable of these being that on 13 November 1985, when Mrs Thatcher in true Lincolnian style rejected British membership of the ERM (although the meeting was six to two in favour), and the meetings between the prime minister, chancellor and foreign secretary on the same subject prior to the Madrid Council in June 1989, which Mrs Thatcher describes as 'an ambush'.[54]

Increasingly Mrs Thatcher relied on advice in such matters from two hard-line monetarists, the head of her Policy Unit, Professor Brian Griffiths and Professor Alan Walters, who had been recruited to Downing Street in 1980 and quickly won her confidence in the run-up to the 1981 budget. Although he took up an American academic post in 1984, he continued to advise her informally. His formal return to No 10. in May 1989 coincided with growing public awareness that policy towards sterling was a matter of dispute between No. 10 and No. 11. Mrs Thatcher's belief that the market could not be bucked was so clearly at odds with the chancellor's wish to use the exchange rate to discipline inflation that, even without their increasingly public row over the ERM, it could well have led Lawson to resign much earlier. The actual occasion in October 1989 was the impossibility, as Lawson saw it, of conveying to the markets an agreed policy line so long as Walters was at No. 10. Lawson wrote to Mrs Thatcher, 'the successful conduct of economic policy is possible only if there is, and is seen to be, full agreement between the Prime Minister and the Chancellor.'[55] and that no longer obtained.

To lose one chancellor might be taken as misfortune, to lose two in short measure would rightly be seen as bad management. Inevitably the resignation or dismissal of a chancellor strengthens the hand of his successor: if he is not given a fair run, the prime minister would be confessing to a serious error of selection on his or her part. Lawson's successor, John Major, was able to use his much stronger position in regard to No. 10 not only to persuade the prime minister to give her consent to entry to the ERM in June 1990 but to secure her endorsement of an alternative route to monetary union, the so-called 'hard ecu plan'. Both moves were accomplished without in any way prejudicing Major's position as Mrs Thatcher's favoured successor.

Prime ministers have an inbuilt tendency to interfere in interest rate policy and political considerations ensure that their bias is to see them lower. It was no doubt this which prompted Kenneth Clarke to move to a situation where the minutes of his discussions with the Governor of the Bank of England became public after a few weeks' delay. Although the prime minister knew what line the chancellor would take in the discussion, nothing short of giving the job to an independent central bank could have been better calculated to take undue pressure from No. 10 out of the equation. Kenneth Clarke was self-evidently his own man at the Treasury, resisting, for example, pressures from No. 10 to abandon VAT on fuel. In general his relationship with the prime minister was easy. There was genuine goodwill between them, which proved one of the government's strengths in troubled times, not least the months when Clarke himself was widely seen as Major's inevitable successor. Differing, so it is believed, on the likelihood of early British membership of a single currency, they agreed a compromise, promising a referendum should the government decide to join it.

This confirms Lawson's view that there are two main checks on the power of the prime minister, the first being the damaging effect of a resignation, the effect being cumulative. More important to the day-to-day operation of government is what he describes as a mutual blackmail system...By that I mean that if a Minister wishes to do something within his own field which the Prime Minister profoundly disapproves of, then the Prime Minister has a blackball which he or she can cast...Equally, however, unless the Minister concerned is absolutely spineless...then if the Prime Minister wants something done in a particular area, and the Minister responsible disagrees with it, then it will not happen...he has a blackball too.[56]

In contrast to the prime minister's relationship with the foreign secretary post-war, his relationship with the chancellor suggests continuity rather than change. While they cannot escape the need to work hand in glove, the relationship will vary with the personalities involved and, even with the same incumbents, may change over time. Lawson's relationship with Margaret Thatcher, for example, began in mutual confidence to the point where he was not even disposed to take her ERM veto to cabinet or resign. It was more than four years (September 1987) before it began to deteriorate. Many variables are involved, not least personal chemistry, their relative economic expertise and their relative political standing. Wyn Grant identified four possible relationships (see Table 5.2). However, he ignored the possibility of a close working relationship amounting to partnership. The Thatcher/Howe tandem and, to a lesser extent, the Macmillan/Maudling relationship suggest that such a partnership can exist.

The Economic Policy Committee, more recently known as Economic Affairs (EA) and, under John Major's chairmanship, as Economic and

Table 5.2   Relationship between Prime Minister and Chancellor

	Chancellor a major politician	Chancellor lacks independent base
Harmonious relations	Chancellor largely autonomous with PM's support, e.g. Healey, Clarke	Chancellor executes PM's policy, e.g. Amory, Lamont
Difficult relationship	Relationship under strain with regular clashes, e.g. Lawson	PM feels able to sack after losing confidence, e.g. Lloyd

Domestic Policy (EDP), has, like the Overseas and Defence Committee, been attributed a rather larger role in the formation of policy than it actually enjoys. Mrs Thatcher's memoirs, when taken together with those of Howe and Lawson, make it clear that in the conduct of macroeconomic policy she had no need to rely on EA. Indeed there are very few mentions of the committee in Lawson's very full *View from No. 11*. The cabinet was in practice marginally more important since the control total and final public expenditure packages were always discussed there. Bilateral discussions between the Chief Secretary and the spending ministers and on occasion appeals to the 'Star Chamber', a special cabinet committee set up to hear them, had usually settled its content, but in 1980, 'after three exceptionally long discussions', Mrs Thatcher and Howe suffered a cabinet defeat over the proposed cuts and the chancellor had to retrieve the position by increasing national insurance payments.[57] After the dismay expressed when the cabinet was faced at the last moment with the exceptionally controversial (although ultimately successful) 1981 budget, Howe arranged with Mrs Thatcher for there to be some discussion of economic policy not only when the public expenditure control total was settled in July, but also some weeks in advance of the budget.[58] However, a more recent chancellor observed that the discussion is 'rather general and not particularly useful', not least perhaps because the chancellor does not take an active part.[59]

The conduct of economic policy remains very much a matter for prime minister and chancellor, with the Economic Policy Committee being used to take decisions on individual questions like the future of Westland, the abolition of the price commission, energy pricing or the decision not to sell Rover to an American buyer. That is not to minimise the committee's importance, simply to say in contradiction of Burch that this not the way in which 'economic policy has effectively been hived off from the scrutiny of the whole Cabinet.'[60] Indeed it would be wrong to suppose that the way in which macroeconomic policy was conducted in Mrs Thatcher's governments differed in any major respect from the way it was conducted by her predecessors and immediate successor. There were fewer sterling crises, however, and it was at times of crisis that, under earlier prime ministers, cabinets became involved in genuine policy discussions, for example in 1957 and 1966. It is worth observing, however, that the packages to deal with successive crises were rarely the product of such discussion.

In July 1965 Wilson, Brown, Callaghan and Jay settled the main features of the necessary package, the details were worked out by officials and the proposals discussed with the ministers involved in the cuts at a meeting in No. 10 on 26 July, with Wilson, Brown and Callaghan settling the final details that night. Both the Americans and the press had already been briefed by the time the cabinet received the package that they were to discuss the next morning, 27 July. 'What happened then was as near to central dictatorship as one is likely to get in a British Cabinet . . . we were not given time either to discuss the underlying strategy or even to consider the document as a whole.'[61] There was more room for cabinet discussion in 1966, since the need for a package was broken to the cabinet on 14 July, devaluation discussed and rejected on the 19th and the package agreed on the 20th. But the results were much the same. 'The Treasury papers before us, making precise proposals and not offering alternatives, had only been in ministers' hands about thirty hours. This was a mockery of sensible government. . . .'[62]

Increasingly, if there was collective discussion, it took place in committee, cabinet ratifying the result. The 1967 devaluation discussions were confined to an informal airing of the issues at the Steering Committee on Economic Policy on 8 November, two meetings between Wilson, Brown and Callaghan, the decision to go ahead which was taken by Wilson and Callaghan late on the 13th, ratified and taken forward by the 'Tuesday Club' (prime minister, chancellor, Foreign Secretary, First Secretary, Commonwealth Secretary, Defence Secretary and President of the Board of Trade) at two meetings on the 14th and 15th, whose main purpose was to settle details of the accompanying economic package. The cabinet, faced with the decision and package on 16 November, would have found it difficult to do other than 'confirm' the decision already reached. The creation of the Steering Committee on Economic Policy in September 1966 had been meant to allow the Wilson government to predigest vital economic matters, but it was not allowed to discuss devaluation, even informally, until 8 November 1967, more than a year after it was formed, and did not meet again until the decision had been taken, when its role was to consider Callaghan's post-devaluation statement. The evidence suggests that Heath, too, used his economic policy committee to prepare for departures from previous policies over industrial intervention and prices and incomes control, although the key decisions were always ratified by cabinet. The Labour governments of 1974–9 certainly used the Ministerial Committee on Economic Strategy in this way, although not to any great extent until the European issue was off the agenda.[63] Wilson also used a smaller committee, MISC 91, to pave the way for an incomes policy in June 1975, as well as to monitor its implementation.[64] Donoughue credits the Cabinet Secretary, Sir John Hunt, with the decision to replace both these committees and the parallel official committee (PIO) with 'a single strategic economic Cabinet Committee which would cover the whole broad economic field and would be serviced by various committees concentrating on particular micro areas of policy'.[65] Clearly it was used by Callaghan and his chancellor in exactly the same way as the earlier committees, so much so that Healey was discommoded when it was agreed in cabinet on 18 November 1976 that continued discussion of the IMF terms would not take place there but at the full cabinet.[66] Callaghan's use of the cabinet for a genuine consideration of the alternatives to a settlement with the IMF has attracted much attention. However, not only is it very much the exception to the general pattern, but in fact it confirms that if prime minister and chancellor stick together, they usually win. When Callaghan came down in favour of his chancellor, a majority of the cabinet was against them. They had no need to threaten resignation. Thoughts of press stories that they had been overruled were sufficient to bring the cabinet into line.

In reflecting on 'Cabinet Government in the Thatcher Years',[67] Lawson emphasised that he did not see fiscal and monetary policy as matters for collective decision-making and, in a later seminar on Labour cabinets, Edmund Dell agreed. Indeed it became part of his ongoing argument that collective responsibility is a myth and should be abolished: 'Read Lady Thatcher's account of her dealings with Howe and Lawson over joining the ERM. Not a whiff of collective responsibility in it. The three of them were going to take the decision. When we did join the ERM in October 1990 it was not a Cabinet decision.'[68] During the Thatcher years, the chancellor and prime minister handled runs on sterling without any consultation of colleagues,[69] although there was discussion within the framework of the G7. Nor did the cabinet choose to debate Major's strategy when, in the summer of 1992 and again in the autumn, he outlined the considerations that had led the chancellor and himself to dismiss devaluation and seek a support package for the pound. On 'Black Wednesday', when Britain was forced out of the ERM, the decisions were taken by the prime minister and chancellor in consultation with a group consisting of Clarke, Hurd, Heseltine and the Chief Whip. It had been convened to discuss contingency plans for the aftermath of the French referendum, but the decision to involve them was deliberate. The prime minister wished to ensure that his senior colleagues were fully involved – 'dipping their hands in the blood', as Clarke put it – but the nexus between prime minister and chancellor remained the heart of the meeting.

Prime ministers have sought from time to time to enhance both their capacity and their role in the making of economic policy. Where Attlee was content to rely on Douglas Jay and did not replace him in No. 10 when he entered parliament, Churchill incorporated Lord Cherwell in the Downing Street set-up and asked him to recreate the Statistical Section that had served him during the 1939–45 war. However, this arrangement petered out after a couple of years. Neither Eden nor Macmillan looked beyond their private office for inside advice, although the latter was always ready to canvass the Treasury for comment and reply to what amounted to a running critique by Sir Roy Harrod of its conduct of affairs. Wilson lodged the Oxford economist Thomas Balogh, a close friend, and the economist Michael Stewart (not to be confused with the Foreign Secretary) in the Cabinet Office to provide him with economic advice and, when the civil service appeared to get in the way of constructive communication, he then brought Balogh into No. 10. Briefly he also took charge of the Department of Economic Affairs himself in 1967 with Peter Shore working to him. However, the Department was abolished in 1969. Heath appointed Brian Reading, who had advised him in opposition, to the Cabinet Office, but the creation of the CPRS and the existence of the Civil Service Department under a former Permanent Secretary to the Treasury gave him more potent alternative sources of advice. When he returned to office in 1974, Wilson could rely on his new creation, the Policy Unit, which contained economists of the stamp of Gavyn Davies. Callaghan also looked to the CPRS and eventually made its head, Sir Kenneth Berrill, Chief Economic Adviser. Both he and his predecessor also looked to Harold Lever for an input into economic policy and they were rarely disappointed. Initially Mrs Thatcher sharply reduced the staff and inevitably the scope of the

No. 10 Policy Unit, but in 1980, as we have seen, she added Alan Walters to the No. 10 strength. When she expanded the Policy Unit after the abolition of the CPRS in 1983, she had other sources of economic advice to draw on, most notably Brian Griffiths of the LSE and City University, who was its head from 1985 to 1990. Major took Judith Chaplin with him from the Treasury to No. 10, but his choice of Sarah Hogg to head his Policy Unit was more significant. She was an outstanding economic correspondent. However, with the exception of the set-up under Heath and, more questionably, Mrs Thatcher's arrangements, the prime minister has rarely been in a position to make a sustained and effective challenge to the Treasury.

An increase in prime ministerial involvement does not automatically amount to an increase in prime ministerial power. Rose's salutary reminder about the degree of international interdependence in economic and foreign affairs can be reinforced by reference to the interdependencies which exist between the prime minister and his most senior ministers. The former holds high cards, and his place in the European Council may well allow him to run the most significant part of the international agenda. But the time given to that part of his job may well mean that he exercises less control over prioritisation in domestic policy. One of the more significant innovations made by the Major government, the creation of a cabinet committee (EDX) chaired by the chancellor to steer the bilaterals and settle public expenditure disputes, did improve the coherence of government strategy, but it also strengthened the chancellor's hand in that process. In the actual conduct of economic policy the prime minister's role is more 'hands on' and much will rest on the relative balance of expertise, confidence and political standing. The prime minister's power to shift and to sack remains a double-edged sword. In the short run it may enable him or her to evade a policy urged by chancellor and foreign secretary but, as Mrs Thatcher found, that in turn can render him or her virtually a prisoner of whoever takes their place, that is unless success and high political standing give fresh authority to the prime minister's position. John Major found his own solution, institutionalising the interdependencies by bringing senior ministers together in an informal inner Cabinet where there could be a genuine pooling of minds. That was a measure of the need both for an overarching strategy linking these fields and skilful prime ministerial politics in dealing with the 'biggest beasts in the jungle'.

Notes

1. R. Rose, 'British Government: the Job at the Top', in R. Rose and E. Suleiman (eds), *Presidents and Prime Ministers* (Washington, DC: American Enterprise Institute), 1980, p. 49.
2. M. Williams, *Inside Number 10* (London: Weidenfeld & Nicolson, 1972), pp. 40, 153.
3. D. Hurd, *An End to Promises* (London: Collins, 1979), p. 121.
4. Note Mrs Thatcher's worry 'that summits took up too much time and energy, particularly when there was so much to do at home' (*The Downing Street Years* (London: HarperCollins, 1993), p. 67).
5. H. Wilson, *The Governance of Britain* (London: Weidenfeld & Nicolson/Michael Joseph, 1976), p. 119; H. Wilson, *Final Term* (London: Weidenfeld & Nicolson/Michael Joseph, 1979).
6. Thatcher, op. cit., pp. 66–7.
7. Sir Robert Armstrong in seminar.
8. 'Britain and the World', in D. Kavanagh and A. Seldon, *The Thatcher Effect* (Oxford: Oxford University Press 1989) p. 160.
9. Ibid., p. 119.
10. H. Macmillan, *Riding the Storm* (London: Macmillan, 1971); CAB 128/31 CC74 (57) 2, 21 October 1957.
11. H. Macmillan, *At the End of the Day* (London: Macmillan, 1973).
12. H. Wilson, *The Labour Government, 1964–1970* (London: Weidenfeld Nicolson, 1971), p. 40.
13. P. Hennessy, 'Planning for a Future Nuclear Deterrent', *The Times*, 4 December 1979.
14. Private information.
15. N. Henderson, *Mandarin: The Diaries of an Ambassador* (London: Weidenfeld & Nicolson, 1994), p. 316.
16. Henderson's diary entry for 3 December 1979 is worth reading in this regard, ibid., pp. 316–17.
17. H. Macmillan, *The Past Masters: Politics and Politicians, 1906–1939* (London: Macmillan, 1975), pp. 136–7.
18. D. R. Thorpe, *Selwyn Lloyd* (London: Jonathan Cape, 1989), p. 274.
19. Home in interview with Kenneth Young, *Sir Alec Douglas-Home* (London: Dent, 1970) p. 124.
20. G. Howe, *Conflict of Loyalty* (London: Macmillan, 1994), p. 394.
21. Quoted in A. Sampson, *Anatomy of Britain* (London: Hodder & Stoughton, 1962), pp. 332–3.
22. S. Jenkins and A. Sloman, *With Respect, Ambassador* (London: BBC Publications, 1985), p. 117.
23. M. Stewart, *Life and Labour: An Autobiography* (London: Sidgwick and Jackson, 1980), p. 274
24. R. Crossman, *The Diaries of a Cabinet Minister*, vol. I (London: Jonathan Cape, 1976).
25. A. Shlaim et al., *British Foreign Secretaries since 1945* (London: David & Charles, 1977), Chapter 7 and Postscript; J. Campbell, *Edward Heath*

(London: Jonathan Cape, 1993), chapter 16; H. Kissinger, *Years of Upheaval* (London: Weidenfeld & Nicolson/Michael Joseph, 1982), pp. 140–2.

26. Philip Ziegler's authorised life, *Wilson* (London: Weidenfeld & Nicolson, 1993), chapter XXI, provides a brief account.

27. R. Jenkins, *A Life at the Centre* (London: Macmillan, 1991), p. 494.

28. J. Dickie, *Inside the Foreign Office* (London: Chapmans, 1992), p. 285.

29. P. Junor, *John Major: From Brixton to Downing Street*, rev. edn (Harmondsworth: Penguin, 1996), p. 214.

30. C. Hill, *Cabinet Decisions on Foreign Policy: The British Experience, October 1938–June 1941* (Cambridge: Cambridge University Press, 1991).

31. On the latter see R. Lamb, *The Macmillan Years, 1957–1963: The Emerging Truth* (London: John Murray, 1995), pp. 387 ff.

32. Wilson, op. cit., p. 396.

33. A. Adamthwaite, 'Introduction: The Foreign Office and Policy-Making', in J. W. Young (ed.), *The Foreign Policy of Churchill's Peacetime Administration, 1951–55* (Leicester: Leicester University Press, 1988), p. 21.

34. J. Barnes, 'Suez: a Case of Cabinet Government', Churchill Archives Lecture, 1990.

35. Cmnd 20997, July 1963.

36. R. Crossman, *The Diaries of a Cabinet Minister*, vol. II (London: Jonathan Cape, 1977), p. 397.

37. D. Owen, *Time to Declare* (London: Michael Joseph, 1991).

38. Howe, op. cit.

39. Junor, op. cit., p. 255.

40. Note, for example, Macmillan's interest in the problems of world liquidity. See R. Maudling, *Memoirs* (London: Sidgwick and Jackson, 1978).

41. Chamberlain's judgement; Nigel Lawson, *The View from No 11: Memoirs of a Tory Radical* (London: Bantam Press, 1992), p. 586.

42. Lawson in *Hansard*, 29 June 1983.

43. J. Callaghan, *Time and Chance* (London: Collins, 1987), p. 399.

44. P. Hennessy, *Cabinet* (Oxford: Blackwell, 1986), p. 64; Young, *Sir Alec Douglas-Home*, p. 179.

45. A. Seldon, *Churchill's Indian Summer: The Conservative Government, 1951–55* (London: Hodder and Stoughton, 1983) underplays Churchill's contacts with Butler, rightly perhaps since their content was increasingly more political than economic.

46. Jenkins, op. cit., p. 248.

47. D. Healey, *The Time of My Life* (London: Michael Joseph, 1989), p. 389.

48. Ibid., p. 450.

49. Howe, op. cit., p. 142.

50. Campbell, op. cit., p. 303.

51. P. Whitehead, *The Writing on the Wall: Britain in the Seventies* (London: Michael Joseph in association with Channel 4, 1985), pp. 82–4; Sir Leo Pliatzky, *Getting and Spending*, 2nd edn (Oxford: Blackwell, 1984), pp. 103–7.

52. Howe, op. cit., pp. 146–7.

53. Lawson, *The View from No. 11*, p. 383.
54. Thatcher, op. cit.
55. Lawson, *The View from No. 11*, p. 964.
56. *Contemporary Record*, vol. 8, no. 3 (1994), p. 444.
57. Howe, op. cit., pp. 189–90.
58. Ibid., p. 169.
59. Private information.
60. M. Burch, 'Mrs Thatcher's approach', in M. Burch and B. Wood, *Public Policy in Britain* . . . (Oxford: Blackwell, 1990).
61. Crossman, *Diaries of a Cabinet Minister*, vol. i, p. 290.
62. Douglas Jay, *Change and Fortune:A Political Record* (London: Hutchinson, 1980).
63. Tony Benn, *Against the Tide: Diaries 1973–76* (London: Hutchinson, 1989), pp. 324–6, 329; B. Castle, *The Castle Diaries, 1974–76* (London: Weidenfeld & Nicolson, 1980), p. 649.
64. The head of the Prime Minister's Policy Unit, Bernard Donoughue, records two meetings of this committee on 26 and 30 June. B. Donoughue, *Prime Minister: the Conduct of Policy under Harold Wilson and James Callaghan* (London: Jonathan Cape, 1987), pp. 65–7.
65. Ibid.
66. K. Burk and A. Cairncross, *'Goodbye, Great Britain': The 1976 IMF Crisis* (Harvard: Yale University Press, 1992), provide a full account. See Benn, *Against the Tide*, pp. 575, 579–80, 588–9, 636–8, 640–1; Benn, *Conflicts of Interest, Diaries 1977–80* (London: Hutchinson, 1990), pp. 59, 191–2, 256–7, 259, 389 for the use of EY.
67. *Contemporary Record*, vol. 8, no. 3, (1994).
68. *Contemporary Record*, vol. 8, no. 3 (1994), p. 462.
69. See, for example, Thatcher, op. cit., p. 394, and Lawson, *The View from No. 11*.

6
Television Premiers

Michael Cockerell

There was an extraordinary scene on College Green on 4 July 1995. College Green is the strip of grass opposite the House of Commons where television crews congregate when there is a big political story. As television cameras are not allowed to film interviews inside the Commons, it is the nearest spot to Westminster where one can get a shot with a suitable backdrop of Big Ben. The TV people were awaiting the result of the Tory leadership election which John Major had surprisingly announced to the television cameras in the rose garden at No. 10 a fortnight earlier.

That morning the newspapers had been unanimous with their guides to the number of votes Major needed to stay in office. Any figure lower than 220 and he was in deep political trouble, the press agreed. Waiting on College Green were scores of television crews and reporters: from BBC, ITN, Channel 4, regional TV, Sky News and many foreign networks. But also waiting on College Green were squads of Major loyalists – from cabinet ministers like Michael Howard and Gillian Shephard downwards – who had all been primed to go on to any TV channel that was available to them.

I talked to a minister just before the result was announced. He had a card that was marked with a range of different soundbites for every result. If Major received the barest majority of 165, 'A win is a win, is a win'. Anything more than that up to 185, 'well over half the party'; 185 and over: 'more than Major got last time'; over 195: 'a higher percentage than voted for Tony Blair'; over 202, 'more than any Conservative Leader has ever received in a serious election contest'. And anything over 210, a stunning victory: 'any leader in the

Western world would be delighted with two-thirds of the vote'. (This latter of course conveniently ignored that Major was seeking the vote of those who were nominally his own supporters, not the electorate as a whole; but the first law of statistics – compare like with like – was conspicuously lacking from the prepared soundbites.)

When the result was announced – Major 218, Redwood 89, abstentions 22 – the ministers duly trooped onto every available outlet to pronounce the great victory. First impressions can be everything in politics and the Major camp had produced its own verdict; the much heralded danger zone for the prime minister had melted away along with the Tory rebels. It had been a skilfully organised pre-emptive media strike. Working discreetly behind the scenes in John Major's election campaign team were a significant number of political public relations men – or spin doctors – who seek to impart a specific angle or spin to a story. Among them were Tim Collins, until recently Director of Publicity at Conservative Central Office and now Head of the No. 10 Policy Unit; Howell James, now Chief Policy Adviser to Major but formerly a corporate media relations man; and Peter Gummer, Chairman of Shandwick, the biggest public relations and lobbying firm and brother of cabinet minister John Gummer – one of the Major loyalists who took immediately to the airwaves once the result was known.

Collins, James and Gummer form part of the burgeoning breed of media gurus and electronic image consultants who have become close to successive prime ministers. Such men were unheard of fifty years ago when political television was in its infancy.

In 1948 both the prime minister and the Leader of the Opposition were agreed that television had no part to play in the political process. When the BBC invited Clement Attlee and Winston Churchill to make separate television broadcasts to the nation, the two men turned the offer down flat. 'When I was very young,' explained Churchill, 'if one said something in one's constituency which might have led to trouble if it was spread abroad, nothing happened. Now one has to weigh every word knowing all the time that people will be listening all over the country. It would be intolerable if one also had to consider how one would appear – what one would look like all over the land.' For his successors, how they look on television has become a prime consideration. Although Churchill still felt he could ignore the cameras on his return to No. 10 in 1951, during his final term the potential audience rose from a few hundred thousand to over 12 million. Since he retired, the small screen has transformed the art of political communication. In the struggle to come to terms with it, every modern prime minister has loved, hated and feared television: some have done all three.

Even Churchill himself considered using television to announce his retirement. In strictest secrecy he arranged a screen test. His contempt for television comes over clearly: 'I am sorry to have descend to this level, but we all must keep pace with modern inventions and it is just as well to see where you are in regard to them.'[1] But Churchill hated what he saw. 'I should never have appeared on television', growled the Grand Old Man.[2]

Harold Macmillan was likewise unimpressed by his own early efforts: 'I presented the appearance of a corpse looking out of a window.'[3] Macmillan had become prime minister in 1957 with trousers that disgraced his tailor, an unkempt moustache and teeth in disarray. Some eighteen months later, according to his biographer Alastair Horne, a new self-confident Macmillan appeared on the screen:

> The schoolmasterly glasses have disappeared, the disorderly moustache has been rigorously pruned, the smile is no longer toothy and half apologetic and he is wearing a spruce new suit. The first incumbent of Number 10 to emerge as a TV personality has arrived and the success is almost immediate.[4]

At the age of 62, Macmillan realised he had to alter the techniques of public speaking that had served him throughout his political life. 'People of my age were brought up on the hustings where something comes back to you from the audience all the time', said Macmillan in an interview after he retired. 'Now with television, it is like playing lawn tennis and there isn't anybody to hit the ball back from the other side of the net. And it took me a long time to learn – I think I got a little better towards the end. And I remember someone once said to me "There will be twelve million people watching tonight." And I just had the sense to say to myself: "no, no, no, two people – at the most three". Television is a conversation, not a speech.'[5]

Macmillan began a party political broadcast in 1962 with the mechanics of production – normally so carefully concealed –

deliberately on display: 'Well, there you are, you can see what it's like: the camera's hot probing eye, these monstrous machines and their attendants – a kind of twentieth-century torture chamber, that's what it is like. Well, I must try to forget all this paraphernalia and imagine that you are sitting here in the room with me.' He was the first prime minister to face a hostile television interviewer – the youthful Robin Day with his 'cruel glasses' – and he learned ways to project himself favourably. But he discovered that, like a delicate adjustment of focus on a camera, the viewers' perception of a prime minister can subtly alter. Macmillan's unflappability, showmanship and Edwardian *élan* came to appear complacent, contrived and out of touch.

Harold Wilson – the TV doctor

The chief beneficiary was Harold Wilson. 'Television had one great advantage for the Labour Party', Wilson told me. 'Most of the press were against us and if the right-wing press were tempted to say about me: "this is a terrible man, looks like an ogre, his voice is terrible", then you go on television and the people say: "he is an ordinary chap like the rest of us".'[6] To play up his ordinariness the former Oxford don and ex-President of the Board of Trade appeared on the screen as the man in the Gannex raincoat – with a pipe in the place of the cigars he smoked in private, a well-publicised love of HP sauce and a Yorkshire accent still carefully preserved.

Wilson prided himself on his television professionalism. 'If a cameraman asked him to walk down the garden steps from the Cabinet room across the lawn and stop on a certain leaf facing in a certain direction, he did it without any sense of condescension and got it right first time',[7] wrote John Whale, then ITN's chief political reporter. Wilson drew on many influences for his small screen persona – Baldwin, Churchill, J. F. Kennedy and J. B. Priestley among them.

'Harold Wilson told me', said the Irish Taoiseach, Sean Lemass, 'that a Prime Minister should try to look on television like a family doctor – the kind of man who inspires trust by his appearance as well as by his soothing words and whose advice is welcome'. But Wilson discovered that those who live by the 'box' can perish by the 'box'. His 1967 devaluation broadcast, where he denied that 'the pound in your pocket or purse or bank', had been devalued, did him more harm than any other appearance. The Conservatives had spent nearly five years seeking to demolish Wilson's homespun credibility on television. Ironically, the prime minister's own autocued words did it for them.

Ted Heath – anti-image man

Ted Heath, Wilson's chief adversary over a decade, never came to terms with the cameras. There were people who talked about 'the natural Heath' as against 'the Heath who appears on television'. But, says Heath, 'they discovered there was nothing they could do about that'.[8] It was not for want of trying. Heath took on a cast of media advisers from the advertising, film and TV worlds. One was the director Brian Forbes: 'I watched Ted Heath making a broadcast to camera and just bled for him. I thought it was nothing but him staring into the camera with the reflection of the firing squad in his eyes. All they were photographing was varying degrees of fear.' Heath was put through endless sessions on closed circuit television to try to improve his performance. 'But they gave up in despair', he says resignedly.

As prime minister, Heath did not believe that a confrontation with Robin Day on *Panorama* was necessarily the best way to put his policies across. He came up with the idea of staging grand televised press conferences *à la* de Gaulle in the marble and gilt splendour of Lancaster House. But these intensified Heath's image as a remote authority figure and did nothing to create any personal bond with his audience. When he sought to appeal directly to the viewers during the 1974 miners' strike, his suddenly personalised broadcasts found little response. His friend Sir Ian Trethowan, later to become BBC Director General, wrote: 'Heath's curious inability to project his private charm had a decisive and damaging effect at a moment critical not only for himself but for his country.'[9] Asked today what he feels about that judgement, Heath replies: 'But I don't think a miners' strike is the time to come on television and ooze charm, do you?'

Margaret Thatcher – action woman

When Margaret Thatcher first became Tory leader she seemed to react to the sight of a TV crew almost in the manner of an African tribesman faced with a white man's camera: it was as if her soul might be taken away. The feeling persisted throughout her time at No. 10. Asked during the 1987 general election what she thought about big set-piece television interviews, the then prime minister replied: 'I hate them, I hate them, I hate them.'

After each of her early broadcasts as Leader, Mrs Thatcher's media adviser Gordon Reece (later knighted) commissioned private opinion polls. The findings were conflicting: many viewers said her voice was too shrill and upper class, her style too hectoring, her appearance too austere and school-marmish – yet they approved of the strength of her character and of what she had to say. Unlike Heath, Mrs Thatcher believed in taking on television interviewers on their own terms: 'This animal, if attacked, defends itself. So when I come up against somebody who is obviously out to do a very belligerent interview, I say to myself "By God, anything you can do, I can do better" and I'm belligerent back.'[10]

Reece, however, decided that in Opposition this approach did Mrs Thatcher no good and kept her away from hostile interviews. He also effectively gave her reverse elocution lessons and softened her clothes and hair style. She took humming lessons to bring down the pitch of her voice and her media adviser introduced the 'photo-opportunity' – beloved of American presidential candidates – to British elections. Until 1979 no previous aspirant to No. 10 had given a press conference clutching a two-day-old calf in a meadow. As prime minister, Mrs Thatcher was for a long time an extremely effective screen figure. Photogenic actions often replaced words – as when she flew to Crossmaglen after the murder of Mountbatten and defiantly donned a red beret of the Parachute Regiment; or when she suddenly arrived in the Falklands six months after the victory there and six months before the 1983 general election. On successive nights the peak-time news bulletins on BBC and ITN showed her windswept on a hillside battleground, taking the salute on board ship, genial with grateful villagers, firing a 105-mm gun and tearful as she placed wreaths on the graves of fallen soldiers. 'The pictures provided some of the most potent pre-election help the Prime Minister was likely to receive from the small screen',[11] claimed an early biographer.

But, like Macmillan before her, Mrs Thatcher discovered the fragility of a television image. After her 1983 election triumph her celebrated conviction politics and iron resolution blurred into charges of pig-headedness and lack of compassion. She blamed the electronic messenger. 'We live in a television age and television is selective', said Mrs Thatcher in a speech to the Conservative Council in 1986. She went on:

> One camera shot of a pretty nurse helping an elderly patient out of an empty ward speaks louder than all the statistics in Whitehall and Westminster. Never mind that the hospital is being closed because it is out of date. Never mind that a few miles away a spanking new hospital is being opened with brighter wards, better operating theatres and the very latest equipment. In today's world selective seeing is believing; and in today's world, television comes over as truth. I remember myself opening a beautiful new hospital. Virtually the only publicity was a demonstration outside – about cuts.

Against that, Mrs Thatcher and her advisers themselves became increasingly skilled at staging prime ministerial charades which the cameras willingly filmed. Skilled at inconsequential small talk for the boom microphones to make her sound more down-to-earth and 'caring', she was also an expert in the art of hijacking interviews. Robin Day joked that he planned to begin a No. 10 interview: 'Prime Minister, what is your answer to my first question?'

'Do I enjoy television broadcasting?', pondered the prime minister during the 1987 general election. 'In retrospect, sometimes yes. But in prospect I'm – one doesn't have nerves of steel, you know – one is frightened to death one won't do as well for your cause as you should.'[12]

In her decade at Downing Street, Mrs Thatcher played many parts on the small screen: tearful mother, Iron Lady, wide-eyed *ingénue*, war leader, simple housewife and world statesman. A medium that in any case tended to magnify personalities had been faced with a giant one. Although the prime minister's screen presence sent some viewers screaming from the room, she spoke a populist language that attracted many others. Mrs Thatcher told broadcasting chiefs at a meeting in No. 10 in 1988: 'Television is the most powerful form of communication known to man.' She had every intention of continuing to harness its power to her purposes. But over the Thatcher years in Downing Street she grew increasingly out of touch and when I last interviewed her in No. 10 shortly before her downfall, I had the eerie feeling I was talking to someone who was hearing voices.

John Major – off-camera man

Her chosen successor John Major at first eschewed the TV image consultants and spin doctors. 'I will remain the same plug-ugly person I've always been', he claimed. But after five years in power he had become increasingly reliant on them. He has suffered more than any of his predecessors from confiding to television interviewers his genuine thoughts while he thought the microphones had been switched off. His notorious designation of three of his cabinet colleagues as 'bastards' came in a discussion with Michael Brunson, the political editor of ITN, at the end of an interview. But the interview was being fed down the line to various broadcasting organisations and a copy was recorded and made public.

I had personal experience of John Major's lack of awareness of the presence of the cameras when I was filming in No. 11 Downing Street for a TV profile of Ken Clarke. We knew that there was to be a photocall in the garden for all previous living chancellors. We had been given permission to film it, but suddenly the No. 10 press office vetoed our filming. That morning former Chancellor Norman Lamont, who was coming to the photocall along with Major, had vehemently attacked the prime minister on the BBC radio *Today* programme. No. 10 judged it 'unhelpful' for the PM to be filmed together with Lamont. After pressure, they reluctantly agreed that we could have a locked-off camera in a fixed position in the hallway of No. 11, so we could film the ex-chancellors as they filed past; but there would be no chance of a shot of Lamont and Major together as the PM would arrive for the photocall separately from the No. 10 garden. But, as our luck would have it, after the photocall, Major – obviously not realising that we were still filming – emerged into the hallway asking rather irritably what had happened to the drinks for the ex-chancellors. It was a telling piece of film that tended to give the impression that the prime minister might have some difficulty organising a party in a brewery.

But as Mr Major would say: 'I am still here.' And as he said in an unguarded moment to a TV microphone: 'If they want to get rid of me, they will have to prise my fingers off the doorknob of Number

Ten.' And the skilled way he organised his 1995 leadership campaign, with the help of some of the most sophisticated media gurus in the business, vividly demonstrates that he is an opponent it can be dangerous to underestimate – even though on television he can sometimes give the impression that he is Mr Angry coming to Woolworths to complain about a faulty pop-up toaster.

Notes

1. 'Television and Number 10', transmitted BBC2, November 1986.
2. Martin Gilbert, *'Never Despair': Winston Churchill, 1945–65* (London: Heinemann, 1988), p. 1119.
3. Harold Macmillan, *Riding the Storm* (London: Macmillan, 1971), p. 196.
4. *Harold Macmillan: A Life in Pictures* (London: Macmillan, 1983).
5. Interview with Robert Mackenzie, transmitted BBC1, 1972.
6. Interview with the author.
7. J. Whale, *The Half-Shut Eye* (London: Macmillan, 1969), p. 96.
8. Interview with the author.
9. I. Trethowan, *Split Screen* (London: Hamish Hamilton, 1984), p. 57.
10. K. Harris, *Thatcher* (London: Weidenfeld & Nicolson, 1988), p. 83.
11. G. Brock and N. Wapshott, *Thatcher* (London: Futura, 1983), p. 255.
12. *The Times*, 9 June 1987.

7

The Judges into Politics: the Rise of Judicial Review since 1945[1]

Simon James

An inexplicable fault line in contemporary scholarship separates public lawyers from students of politics. British texts on administrative law pay scant attention to the executive landscape beyond perhaps a (usually perfunctory) treatment of ministerial responsibility. Conversely, works on politics and administration scarcely touch on the role of the courts. Fifty years ago, when public law scarcely existed, this apartheid was understandable. Today it is indefensible: administrative law is a vigorous discipline in its own right, and our courts pronounce daily on the validity of government decisions.

This essay makes a modest attempt to bridge the gap, selecting the most sensitive point at which law connects with government: the extraordinary expansion in the past 30 years of judicial review, the process by which judges scrutinise the decisions of public officials to decide whether they are lawful. In the early postwar period applications to the courts to review administrative decisions were rare, and successful applications even rarer. But by 1974 the number of annual applications in England and Wales had reached 160; that figure rose to 1230 in 1985, and to over 2600 in 1992. While the number of cases fluctuates from year to year, the overall trend is unquestionable.[2] A similar development has been apparent in Scotland, although this paper will rarely venture north of the border. And these figures do not include cases brought by citizens before the European Court of Human Rights or the European Court of Justice. I have elsewhere analysed judicial review in terms of its impact on constitutional arrangements, the behaviour of public administrators and the political science of government.[3] In this article I consider two historical aspects of the issue: why the judges moved from quietism to activism in this area, and why politicians did not react earlier and more vehemently. I will concentrate on the impact at national government level, although it should be noted that there are as many if not more cases brought against local authorities and tribunals. The chapter starts from the assumption that the reader knows little of judicial review; those with a working knowledge of the case law can skip the next few pages.

Probably the most vivid way of illustrating the scale of the change in judicial attitudes is to compare two sets of legal decisions half a century apart. To start in 1994: in successive days in November of that year the lead stories in most newspapers were, first, the Appeal Court's declaration that the home secretary's remodelling of the criminal injuries compensation scheme had been unlawful and, second, the High Court's decision that overseas aid for the Pergau dam in Malaysia, approved by the foreign secretary in conjunction with the prime minister, had also been illegal.[4] Now go back to the Second World War. In 1942 one Liversidge was interned by the home secretary under wartime regulations as having 'hostile associations'. He argued that there was no objective evidence to support this. The House of Lords, however, held that the law gave the minister an absolute discretion, and would not question his decision.[5] The difference in underlying legal ethos between the courts' self-denying quiescence in 1942 and their active intervention today is striking.

In the aftermath of the Second World War, however, Britain had no administrative law. Law lecturers told their students so, and their adamant teaching was verified by contemporary – if negative – evidence: there were very few cases in which citizens sought to restrain public authorities, and still fewer in which they succeeded. Successive generations of lawyers had been influenced to an extraordinary degree by that unstable partisan A. V. Dicey who, in his monumental *Law of the Constitution*,[6] had heaped odium on the alien fallacy of 'droit administratif'. The courts flinched away from any suggestion that they should review the behaviour of public authorities. The only circumstance in which the courts would strike down a decision was if it was a blatant breach of the law – and naturally flagrant breaches were very rare.

The implications of this narrow approach were demonstrated alarmingly in the 1956 case of *Smith* v. *East Elloe RDC*,[7] in which a landowner challenged a compulsory purchase order on the grounds of fraudulent behaviour by municipal officials procuring the order. The statute provided that any legal proceedings against the decision had to be instituted within six weeks of the decision, but in this case the misconduct had not come to light until after that period. The House of Lords refused to rectify matters, holding not only that the six-week statutory period for challenge was an absolute bar to proceedings after that point, but also – and more alarmingly – that even within those six-weeks they would have struck down the decision only if it could be proved that the minister had exceeded his powers, regardless of any earlier irregularity.

This attitude persisted for a good 20 years. Then the 1960s saw a series of cases of which three, in their different ways, made clear how the courts would mark out the territory of judicial review. In *Ridge* v. *Baldwin*, the courts reiterated the rules of natural justice – in this case, the right to a hearing – and applied them to a public authority: the Brighton police committee had acted unfairly in dismissing their chief constable without informing him of the charge or allowing him a hearing.[8] In *Padfield* v. *Minister of Agriculture*, they set limits to the exercise of a discretionary power. In this case the minister had refused to refer a request for a review of milk prices to a statutory committee of investigation, because he feared that the likely consequence – an increase – would cause political ructions. The House of Lords struck down the decision, holding that this was an invalid reason and frustrated the intention of the legislation.[9]

In the third case the House of Lords made clear they would resist to the utmost any attempt to exclude the courts from reviewing a decision. Periodically parliament wrote into statutes clauses which sought to oust the jurisdiction of the courts, generally worded 'The decision of X shall not be called into question in any court of law.' The judges naturally disliked such 'ouster' clauses, and in *Anisminic Ltd.* v. *Foreign Compensation Commission* the Lords ingeniously held that, since the Commission had exceeded its jurisdiction by considering factors outside the scope of the legislation, its determination against Anismicic was no determination at all, and so could be challenged at law.[10]

The landslip had started. And in the 1970s a procession of well publicised cases under the Labour government imprinted this new interventionist role of the courts on the public mind. The home secretary had exceeded his power in revoking the television licenses of people who had renewed them just before the price went up. The trade secretary had invalidly revoked the licence for Freddie Laker's transatlantic Skytrain service. And the education secretary had erred in overruling Tameside council's postponement of its plans to introduce comprehensive education.[11] As if to prove they were even-handed, in the following decade the courts meted out similar treatment to a Conservative government, and to local government and health authorities as well.

What, in practice, did the courts' intervention mean? Judges like to say that judicial review is not an appellate jurisdiction, but a supervisory jurisdiction. In other words, the courts are not an all-purpose appeals tribunal; they merely review the work of decision-makers to ensure that it meets basic criteria of fairness and lawfulness. In practice these criteria can be grouped under three headings, helpfully identified by Lord Diplock in his judgement in the GCHQ case (and incessantly cited since).[12] The first is the defect of a decision-maker simply acting outside his legal powers, which these days the courts are prepared to apply in a less mechanistic way than in the East Elloe case. The second is the requirement to observe the rules of natural justice, considerably developed since their use to grant a right to a hearing in *Baldwin* v. *Ridge*: successive judgements, including the GCHQ case, have held that a person must be consulted about a decision before it is taken either if they had a 'legitimate expectation' that this might happen.

The third criterion is that the decision-maker should behave 'reasonably'. This is quite tightly drawn: 'irrationality' was quite stringently defined in Lord Diplock's GCHQ judgement as a decision 'so outrageous in its defiance of logic or accepted moral standards that no sensible person who had applied his mind to the question to be decided could have arrived at it'. This is 'Wednesbury' unreasonableness, named after the leading case in which a cinema company unsuccessfully challenged Wednesbury Urban District Council which, zealous against moral turpitude, would allow it to show films on Sunday only if nobody under 15 were admitted under any circumstances.[13] But in recent years judges have often applied a more expansive interpretation of reasonableness: 'broad' Wednesbury has often (but not always) replaced 'narrow' Wednesbury, and some of the growth in judicial review is due to this.

The development of judicial review is not due to any decision of parliament to create a framework of restraint on decision-makers. The judges have done it off their own bat, developing case by case a template for the striking down of decisions which they regard as iniquitous. Why have they become so adventurous since the judicial nadir of the 1950s?

Two essential preconditions existed within the legal system. One was a system of adaptable principles – the common law – which affords enormous discretion to judges who wish to make adventurous use of it. Two contemporary cases from outside the administrative sphere well exemplify this remarkable flexibility and the pragmatism with which the courts can exploit it if they wish. Most readers will recall the 1992 case in which the House of Lords reformulated the common law to provide that rape within marriage is a crime.[14] The public at large rightly welcomed this change; the only complaint was that it was scandalously belated. Few stopped to consider that the judges had, on their own authority, effectively created a new criminal offence, and one with a retrospective element at that – something the judiciary had studiously avoided doing for decades. It set a potentially dangerous precedent. A second case, which illuminates the political realism with which judges will refashion the law, was brought by the Woolwich Building Society against the Inland Revenue. The Woolwich had paid tax in advance under regulations later ruled to be unlawful. The Revenue repaid the money, with interest, from the moment the regulations were struck down. The Woolwich wanted interest backdated to the time of payment, and asked the courts to reformulate the common law to that effect. The Inland Revenue objected that this went against common law precedent, and that any change should be left to parliament. The House of Lords found for the building society, however, arguing (amongst other entertaining grounds) that 'however compelling the principle of justice might be [in this case] it would never be sufficient to persuade a government to propose its legislative recognition by Parliament; caution, otherwise known as the Treasury, would never allow this to happen'.[15]

The second precondition for the expansion of judicial review was a high-calibre judiciary. That is no idle flattery. In the United States in recent years, the most alarming aspect of the pantomime surround-

ing nominations to the Supreme Court has not been the media hoo-
ha surrounding the congressional hearings, but the revelation that so
many candidates were, frankly, mediocre lawyers. In Britain, the 35-
year expedition into the heart of administrative power has been a
hazardous enterprise, demanding scholarship and intellectual resili-
ence. We take the calibre of our High Court for granted.

But if these were the preconditions, the key ingredients of change
were, firstly, a change in the outlook by judges about the social
purpose of law; secondly, changes of procedure within the legal
system; and, thirdly, a shift in judicial perceptions of the adequacy
of parliamentary restraint on administrative action. To start with the
change in judicial attitudes about the purpose of the law: judicial
psychology and ethos have never been static. In the Victorian era the
judiciary were robust in their forays against political authority, yet
they retreated in the early years of this century. Between the wars
they again rode out to overrule the actions of local and national
government, this time in the field of property law, by protecting
property owners against compulsory purchase and slum clearance.[16]
But during and after the Second World War they once again shrank
into the most extraordinary timidity.

The postwar political ethos certainly discouraged judicial intervention. Wartime had accustomed the public to regulation. The Beveridge report had recommended using administrative tribunals rather
than the courts in social matters like industrial injury. The welfare
and nationalisation legislation of the Attlee government vested arbi-
tration of disputes in ministers rather than judges (mark you, the
same had been true of Butler's 1944 Education Act.) Ministers were
bullish: Aneurin Bevan bluntly told the Commons that the government would not tolerate 'judicial sabotage'.[17] Attlee's Lord Chancellor, Jowitt, firmly discouraged judicial creativity: the task of the
lawyer was 'not to consider what the social and political conditions
of today require . . . that is the task of the legislature. It is quite possible that the law has produced a result that does not accord with the
requirements of today. If so, put it right by legislation. [The lawyer] is
far better employed if he puts himself to the much simpler task of
deciding what the law is.'[18]

Jowitt was not necessarily moved by a partisan spirit. The dominant judicial ethos of the era opposed a broad interpretation of the
courts' role. Viscount Simonds, Lord Chancellor in Churchill's peace-

time administration, declared 'the task of the courts is to consider what the law is, not what it ought to be'[19] and in the early 1950s led the Law Lords in a highly restrictive approach, characterised particularly by adherence to literal verbal interpretation of statutes, not attempting to interpret parliament's intention or tempering statutes with broader notions of common law fairness.[20] A notorious example of this practice was the East Elloe case mentioned disparagingly above. But in the later 1950s judicial thinking began to shift towards a more creative approach, interpreting the intention of the law. There had always been partisans of this view: in *Liversidge* v. *Anderson*, the wartime internment case, Lord Atkin entered a powerful dissent in which (despite Lord Chancellor Simonds' attempt to tone down his remarks)[21] he protested vigorously at the attitude of his colleagues, 'judges who on a mere question of construction when face to face with claims involving the liberty of the subject show themselves more executive-minded than the executive'. In *Smith* v. *East Elloe* Lord Reid entered an equally spirited dissent against reading the words of the statute literally, to the detriment of a general legal principle: 'Courts have held that general words are not to be read as enabling a deliberate wrongdoer to take advantage of his own dishonesty. Are the principles of statutory construction so rigid that these general words must be so read here?'[22]

At a political level, a lead in the opposite direction was given by Simonds' successor, Lord Kilmuir, who told the House of Lords that the law was 'a dynamic force [that] should be brought in to help in the solutions of the great problems of a modern state'.[23] Kilmuir went to some lengths to persuade his fellow judges of his views: he was a party to transferring powers from the Monopolies Commission to a Restrictive Practices Court in the mid-1950s and, when judges expressed worry at being drawn into political decisions, he called them to a meeting to talk them round.[24]

Some judges took up this cause. Most enthusiastic were Lords Reid and Denning, followed at a circumspect distance by the likes of Lords Devlin and Ratcliffe. Their efforts were initially frustrated in the late 1950s by Simonds, now senior Law Lord, who acted as a drag anchor on judicial creativity and engaged in a protracted and rather personalised duel with Denning.[25] But Simonds' retirement in 1962 coincided with an unexpectedly brisk turnover of personnel in the Lords which brought in a transfusion of adventurous spirit.

Simonds' replacement, Reid, exercised a tremendous influence over subsequent judicial developments, leading his colleagues in a string of innovatory judgements, some laying the foundations of the contemporary system of judicial review. As Professor Griffith has observed, in the seven most significant decisions of the 1960s which extended judicial activism, the push forwards was achieved by the House of Lords overruling the Court of Appeal.[26] Truly, this was leadership from the front. One of the Lords' most liberating decisions was their landmark pronouncement in 1966 that they would no longer be bound by their past decisions, which scraped away the legal barnacles of centuries.

Of course, judicial opinion does not evolve in isolation. It is influenced by shifts in public opinion: perhaps only partially, often with a time lag, but there is an influence. And from the 1960s onwards, social attitudes changed. People became less deferential and more willing to argue the toss with officialdom. Judges reflected that change in national temperament.

Turning now to the second significant factor in the change in legal attitudes, the technical changes in the legal system: the most significant of these was undoubtedly the overhaul of the regulations governing judicial challenge to administrative action in the 1970s. Until then challenge had been fraught with procedural hazard, and sound challenges were vulnerable to rejection on technical grounds. In 1977 these complex and arcane rules were greatly simplified. Judicial review cases were concentrated in a 'Crown cases list', creating a cadre of judges specialising in the field. The expertise of that cadre has been reinforced by the practice of appointing Treasury Counsel – QCs who give up a lucrative practice to work exclusively as Crown advisers – to the bench when their stint as Treasury Counsel ends, a practice which has brought onto the bench some of the more notable luminaries of judicial review, including Lord Woolf, Lord Justice Simon Brown and Mr Justice Laws. They often end up hearing judicial review applications, and it would be a mistake to expect them to be automatically sympathetic to the government; if anything, their experience of advising the Crown reputedly makes them more sceptical of the case advanced by public authorities. Humour is a good indicator of perceptions, and a popular current legal joke tells of a former Treasury Counsel promoted to the bench who is told by a senior colleague: 'Look, you've been a judge for over a year; it would be quite all right for you to decide the occasional case in the Crown's favour now, you know.'

These changes, coinciding with a number of high-profile decisions against the Labour government of the 1970s, contributed substantially to a boom in challenges. Since nothing succeeds like success, lawyers and others began to appreciate the potential of this means of challenge. Pressure groups used it to challenge government: for instance, the Child Poverty Action Group adopted a test case strategy in the 1970s to contest social security regulations. In the 1980s, as the consensus about the role and values of local government fractured, local councils showed increasing willingness to challenge Whitehall in the courts. And commercial interests began to exploit judicial review: several leading cases concerned government refusal to provide industrial development grants.

The third significant factor in changing judicial attitudes was a combination of shifts in Britain's constitution that had deep implications for judicial restraint of the executive. Paramount amongst these was a growing realisation that the traditional reliance on political safeguards was inadequate. Traditionally the British citizen's recourse against misgovernment had been political: complaint to his MP.[27] In the immediate postwar period the judiciary relied for justification of their restraint on the responsibility of ministers to parliament: in *Liversidge* v. *Anderson*, Lord Macmillan emphasised that the home secretary was 'one of the high officers of State who, by reason of his position, is entitled to public confidence in his capacity and integrity; who is answerable to Parliament for his conduct in office'.

Those were the days! But as the complexity of administration grew, it outstripped parliamentary control. Besides, the MP might not be interested; he might get nowhere; parliament or government might view his representations in partisan terms. The proliferation of ombudsmen was tacit acknowledgement of the limitations of parliament. A dramatic exposition of this malaise came in the Crichel Down case, which exposed the limitations of ministerial responsibility for officials' behaviour. A tenacious myth holds that the minister, Sir Thomas Dugdale, resigned because he accepted responsibility for the misdeeds of officials over the disposal of farm land in Dorset. That is untrue: he was compelled to go because of his own political ineptitude, and the Home Secretary, Maxwell–Fyfe, concluded the affair by propounding a rather attenuated version of ministerial accountability, under which a minister was not responsible for reprehensible conduct in his department of which he was unaware.[28] The Maxwell–Fyfe rules remain the formal constitutional position today. And Maxwell–Fyfe was the same man who, appointed Lord Chancellor as Lord Kilmuir a few years later, so vigorously promoted intervention by the judges 'to help in the solution of the great problems of a modern state'. Kilmuir was a clear-minded man, and his two pronouncements were, evidently, opposite sides of the same coin.

In short, judges came to the conclusion that political institutions provided inadequate remedy for the citizen. Lord Scarman spoke for many when he said:

> The social, constitutional, legal and administrative developments of the past thirty years are overwhelming the old structure of essentially political safeguards and remedies for the citizen and introducing a new world in which there are also legal safeguards and remedies developed judicially and enforced through the courts.[29]

Some politicians agreed. When the home secretary lost the television licences case in December 1975, the Conservative MP and QC Ronald Bell observed percipiently in the Commons that the courts were moving in because parliament was failing to keep an adequate check on ministers.[30] Today, it seems to be commonly accepted that the two mechanisms of accountability operate concurrently. In 1994 it was held that the parliamentary ombudsman, despite being accountable to a select committee of the House of Commons, was also subject to judicial review, Lord Justice Simon Brown observing, 'Many in government are answerable to Parliament and yet answerable also to the supervisory jurisdiction of this court.'[31] This seems to be accepted by the government: for example, the Minister of State at the Home Office in June 1995 (doubtless making a virtue of necessity) stated explicitly that the home secretary was not only accountable to parliament for his decisions on tariffs for murder sentences, but 'he is also subject to judicial review which is yet another check and balance in the system'.[32]

The proliferation of administrative authorities only fuelled this apprehension as the 1950s and 1960s progressed. Crichel Down caused, rather illogically, the establishment of the Franks inquiry into administrative tribunals, which led to a strengthening of the courts' powers over these bodies in the Employment and Tribunals Act 1956 and to the creation of the Council on Tribunals in 1958. (Even so, these bodies are frequently the target of legal challenge.)

Criticism grew steadily of the shortcomings in parliament's function of calling the executive to account for its actions: hence the introduction of ombudsmen and select committees. But judicial opinion is likely to have been affected as much by failings in parliament's legislative function. There are two main problems. Firstly, lack of parliamentary time. Even where there is a consensus in favour of changing the law, the ever-increasing pressure on the legislative timetable makes it difficult to find parliamentary time. Understandably, governments give priority to politically sensitive measures, and many modest, uncontentious reforms languish for lack of time. In 1993 the then Master of the Rolls, Sir Thomas Bingham, pointed out that 36 proposals for law reform from the Law Commission, to which the government had no objection, 'gather dust not because their value is doubted but because there is inadequate time to enact them'.[33] There is an obvious opening, not to say temptation, for the judges to supply through the common law what the politicians will not provide by statute.

Secondly, there has been a huge growth in delegated legislation. This was for a while a hot topic between the wars. The redoubtable, choleric Lord Chief Justice Hewart published in 1929 *The New Despotism*, a book which attacked delegated legislation as a bureaucratic conspiracy, particularly the use of 'Henry VIII clauses' by which ministers could by order amend or repeal primary legislation. A government inquiry calmed these exaggerated fears and the Second World War habituated the public to regulations: it is significant that Attlee's government saw no need to extend its Parliament Act of 1949 to secondary legislation. But today some 2000 sets of regulations are made by ministers each year, compared to 100 Acts of Parliament. At the same time, parliamentary arrangements for scrutinising secondary legislation are limited: in the late 1980s only a third of regulations were debated by parliament. Even then debates are often brief and the choice is between approval or rejection since there can be no amendments.

Today the courts take careful and practical account of this patchy scrutiny. There is a marked propensity to intervene less when statutory instruments have been debated and approved by parliament, as opposed to regulations merely signed off by a minister: for example, when the Lords rejected an appeal by Bradford City and Nottingham County Councils in 1985, Lord Scarman stated that where parliamentary approval was required and given, the courts would not intervene unless the minister had actually misconstrued the statute or misled parliament.[34]

Yet the whole phenomenon of delegated legislation is still regarded warily by the judiciary: current and former Law Lords have been active members of the Joint Committee on Statutory Instruments, set up in 1973 to scrutinise all delegated legislation. Furthermore, a new Delegated Powers Scrutiny Committee was set up by the House of Lords in 1993 as a check on the granting of excessive delegated power to ministers. The new Committee's first report[35] was devoted to the evils of 'Henry VIII' clauses (Hewart lives!) and subsequent reports have sharply criticised the conferring of broad discretion on ministers – for example the 1995 Jobseekers Bill, which left ministers to decide what is meant by 'available for employment' or 'actively seeking employment'.[36]

Further spice was added to this constitutional stew by the evolution of a European dimension to domestic law. As early as 1965 British citizens gained the right to petition the European Court of Human Rights, and its attendant Commission. While (unlike all other signatories except Sweden) Britain refused to make the convention enforceable in the domestic courts, it was a development on which the legal profession kept an eye. And when in 1973 Britain joined the European Community, the judges absorbed faster than anyone the warnings of Mr Powell and Mr Benn – unheeded by the public – that henceforth Community law would override domestic law. The British parliament was no longer supreme, even if it took 20 years of evasion before the Factortame fisheries case made this explicit.

Finally, we must recognise that the judiciary appears to have become a great deal more sensitive to the ambient political temperature. Judges have learned a lot about the work of government by their appointment to conduct a string of inquiries into public problems and disasters.[37] The practice stretches back at least as far as the Denning report on the Profumo affair, and in the 1960s senior judges often headed enquiries to settle industrial disputes. But it was particularly in the 1980s that some of our leading judges attained fame by conducting public inquiries: the Bingham report on BCCI, the Taylor report into football, Woolf on prison riots, Scott on Matrix-Churchill, and so on. Heading an enquiry now seems almost an essential element of the curriculum vitae of a judge destined for higher things.

Although many on the bench had misgivings about involvement in such enterprises as Heath's Industrial Relations Court, there has been a marked willingness by some judges to voice in their judgements opinions on live issues of the day – most notoriously Lord Denning's comments on election manifestos in the GLC 'Fares Fair' case. In a more temperate vein, Law Lords and Lords of Appeal have used their seats in the upper house to express views on an variety of subjects impinging on legal life. For example in June 1995 the Lord Chief Justice led 12 current and former Law Lords in voting against clauses in the Criminal Appeals Bill,[38] and the following year many Law Lords vehemently denounced the proposed introduction of minimum sentences.[39] When the government appealed to the Judicial Committee of the House of Lords in the criminal injuries compensation case, there was some difficulty in assembling five Law Lords to hear the appeal, since so many of them had spoken against the proposals in parliament.

Out of these seismic shifts in our constitutional arrangements, the unease about the adequacy of democratic safeguards on administrative power, and the more creative conception of the judges' role which they encourage, there appear to have emerged – sometimes implicit, often unlabelled – two strands of judicial thinking about the role of judges in modern society. The first and more circumspect of the two, reaching back to the constitutionally fundamental pronouncements of Lord Chief Justice Coke in the sixteenth century, is the concept of protecting private right against public power, to maintain a constitutional balance between the ability of government to govern and the right of the individual citizen. And since the central executive has extended its power, the trend of recent decisions has been to tip the scales back in favour of the citizen. This was undoubtedly the spur to judicial reassertion in administrative law from the 1960s onwards, and remains a powerful motivation today, asserted through common law principles. But it has more recently been supplemented by a second, more radical line of thought: a concept of fundamental law, effectively superior to parliamentary authority. Protagonists of this second concept have found the common law an equally flexible vehicle through which to imprint their views, but have also in recent years looked to the importation of the principles of the European law, and particularly the Convention of Human Rights, as a way of advancing their views.

Attributing the views of judges to one or other of these camps is not easy: their judgements, their *obiter dicta*, even their public writings and public lectures often combine an exemplary lucidity with a remarkable degree of code. Certainly into the former, more cautious camp would fall the pragmatic master architects of postwar administrative law like Lord Reid and Lord Diplock, and an individual such as Lord Salmon who stood so staunchly by the preservation of personal property rights. Into the latter would probably fall those like Lord Scarman, who has made repeated calls for a bill of rights, the present Lord Chief Justice, Lord Bingham, who favours incorporation of the European Convention on Human Rights into British law[40] and practising radicals like Mr Justice Laws.[41] Categorising judges by their views is a perilous exercise: they are an individualistic lot. But the sizeable number of Law Lords, led by such as Lord Woolf (now Master of the Rolls) who supported Lord Lester's Human Rights Bill in early 1995, suggests that support for the more radical fundamental law view has grown in recent years.

Perhaps the most extraordinary aspect of the growth of judicial review is the muted political response. We might have expected politicians to resist fiercely the judges' extension of their power to strike down government decisions. Yet until very recently there has been little evidence of political opposition to this development, or even of political awareness of what is happening. Why? There is a combination of reasons. Firstly, British politicians are usually indifferent to constitutional matters: interest in a bill of rights, reform of parliament or the separation of powers has until recently been very much a minority interest. Nor does the nebulous character of our largely unwritten constitution make for clarity of discussion. Politicians are usually interested in constitutional issues not for their own sake, but as instruments to be used in the party battle. So a government defeat in the courts is greeted with cheers by the Opposition, whichever party is in power, and whatever the constitutional implications.

Following from that, a second consideration is that all major political parties have over the years gone on record as supporting some judgement or other against the government of the day. Once, for example, Conservative front-benchers had encouraged a Conservative council to take the Labour Education Secretary to court and had acclaimed the courts' intervention as a victory for liberty[42] it became difficult for them once in government to denounce judicial review as illicit. The same would presumably be true of a future Labour government, given their support for judicial review applications sought by councils and unions against the Thatcher and Major governments, and their acclamation when the government lost.

Thirdly, from 1964 to 1987 the Woolsack was occupied by three Lord Chancellors – Gardiner, Hailsham and Elwyn-Jones – who all favoured judicial activism, which could explain the lack of resistance displayed by governments towards the development of judicial review. Fourthly, some intervention has been wished on judges by politicians – the most notorious example being the Industrial Relations Court of the early 1970s. Fifthly, although in retrospect the development of judicial review over three decades now seems a logical, almost inexorable process, at the time nobody imagined how far the process would go (including, probably, many judges). It was like a game of grandmother's footsteps: after every innovative decision the judges would have inched a little farther forward, but would be standing virtuously still, giving no indication how much farther forward they would eventually move. Nor was there ever a case which allowed ministers to pick a fight with the judges over the constitutional propriety of judicial review: the judges never overruled the government in a way that presented ministers with a politically defensible *casus belli* against them. There were two crucial periods. The first was the Labour government of 1974–79, and the most crucial case was that on television licences: chronologically the first, and the one in which the political, if not legal, omens were most favourable. Here the government seemed momentarily to run up the flag of constitutional combat: in the course of argument counsel for the Crown, Roger Parker, said: 'If the court interferes in this case it would not be long before the powers of this court would be called into question.' Delivering judgement against the government, Lord Denning commented, 'We trust that this was not said seriously but only as a piece of advocate's license.' It was certainly taken seriously within the government, where the decision was taken to climb down publicly: the court reconvened specially to hear an apology from Mr Parker, who assured the court there had been no intention by the home secretary to threaten that the powers of the court would be curtailed. On the same day the home secretary Roy Jenkins gave the same assurance to the Commons and announced that he would not appeal to the House of Lords.[43]

In this case the government could have fought further. There was an arguable case before the House of Lords. A degree of antagonism towards the judiciary, partly a hangover from Heath's Industrial Relations Court, was shared by a number of Labour ministers. Nor would there have been a colossal political cost in taking the battle further: it was the 50 per cent increase in the television licence that riled the public, rather than the crackdown on those who had sought to save money by renewing their licences prematurely. But what surprises is the comprehensive, almost abject nature of the climbdown. If the government had merely wanted to cut its losses, it could have done so more discreetly.

The answer may well lie in Jenkins' personal views: he was at that time rare amongst politicians in his personal interest in constitutional principles, and his later career as leader of the Social Democratic Party showed him to favour constitutional reform, including a bill of rights enforceable in the courts. Given his sense of constitutional history, he may particularly have been wounded by Lord Denning's declaration that a demand for tax without parliamentary sanction was a violation of the 1689 Bill of Rights – one of our few scraps of written constitution. Perhaps he was also influenced by his special adviser, the civil rights lawyer Anthony Lester, also an enthusiast for a bill of rights. But the clinching point was probably that at this time Jenkins was firmly resisting demands from the Labour left to release the 'Shrewsbury Two', jailed for picketing offences, on the grounds that politicians should not interfere in the administration of justice. Against that background, a fight with the Court of Appeal over constitutional supremacy was politically impossible. Certainly it helped to queer the pitch for the politicians' next best hope of seeing off the courts: the Laker Skytrain case. There is a sizeable body of opinion that the Court of Appeal – led, again, by Lord Denning – got the law wrong when it declared invalid the decision to revoke Laker's transatlantic licence (the court appears to have confused the power to issue guidance with the power to issue a directive). The government seriously considered an appeal to the Lords. But in this case, as the

trade secretary Edmund Dell has recorded,[44] there were many conflicting considerations including public support for Laker's attempt
to reduce transatlantic air fares, and eventually the government
called it quits. But it is interesting to note, from Dell's account, that
there was none of the sense of affront that counsel in the television
licences case had voiced a year earlier at the courts overruling a
minister. Even though the government's legal case in the TV licences
case had been weaker, that had been the point where the psychological pass had been sold.

The second crucial period in which the courts might have been
challenged followed the case in which the Divisional Court struck
down a reduction in Brent Council's rate support grant because the
environment secretary had refused to listen to further representations made by the council.[45] Nothing could have been better calculated to infuriate Mrs Thatcher, hostile to both local councils and
public spending. This author worked at the time in local government
in London and recalls the widespread rumours that the government
would legislate to clip the courts' wings. But it never came to pass; in
all probability, the government decided that parliamentary resistance, technical difficulty and the judges' determination to get
round any restriction placed on them (*à la* Anisminic) made legislation hazardous and futile. Instead, Whitehall resorted to prevention:
production of the pamphlet *The Judge over Your Shoulder* on how to
avoid legal challenge, and better legal training for civil servants.

The immediate aftermath suggested that the government had less
to fear from the courts than it might have anticipated. In the early
and mid-1980s the most newsworthy judicial review decisions were
favourable to the government, notably on local authority finance
and rate-capping, and on GCHQ. A series of judgements on local
government pleased ministers by striking down the radical policies
of Labour councils, including the Greater London Council's cheap
fares policy, the banning of a rugby club that toured South Africa, and
the blacking of newspapers produced by Times Newspapers, which
was involved in an industrial dispute.[46] Outside the sphere of judicial
review, the courts turned in a number of significant judgements
against trade unions in the field of industrial relations (including
judgements at the time of the 1984–85 miners' strike) and in favour
of the government in such cases as the Sarah Tisdale leak to the
Guardian and the *Spycatcher* injunction.[47] The Thatcher government's

relative complaisance towards the activist behaviour of the judiciary can be measured by the large number of public enquiries on politically sensitive issues confided to senior judges.

Still, beneath the phosphorescence of these politically lively cases there was a powerful technical undertow. The same development principles being developed in local government cases would eventually be turned against central government. A string of unglamorous but technically significant defeats in areas like immigration and the requirement to consult was opening the eyes of lawyers to the potential of judicial review as a way of challenging central government.[48] Access to judicial review was made easier by the virtual abolition in England and Wales of the requirement for a challenger to show a direct interest in the decision at issue: so Sir William Rees-Mogg was allowed to challenge the implementation of the Maastricht Treaty because of his 'sincere concern for the constitutional issues'.[49] (The Scottish courts still insist quite stringently that litigants prove 'title and interest'.) Most significant of all, when the euphoria of winning the GCHQ case subsided, ministers woke up to the full implications of their Pyrrhic victory: although the Lords had found for the government on the issue of national security, they had also held, firstly, that actions under the royal prerogative were susceptible to judicial review; and secondly, that the doctrine of a legitimate expectation to be consulted on a decision affecting you now permeated the entire administrative law, with colossal implications for the freedom of action of central government.

In the 1990s central government began to feel the full force of the developments in judicial review that had evolved over the previous decade. Particularly prominent was the foreign secretary's defeat in the Pergau Dam case – a decision to which the prime minister had been party.[50] But the environment and home secretaries suffered most at the hands of the courts. The review of local government structure led to a series of judicial reviews, some of which went against the environment secretary.[51] The home secretary's remodelling of the criminal injuries compensation scheme was declared illegal,[52] requiring a new act of parliament, and the entire immigration system came under intense pressure from a veritable tidal wave of judicial challenges.

Most irksome to all ministers, however, was the home secretary's defeat in the case of 'in re. M'. As the result of an honest misunderstanding, M – a citizen of Zaire challenging by judicial review his deportation – was deported in mid-hearing. A furious judge ordered his immediate return to Britain, but the then home secretary, Kenneth Baker, refused, contending that judicial injunctions were not binding on the Crown (a correct reading of previous case law). On his return to Zaire M contacted the British authorities and asked for readmission, but then vanished and has not been heard of since. The courts, however, pursued the issue and eventually the House of Lords unanimously reversed their earlier judgements to hold Mr Baker to be in contempt of court, Lord Templeman declaring resolutely that 'the proposition that the executive obeyed the law as matter of grace, not of necessity... would reverse the result of the Civil War'.[53] Under the circumstances the court imposed no penalty on Mr Baker, by then dropped from the government, but the ability of applicants for judicial review to injunct the Crown from pursuing its policies while their cases are pending has proved a nuisance to the government in England and Wales ever since. (In Scotland the Crown may not be injuncted, but in practice the Crown will not proceed with a controversial action which is the subject of judicial challenge.)

It is worth repeating that central government was not the only target. This epoch saw a general upsurge of judicial activity restraining public authorities across the board. The wave of immigration cases brought against the Home Office found its municipal counterpart in a huge volume of homelessness cases brought against local councils, who also found their powers to restrict discretionary grants and to charge for services clipped.[54] The courts showed themselves willing to extend judicial review to quasi-public bodies such as university visitors, financial regulatory bodies and the regulatory bodies of sports.[55]

Equality of misery across the public sector was no comfort to the politicians, however. Some, like foreign secretary Douglas Hurd, took defeat gamely: of his antagonists in the Pergau Dam case, he admitted ruefully, 'The World Development Movement was entirely entitled to act as it did and it showed considerable perseverance and skill in doing so' – even though their victory had driven him to the point of resignation.[56] Other political actors took it less well. The Speaker of the House of Commons took the unusual step, when the courts agreed to consider the Rees-Mogg challenge to the Maastricht Treaty, of making a formal statement to the House warning the judges not to infringe the privileges of parliament by questioning its proceedings.[57] Sir Ivan Lawrence, former Chairman of the Commons Home Affairs Select Committee, has declared, 'It is a disaster. We've opened up a whole field and made it impossible for the Government to take any decision without being challenged.'[58] Possibly there was also some political resentment at the fact that, thanks in large measure to judicial review, legal personalities were beginning to imprint their names on the public consciousness: members of the judiciary like Lord Chief Justice Taylor, his successor Sir Thomas Bingham, Lord Woolf, Mr Justice Laws, and members of the Bar such as David Pannick, Helena Kennedy and Lord Lester of Herne Hill, became known both for their involvement in high-profile cases and for their views expressed in media appearances, articles and interventions in House of Lords debates.

One clear sign of political interest was the front-page lead story carried by the *Daily Telegraph* on 7 December 1995 'as a result of a briefing from an authoritative Government source' (which turned out to be Conservative Central Office) that the Lord Chancellor was to make a speech to judges reminding them the courts were not superior to parliament. A public letter from the Lord Chancellor denied the story, but took the opportunity to make clear his view on the relative authority of parliament and courts: that there is no superior 'fundamental' law by which the legality of statute may be measured; that judicial review is designed to ensure that ministers take decisions within the boundaries of the law; and that the judges remain independent of parliament and government.[59] At almost the same time, the prime minister's press office confirmed that he was to hold informal conversations with the Lord Chief Justice to consider, amongst other things, the constitutional implications of judicial review.[60]

To conclude: it is tempting to write the history of judicial review around the more colourful judicial personalities involved; in the law as much as in politics, personalities count for much, since the beliefs and attitudes of key individuals are crucial elements in determining key decisions. Without Reid or Denning, judicial review would undoubtedly have evolved differently. But personalities alone cannot suffice to explain an outburst of activism that has been sustained for three decades and has visibly gained momentum. While the decline in public deference to authority has affected the atmosphere in which the courts operate, the crucial factor seems to have been the judicial perception that traditional reliance on elected institutions to restrain public authorities has become inadequate: a belief which gathered force in the public mind in the 1950s and which the judiciary – always following public opinion at a circumspect distance – absorbed into its outlook and judgements in the 1960s. The core reason for the rise of judicial review was judges' perception that greater government power, dominance of parliament by the executive, and the proliferation of secondary legislation had outstripped the ability of representative institutions to balance the scales between public power and private right. Therefore they created a second channel of accountability, supplementing but not supplanting that exercised by elected bodies. If constitutional shortcomings drove the judges' action, and common law provided the instrument, the evolving European dimension of our legal and constitutional system offers for the future a new means of expanding their intervention: both by the importation of new principles (the concept of legitimate expectations, for example, is European in origin) and by reference to European Union legislation and the principles set out in the European Convention on Human Rights. We have travelled a long way down the road towards an unknown destination. On one hand, the judges keep advancing; on the other, political irritation has started to show. This chapter is, at best, an interim report on an unresolved conflict.

Notes

1. The author is grateful to John McEldowney of the School of Law, University of Warwick, for his helpful comments on an earlier version of this paper.
2. M. Sunkin, L. Bridges and G. Meszaros, *Judicial Review in Perspective* (London: Public Law Project, 1993), p. 100.
3. S. James, 'The Political and Administrative Effects of Judicial Review', *Public Administration*, vol. 74(4) (1996).
4. National press, 10 and 11 November 1994.
5. *Liversidge* v. *Anderson* [1941] 3 AER 338.
6. A. V. Dicey, *Introduction to the Study of the Law of the Constitution* (first published 1885), 10th edn (London: Macmillan, 1959).
7. [1956] 1 AER 855.
8. [1963] 2 AER 66.
9. [1968] 1 AER 694.

10. [1969] 1 AER 694.
11. *Congreve* v. *Home Office* [1976] 1 AER 697; *Laker Airways* v. *Department of Trade* [1977] 2 AER 182; *Secretary of State for Education and Science* v. *Tameside BC* [1976] 3 AER 66.
12. *Council of Civil Service Unions* v. *Minister for the Civil Service* [1984] 3 AER 935.
13. *Associated Provincial Picture Houses Ltd.* v. *Wednesbury District Corporation* [1947] 2 AER 680.
14. *R.* v. *R* [1992] 1 AC 599.
15. *Woolwich Equitable Building Society* v. *Inland Revenue Commissioners* (No. 2), [1992] 3 AER at 763.
16. J. Griffith, *Judicial Politics since 1920*, 4th edn (Oxford: Blackwell, 1993), pp. 114–15.
17. House of Commons debates, 23 July 1946, col. 1893.
18. Quoted in the *Australian Law Journal*, vol. 25, 20 September 1951, p. 296; citation from B. Abel-Smith and R. Stevens, *Lawyers and the Courts: A Sociological Study of the English Legal System, 1750–1965* (London: Heinemann, 1967), pp. 287–8.
19. *Jacobs* v. *London County Council* [1950] 1 AER at 743.
20. Abel-Smith and Stevens, op. cit., 288.
21. G. Lewis, *Lord Atkin* (London: Butterworth, 1983), pp. 132–57.
22. At p. 868.
23. House of Lords debates, 26 July 1956, col. 350, cited in Abel-Smith and Stevens, p. 288.
24. Viscount Kilmuir, *Political Adventure* (London: Weidenfeld & Nicolson, 1964), pp. 261–3.
25. R. Heuston, *Lives of the Lord Chancellors, 1940–70* (Oxford: Clarendon Press, 1987), pp. 152–5.
26. Griffith, op. cit., pp. 79–101.
27. This is taken so much for granted in the British constitutional psyche that no great literature on the subject exists; but see F. F. Ridley, 'The Citizen Against Authority: British Approaches to the Redress of Grievances', *Parliamentary Affairs*, vol. 37 (1984), 1–32.
28. House of Commons debates, 20 July 1954, col. 284.
29. Lord Scarman, 'Editorial', *Public Administration*, special edition on judicial review, vol. 64(2) (1986).
30. House of Commons debates, 9 December 1975, col. 238.
31. *R.* v. *Parliamentary Commissioner for Administration ex parte Dyer* [1994] 1 AER 375.
32. House of Lords debates, 26 June 1995, col. 553.
33. Sir Thomas Bingham, 'The European Convention on Human Rights: Time to Incorporate', *Law Quarterly Review*, vol. 109 (July 1993), pp. 390–400.
34. *R.* v. *Secretary of State for the Environment, ex parte Nottinghamshire County Council* [1986] 1 AC 240.
35. House of Lords Select Committee on the Scrutiny of Delegated Powers: First Report, Session 1992–3 (London: HMSO, 1993).

36. House of Lords Select Committee on the Scrutiny of Delegated Powers, Fifth Report, Session 1994–5 (London: HMSO, 1995).
37. On the evolution of judicial attitudes towards public administration see J. McEldowney, 'The Courts and Good Administration', paper delivered at the Political Studies Association annual conference, 20 April 1995.
38. House of Lords debates, 26 June 1995, cols 530–56.
39. House of Lords debates, 27 January 1996, cols 967–1074.
40. Sir Thomas Bingham, op. cit.
41. Sir John Laws, 'Is the High Court the Guardian of Fundamental Human Rights?', *Public Law*, Spring 1993, pp. 59–79; 'Judicial Remedies and the Constitution', *Modern Law Review*, vol. 57 (1994), pp. 213–27.
42. National press, 3 August 1978.
43. House of Commons debates, 9 December 1975, cols 233–40.
44. Edmund Dell, 'Collective Responsibility: Fact, Fiction or Facade?', in Royal Institute of Public Administration, *Policy and Practice: the Experience of Government* (London: RIPA, 1980).
45. *R. v. Secretary of State for the Environment ex parte Brent London Borough Council* [1983] 3 AER 321.
46. *R. v. Greater London Council ex parte Bromley Borough Council* [l983] 1 AC 768; *Wheeler* v. *Leicester City Council* [l985] 2 AER 1106; *R. v. Ealing Borough Council ex parte The Times Newspapers Ltd* [1986] 85 LGR 316.
47. See Griffith, op. cit., pp. 157–78.
48. E.g. *R. v. Secretary for State for Social Services ex parte Association of Metropolitan Authorities* [l986] 1 WLR 1; *Bugdaycay* v. *Secretary of State for the Home Department* [l987] 1 AER 940.
49. *R. v. Secretary of State for Foreign and Commonwealth Affairs ex parte Rees-Mogg* [1994] 1 AER 457.
50. *R. v. Secretary of State for Foreign Affairs, ex parte World Development Movement Ltd* [l995] 1 AER 611.
51. E.g. *R. v. Secretary of State for the Environment ex parte Lancashire and Derbyshire County Councils* [1994] 4 AER 16.
52. *R. v. Secretary of State for the Home Department ex parte Fire Brigades Union and others* [1995] 2 AER.
53. [l993] 3 WLR 433 at 541.
54. *McCarthy and Stone (Developments) Ltd.* v. *Richmond upon Thames Borough Council* [1991] 3 AER 897; *R. v. Bexley Borough Council ex parte Jones* [1994] COD 393.
55. *Page* v. *University of Hull Visitor* [1991] 1 AER 442; *R. v. The Jockey Club ex parte Massingberd Munday* [l993] 2 AER 207.
56. House of Commons debates, 13 December 1994. Mr Hurd admitted contemplating resignation on the *Today* programme, BBC Radio 4, 11 November 1994.
57. House of Commons debates, 21 July 1993, cols 351–2.
58. *Spectator*, 17 June 1995.
59. *Daily Telegraph*, 7 and 8 December 1995.
60. *Daily Telegraph*, 5 December 1995.

8
From Character to Culture: Authority, Deference and the Political Imagination since 1945

Ken Young

The focus of this chapter is upon cultural change – changes in the things that people in Britain have commonly said and done during the 50 years since the armistice. It poses the question of to what extent the tacit understandings – for tacit they are – which constitute a 'nation' differ fundamentally in the Britain of 1995 from those of 1945. The question can be posed here but not resolved; comparisons of this sort across time are famously difficult due to the lack of comparable evidence. We must do the best we can with what we have to hand, remaining aware of the limitations of that evidence.

We have first to address the prior question: *how are we to understand these understandings?* Obviously, as 'cultural'. The overused and taken-for-granted term *cultural analysis* so permeates our discourse today that it would be right to say that the concept of culture is itself part of our culture, and the notion of 'political culture' has become a central element in the contemporary political imagination. It follows that the concept of culture can be said to have its own history.[1]

The uses of culture

The history of ideas is studded with paternity claims. Anthropology, the discipline which can lay special claim to the idea of culture as its very own 'fruitful paradox', had to live with disputes as to the identity of the true founding father.[2] Most date the establishment of the term to Sir Edward Tylor's *Primitive Culture*, published in 1871.[3] Some have claimed primacy outside professional anthropology for Matthew Arnold; others reach further back to the Renaissance, while yet others would be content to follow Lévi-Strauss's assertion that it is to Rousseau that we owe the recognisably modern nature/culture dichotomy, and that it is upon him, for this reason, that the founding father title rests.

Closer to home, the use of the term as an organising concept was originated for comparative historians by Arnold Toynbee, beyond whom it scarcely travelled at all until Philip Bagby's distinctively modern *Culture and History* in 1958. This showed that for intellectual historians since the Enlightenment, the exegesis of an idea and of the intellectual ethos in which it was located entailed examining belief systems and their social foundations. Similarly, the long-dominant tradition in constitutional history saw political institutions as the expressive arrangements of a people, habits and folk-ways reflecting time, circumstance and disposition. We have long been the unwitting speakers of the prose of cultural analysis.

All of these distinct concerns could be comfortably related to Tylor's own definition of culture as 'that complex whole which includes knowledge, belief, art, morals, law and custom and any other capabilities and habits acquired by man as a member of society'.[4] Yet, while the history of culture is fed by all these tributaries, it is for all practical purposes – that is to say, for our purposes today – a postwar history. This is so because the postwar period saw the displacement of the ubiquitous concept of *character* by the more exact, specific, complex and flexible concept of *culture* in the discourse of the political classes.

From 'character' to 'culture'

The first thing that distinguishes character and culture is the long-running popular usage of character as a term in sloganeering.[5] Character – specifically *national character* – was often the subject of crude nationalistic appeals of both positive and negative kinds. Character was used to exalt or debase a people as a whole. The term had, on the one hand, a particular utility in an age of competing European nationalisms for both nation-building (before and after the achievement of unification) and for the justification of colonial expansion.

Equally, as the competition for power and influence became more intense, negative characterisations could be employed to stiffen domestic opinion against a truculent rival.

In Britain, the idea of a German national character could be relied upon to evoke a common response throughout the first half of the twentieth century. The need to account for the rise of Nazism and its apparent sway over the German population put a premium on characterological explanations, and Vienna and Frankfurt provided them in full measure. The psychoanalytical conjectures of Reich and Fromm had more impact in Europe than in Britain, where they were seen, if read at all, as almost risible parodies of German national character with its propensity to submission to authority.[6]

The outbreak of war intensified the need to understand, the better to counter, this manifestation of a belligerent 'national character'. Propaganda for the home front was no longer the problematic issue. For this purpose the projection of character in a few bold strokes would suffice (although the entry of the Soviet Union into the war posed a challenge in terms of the rapidity with which a new and benign national character could be invented). Beyond the home front, something more sophisticated and sensitive than crude characterisation was required. First, black propaganda, strategic interpretation, political analysis. Later, planning for military occupation, denazification and the eventual handover to local powers. All owed a great deal to the developing arts of interpreting and acting upon mass belief; in short, on cultural analysis and the management of culture. The dispositions, values, beliefs and habits of what were now seen as authoritarian *cultures* were first to be manipulated, then, following the defeat of the Axis powers, destroyed and replaced. The Allied occupations were exercises in cultural reconstruction that had no parallels elsewhere.

It is not without significance, then, that those scholars who during the 1930s and 1950s contributed to cultural theory, spent much of the intervening decade in these most exotic forms of social planning. Arnold Toynbee, the populariser of cultural explanation in history, who had served in the Foreign Office's political intelligence branch in the Great War, returned to head its research department for the duration of the next. Anthropologists Margaret Mead, Ruth Benedict and Clyde Kluckhohn played important roles in research and policy advice in the United States, and their work then and later was explicitly seen as a practical and purposive dissection of authoritarian cultures and their liberal counterparts.[7] In Kluckhohn's case, the experience was one that led him to predict that when anthropologists 'returned home' they would be able to devote their new insights to solving the problems of the postwar world.[8]

So by the early 1950s the term 'character', had become a casualty of the peace, and was no longer in vogue. Some of its assumptions, however, were to splutter along as a reminder of the prewar world. Most notably, the followers of Fromm and Reich regrouped at Berkeley for a massive study, not of authoritarian character, but of the *authoritarian personality*.[9] Their uneasy fusion of Freud and Marx, of sexuality and social conflict – initially greeted with something approaching adulation – promised to probe deeper than the pragmatic programme of German normalisation and raise the awkward question of whether 'it could happen here'.[10] Too fastidious for such crudities, the lonely Conservative philosopher Michael Oakeshott ploughed a parallel furrow, presenting modern European history as a struggle between the self-transforming individual character and the seemingly ascendant *anti-individual* character, distinguished by ready abdication to the claims of authority and conformity.[11] Intellectual opposites, Oakeshott and the Berkeley school were both dealing with the psychopathology of liberal democracy.

Yet these more sophisticated and subtle reworkings of the idea of character were already out of their time. Attacking the wrong enemy – incipient Nazism – at a time of German rearmament and cold war anti-Sovietism, the authors of *The Authoritarian Personality* themselves fell victim to the very tendency they sought to dissect, this time in the form of the California loyalty oath and professional ostracism.[12] Arguably, though, they were behind their intellectual times too, for the focus on 'personality' was too close to character, too psychologistic, and over-neglectful of the larger issues of cultural fashioning. For a delicious moment, though, serious scholarship fluttered on the cusp between the traditional concept of character and the emerging concept of culture. Mead and Metraux's 1953 *The Study of Culture at a Distance* contained a 20-page bibliography on 'national character', perhaps the last to be published.[13] Less obviously ambivalent was a curious British classic researched in 1950 and published five years later, Geoffrey Gorer's *Exploring English Character*. A mile-

stone in the understanding of postwar Britain, in this case the lan-
guid title was something of a pose.

A serious anthropologist of psychoanalytic disposition who had
made his own wartime contribution, Gorer had contributed importantly to cultural analysis since the 1939 American Historical Association's symposium on *The Cultural Approach to History*. He had already
secured his place in the history of the concept of culture. Gorer was
nonetheless tempted by the opportunities for popular journalism and
large-scale analysis that were offered to him by *The People* newspaper,
which was prepared to sponsor and fund what turned out to be a
massive (10,000 respondent) survey. In this apparently down-market
enquiry into sexual behaviour, child-rearing practices and church-
going, Gorer's prose reveals a hard inner core of serious *cultural
analysis*, even if the term itself never appears in the book.

For example, an appendix sets out a remarkable manifesto for
cultural management, in the guise of 'the transformation of the
character of the mass of the population' through police recruitment
programmes designed to enhance social role modelling. Or consider
this statement from a man ready to be portrayed as an ingratiating
journalist fronting a largely titillating social survey of popular newspaper readers:

> syntax by itself structures the world for its speakers. Ideas of time
> and sequence are largely determined by verbal forms; languages
> which possess gender group objects together in a way which
> would not occur to speakers of gender-less languages. The
> thoughts we can have about the world are to a very great degree
> determined by the words our language possesses to express
> them.[14]

The forgotten Gorer perhaps merits rehabilitation today. His reputation diminished rather than enhanced by *Exploring English Character*, Gorer was nonetheless the emblematic social scientist of Britain
in the early 1950s. And, as we shall see, the impulses behind his
project themselves reveal much about cultural change in postwar
Britain.

Despite – or perhaps because of? – Gorer, the developments in
the culture concept over the next decade or so all came from
the United States. Five years after *The Authoritarian Personality*

was published, political scientist Gabriel Almond was working up what was to prove to be a seminal article on political culture, which asserted that 'every political system is embedded in a particular pattern of orientations to political action'.[15] The framework which he erected on this apparent truism owed its paternity to the work of Talcott Parsons, to such psychoanalytically oriented anthropologists as the Kluckhohns, and to the expanding horizons offered by the social survey as a research tool. This last proved the most powerful impulse; political culture was here to stay.[16]

Its arrival, though, coincided with a revival of great power competition just as clearly as had the earlier usages of national character. Almond's concept was advanced through a series of studies – generically the *Princeton Studies* – of political development. Co-written with James Coleman, *The Politics of Developing Areas* launched the series; Lucien Pye and Sidney Verba followed with *Political Culture and Political Development*.[17] The implicit model of the developed polity which typified these and the following studies was one which embodied Anglo-American values and American institutional arrangements. The Third World was by these means to be secured for democracy against an implied Soviet threat. What was in play here was a contest of strategies for cultural management. Almond was later to conclude that the more exalted expectations of both sides had been falsified by experience. The attempts of communist regimes to manage their political culture to the extent of making a new socialist citizen were uniform failure, and political culture shown to be a phenomenon of 'limited plasticity'.[18]

At the same time, the workings of the more-or-less stable democratic polity were to be more deeply explored using a refinement and elaboration of the concept of political culture. This appeared in 1963 as *The Civic Culture*, a comparative social survey of the USA, Britain, Mexico, Italy and Germany, five countries which were chosen for their contrasting experiences of stability and civility.[19] It was 'a study of the political culture of democracy and of the social structures and processes that sustain it'. The analysis of political culture had taken a new, empirical, turn, and the interpretation of postwar Britain was to play a central role in its further development.

The 'exemplary' character of Britain's civic culture

Space does not permit a full review of *The Civic Culture*'s intellectual apparatus. Of particular importance, though, was the way in which that elusive ideal – the civic culture itself – was defined. It was a tension or balance between opposing forces, sometimes to be found in different groups or classes, sometimes (we might infer) within the individual him or herself. On the one hand, activism, confidence, political assertiveness and ready participation. On the other, deference, moderation, acceptance, acquiesence and trust in authority. A blend of traditional and modern, subject and citizen values. And judged in these terms, Britain was a model of the civic culture; indeed, gushed Almond and Verba, 'the whole story of the emergence of the civic culture is told in British history'.

It would be hard to argue that the publication of *The Civic Culture* made much impact on this 'exemplary' society. Dennis Kavanagh explains this neglect in part in terms of the quite different interests and concerns of the 200 or so political scientists (*sic*) in British universities at the time, of whom only a handful had any familiarity with the theoretical and methodological apparatus on which the study was founded.[20] Clearly, a handful of a mere 200 must be a very small number of readers indeed. Despite this studied ignorance, *The Civic Culture* exercised an unrecognised influence on subsequent research undertaken, for example, by the UK Government Social Survey in the early 1960s.[21] In any case, by the time the number of potential readers had grown with changes in the intellectual orientation of teachers of politics, *The Civic Culture* had come to be seen as embarrassingly naïve and – more pertinent to this discussion – as simply wrong.

Wrong, though, in the authors' judgements and in their predictions, rather than in their own direct evidence. In particular, Almond and Verba's attribution of deference and acquiesence in authority to the British population was sharply challenged. Kavanagh, in an important article, challenged the deference thesis.[22] Alan Marsh's survey-based study of protest behaviour, written in the very middle of the postwar period, adduced additional evidence to the effect that the British were an unruly and undeferential lot.[23] These conclusions evoke Gorer's own startling attribution of Britain's famous tolerance and stability not to a deep and noble civility, but to the anxious repression of a savage, underlying aggression.

Among the most persuasive of the evidence quoted by these and other critics was a series of tables in the *World Handbook of Social and Political Indicators*. These showed that, of 136 countries examined for the period 1948–67, Britain ranked 10th for the incidence of protest demonstrations and 36th for the incidence of riots. Britain's reputation as an orderly polity rested mainly on its placing at about the bottom of the league table for violent, life-threatening political conflict – a ranking that must surely now have changed.[24] These new and critical interpretations were reinforced by other evidence of change away from civility. For no sooner had Almond and Verba established the primacy of political trust and deference in Britain than it appeared to fold up before their very eyes; soon writers were casually referring to the collapse or decline of the civic culture itself.[25]

The changing political culture of postwar Britain

While it might now be said that *The Civic Culture* has been revalued (and in the process shown to have worn better than many predicted) the real value of the study lies in its provision of an evidential benchmark for the discussion of postwar Britain. This can be seen by examining just one dimension drawn from *The Civic Culture*, one which has proved useful in the exploration of social change. A key axiom of *The Civic Culture* was that it rested on a high degree of 'subjective political competence' – the belief that an individual could and would make his or her voice heard in respect of some unwelcome or wrong (specifically, 'unjust or harmful') action on the part of government, central or local. The survey presented respondents with the prospect of such a governmental action, asked them what, if anything, they had done, what they would do, and with what expected effect.

The free responses offered by Almond and Verba's respondents were then categorised as follows: the respondents might contact their MP; speak to an influential person; contact a government department; contact radio, television or newspaper; sign a petition; raise the issue in an organisation to which they belong; go on a protest or demonstration; form a group of like-minded people; or take none of these actions. Since 1983 I have worked with these 'civic culture' categories, suitably grouped, in a number of surveys, national and local.[26] What evidence of cultural change emerges?

As they are ordered here, not as they were presented in the original volume, we see nine options, eight of which are to act, and one of which is to do nothing. Of the eight, the first four (contact with MP, influential person, government department or the media) refer to actions that are essentially personal in their efficacy; that is, they do not depend on others for their logic, but on the power and influence of the individual undertaking them. Items five to eight, on the other hand (signing petitions, raising the issue in an organisation, protesting or demonstrating, forming a group), are wholly dependent for their efficacy on others joining in. Rooted in the logic of collective action, their efficacy is generally supposed to be proportionate to the numbers involved. A petition with a single signature, for example, is hardly a petition, and a one-person protest is something less than a march.

Let us call these responses 'political assertiveness'. Looking again at *The Civic Culture*'s 1960 findings, we discover that when faced with an unjust or harmful government action, 47 per cent of the respondents would have taken some personal action, and 23 per cent some collective action, while 32 per cent would have done nothing and six per cent could not answer. The first comparison to be made comes with the re-running of the question in the 1983 *British Social Attitudes* (BSA) survey, a comparison (see Table 8.1) which is highly suggestive of marked social change.[27]

Table 8.1 Political assertiveness in 1960 and 1983

	Proportions choosing action and inaction	
	1960 %	1983 %
Faced with the prospect of an unjust or harmful law, respondent would:		
Take personal action	47	77
Take collective action	23	77
Do nothing	32	14
Don't know	6	1

Source: G. Almond and S. Verba, *The Civic Culture: Political Attitudes and Democracy in Five Nations* (Princeton, NJ: Princeton University Press, 1963); R. Jowell and C. Airey (eds), *British Social Attitudes: The 1984 Report* (Aldershot: Gower, 1984).

This table has been misinterpreted by other commentators, who overlook the fact that Almond and Verba's question was unprompted – respondents were asked what they would do – while in all subsequent surveys respondents have been invited to choose from among Almond and Verba's post-survey categorisation.[28] Inevitably, then, the changes between 1960 and 1983 are greatly overstated by this question effect. Although it is impossible to estimate the magnitude of the effect, it seems likely that it was greater in the realm of collective than personal action. That is, the possibility of joining with others came less readily to mind than the impulse to 'see somebody about it'.

There is a useful summary statistic that captures the important relationship: that between the (multiple) courses of action chosen, and inaction. A very simple formula gives two indices for personal and collective assertiveness – what may be termed the Personal Assertiveness Index (PAI) and the Collective Assertiveness Index (CAI). The formulae are:

$$\text{PAI} = \frac{P - i}{n} \quad \text{and} \quad \text{CAI} = \frac{C - i}{n}$$

where P is the number of personal actions mentioned, C the number of 'collective' actions, i the number of persons choosing none of the alternatives, and n the total number of respondents. Each has a theoretical maximum value of $+4$ (where all respondents choose all courses of action) and a theoretical minimum value of -1 (where no respondent chooses any course of action). As the index score is quite strongly affected by non-participation and is geared to multiple course of action, it discriminates well between subgroups in the population.

Calculating scores for the 1983 BSA study gives similar scores (as the table would suggest), in this case of 0.64 for PAI and 0.65 for CAI. Calculating scores for the Almond and Verba study (which should not, of course, be done) would give two figures close to zero. Perhaps a rough rule of thumb might be to attribute half of the apparent change to question effect, and half to actual cultural change, giving estimated 1960 figures of around 0.3. Experience has shown that in the 1990s a score well clear of 1 would be considered a high score, and a score well under 0.5 a low score.

Table 8.2 Political assertiveness scores for selected subgroups, 1983

	PAI	CAI
Age of completing full-time education		
19 or over	1.03	1.03
17 or 18	0.78	0.63
16 or under	0.56	0.59
Party identification		
Conservative	0.72	0.60
Alliance	0.74	0.89
Labour	0.60	0.67

Source: R. Jowell and C. Airey (eds), *British Social Attitudes: The 1984 Report* (Aldershot: Gower, 1984).

Table 8.2 illustrates the ways in which PAI and CAI scores vary – in different directions – among different subgroups of the population.

We can now turn to consider the light the PAI/CAI scores cast on social change in postwar Britain. Table 8.3 shows the summary scores for PAI for 1983, 1986 and 1991, broken down by social class. Table 8.4 shows the corresponding CAI scores.[29]

Table 8.3 PAI (Personal Assertiveness Index) scores by social class, 1983, 1986 and 1991

	1983	1986	1991
Social class			
I	0.83	0.96	1.15
II	0.83	1.07	1.07
III non-manual	0.75	0.87	0.95
III manual	0.59	0.69	0.75
IV	0.52	0.67	0.71
V	0.35	0.63	0.52

Source: R. Jowell and C. Airey (eds), *British Social Attitudes: The 1984 Report* (Aldershot: Gower, 1984); R. Jowell, S. Witherspoon and L. Brook (eds), *British Social Attitudes: The 1987 Report* (Aldershot: Gower, 1987); R. Jowell and L. Brook (eds), *British Social Attitudes: The Ninth Report* (Aldershot: Gower, 1992).

Table 8.4 CAI (Collective Assertiveness Index) scores by social class, 1983, 1986 and 1991

	1983	1986	1991
Social class			
I	0.86	1.02	1.06
II	0.76	0.97	1.21
III non-manual	0.55	0.77	1.00
III manual	0.61	0.75	0.98
IV	0.37	0.54	0.76
V	0.36	0.89	1.01

Source: See Table 8.3.

The value of these measures of cultural change and diversity is not confined to the national level. The exercise has been repeated, albeit infrequently, using a question form that refers to *local* political protest. With the benefit of the employment of the same question form in local studies it has proved possible to compare localities with one another, and with the overall national picture. Comparison of results at both levels of government reveals that the propensity to protest against local government actions is higher than that recorded for parliamentary actions, reflecting perhaps the greater closeness of local government to the aggrieved citizen. Like those at the national level, these local-level scores show increases over time: Table 8.5 shows scores drawn from the 1984 *British Social Attitudes* survey, and calculated from a survey conducted for the Joseph Rowntree Foundation in 1990.[30]

Table 8.5 Protesting local council actions, 1984 and 1990

	1984	1990
PAI	1.13	1.32
CAI	0.69	0.79

Source: Alice Bloch and Peter John, *Attitudes to Local Government* (York: Joseph Rowntree Foundation, 1990).

Conclusion

Welcome or otherwise, 'political culture' has become an indispensable element in the modern political imagination. It serves much the same need as the earlier usage of character, and can be accepted as standing in its place. At the same time, it offers a richer and fuller insight, untrammelled by the limits and distortions that come from projecting the moral nature of the individual onto the national scene, so as to stand for the attributes of a people. On the other hand, 'culture' is as readily abused as the term it displaced, not least when it is transposed to some intermediate level between the individual and the nation, as when popular gurus incite aspiring managers to 'shape the culture' of their organisations.[31] To that extent, the idea of culture is as susceptible to expedient and self-serving misuse as was 'character' in, for example, the justification of Britain's imperial 'mission', a comparison that perhaps neatly captures the different worlds of 1945 and 1995.

Culture may be here to stay, but assessing cultural change still presents daunting problems. These figures presented above do not claim to tell the whole story of Britain's changing postwar political culture. They provide no more than a suggestive picture of change – inescapably one with sharper and clearer contours in the foreground of the recent past than in the background of the immediate postwar era. There surely has been an erosion of trust and an increase in political cynicism since 1945, trends that confound the hopes of social reconstruction that drove Labour to victory that year. True, claims to the special quality of British civility were ever overstated. Yet it does seem that Britain has moved further away from the 'exemplary' civic culture towards an assertive and truculent pattern of political behaviour. The 'new politics' is different in kind from the old, which will not now return.

Notes

1. The term is used in this chapter in the larger sociological sense of the attitudinal and behavioural attributes of a way of life, rather than in the narrower sense of the critical interpretation and purposive transmission of those aspects of a way of life which are to be valued.

2. James A. Boon, 'Further Operations of "Culture" in Anthropology: a Synthesis of and for Debate', in Louis Schneider and Charles Bonjean (eds), *The Idea of Culture in the Social Sciences* (London: Cambridge University Press, 1973), pp. 2–3.

3. Edward B. Tylor, *Primitive Culture: Researches into the Development of Mythology, Philosophy, Religion, Language, Art and Custom* (New York: Brentano, 1924 edn). Tylor was elected Oxford's (and Britain's) first Professor of Anthropology in 1883.

4. Ibid., p.1.

5. It might be argued that the more fruitful distinction is to be drawn not between the idea of 'character' and that of 'culture', but between the notion of individual character as a man's moral nature, and the bundles of characteristics that constitute both 'national character' and, later, 'culture'. If this line were followed through, it would become apparent that the notion of national character was a simple mistake – an unwarranted projection of individual character on to larger groups.

6. See especially Wilhelm Reich's 1933 tract, *The Mass Psychology of Fascism*, 3rd edn, trans. Vincent R. Carfagno (New York: Souvenir Press, 1970).

7. See Gabriel Almond, 'The Intellectual History of the Civic Culture Concept', in Gabriel Almond and Sidney Verba (eds), *The Civic Culture Revisited* (London: Sage Publications, 1989), p. 14, note 41.

8. Clyde Kluckhohn, *Mirror for Man* (New York: Whittesley House, 1949), quoted in Lucien Pye, 'Culture and Political Science: Problems in the Evaluation of the Concept of Political Culture', in Schneider and Bonjean, op. cit., p. 66.

9. T. Adorno, E. Frenkel-Brunswik, D. J. Levinson and N. Sanford, *The Authoritarian Personality* (New York: Harper, 1950).

10. For the intellectual history of this school, see Franz Samelson, 'Authoritarianism from Berlin to Berkeley: on Social Psychology and History', *Journal of Social Issues*, 42 (1) (1986), pp. 191–208.

11. Michael Oakeshott, 'The Masses in Representative Democracy', in Albert Hunold (ed.), *Freedom and Serfdom* (Dordrecht: D. Reidel, 1961), pp. 151–70.

12. Samelson, op. cit., pp. 200–1.

13. Margaret Mead and Rhoda Metraux, *The Study of Culture at a Distance* (Chicago: Chicago University Press, 1953).

14. Geoffrey Gorer, *Exploring English Character* (London: Cresset Press, 1955), pp. 28–9.

15. Gabriel A. Almond, 'Comparative Political Systems', *Journal of Politics*, (August 1956), pp. 391–409.

16. Yet it was by no means universally welcomed. For a forcefully argued dismissal of the idea that 'culture' can have any explanatory power, see Brian Barry, *Economists, Sociologists and Democracy* (Chicago and London: University of Chicago Press, 1978).

17. Gabriel A. Almond and James Coleman (eds), *The Politics of Developing Areas* (Princeton, NJ: Princeton University Press, 1965); Lucien W. Pye and

Sidney Verba (eds), *Political Culture and Political Development* (Princeton, NJ: Princeton University Press, 1965).

18. Almond, 'Intellectual History of the Civic Culture Concept', p. 32.

19. Gabriel Almond and Sidney Verba, *The Civic Culture: Political Attitudes and Democracy in Five Nations* (Princeton, NJ: Princeton University Press, 1963).

20. Dennis Kavanagh, 'Political Culture in Great Britain: the Decline of the Civic Culture', in Almond and Verba, *Civic Culture Revisited*, pp. 127–9.

21. See Committee on the Management of Local Government, vol. 3, *The Local Government Elector* (London: HMSO, 1967).

22. Kavanagh, op. cit.

23. Alan Marsh, *Protest and Political Consciousness* (Beverly Hills, Calif.: Sage, 1977).

24. C. L. Taylor and M. C. Hudson, *World Handbook of Political and Social Indicators* (New Haven, Conn.: Yale University Press, 1972).

25. Kavanagh, op. cit.; Anthony Heath and Richard Topf, 'Political Culture', in Roger Jowell, Sharon Witherspoon and Lindsay Brook (eds), *British Social Attitudes: The 1987 Report* (Aldershot: Gower, 1987), pp. 51–67; Roger Jowell and Richard Topf, 'Trust in the Establishment', in Roger Jowell, Sharon Witherspoon and Lindsay Brook (eds), *British Social Attitudes: The Fifth Report* (Aldershot: Gower, 1988), pp. 109–26.

26. Ken Young, 'Shades of Opinion', in Roger Jowell and Sharon Witherspoon (eds), *British Social Attitudes: The 1985 Report* (Aldershot: Gower, 1985), pp. 11–17.

27. Ken Young, 'Political Attitudes', in Roger Jowell and Colin Airey (eds), *British Social Attitudes: The 1984 Report* (Aldershot: Gower, 1984), p. 22.

28. Richard Topf, 'Political Change and Political Culture in Britain, 1959–87', in J. R. Gribbins (ed.), *Contemporary Political Culture: Politics in a Postmodern Age* (London: Sage, 1990), pp. 52–80.

29. Ken Young, 'Race, Class and Opportunities', in Roger Jowell and Lindsay Brook (eds), *British Social Attitudes: The Ninth Report* (Aldershot: Gower, 1992).

30. Ken Young, 'Local Government and the Environment', in Roger Jowell and Sharon Witherspoon (eds), *British Social Attitudes: The 1985 Report* (Aldershot: Gower, 1985), pp. 149–76; Alice Bloch and Peter John, *Attitudes to Local Government* (York: Joseph Rowntree Foundation, 1990).

31. It is a moot point whether 'organisational culture' can truly be said to exist, its taken-for-granted status notwithstanding. For serious discussions of the applicability of the concept at the level of the firm, see L. Smircich, 'Concepts of Culture and Organisational Analysis', *Administrative Science Quarterly*, (28) (1983); L. Smircich, 'Organisations as Shared Meanings', in L. Pondy et al. (eds), *Organisational Symbolism* (Greenwich, Conn.: JAI Press, 1983); and J. Martin and C. Siehl, 'Organisation Culture and Subculture: an Uneasy Symbiosis', *Organisational Dynamics*, (12) (1983).

9
Postwar Broadcasting and Changes in the Character of Political Public Life

Jenie Betteridge

Introduction

In the *BBC Year Book for 1946* Robert Silvey, Director of the BBC Listener Research Department, said:

> When the time comes for the social historian to tell the story of the last six years in Britain, it is to be hoped that he will not omit to record the nation's listening.[1]

Historical discourse generally tends to ignore the media or at best to regard them as a resource. That is, as a passive recorder of history that can be reconsulted and utilised to access history. Conversely, sociological discourse too often ignores history, and is concerned with social relationships regardless of time. This paper aims to show that the media were (and are) active participants in the history-making process; that the particular set of social relationships existent in the postwar period gave rise to a particular set of negotiations in which political broadcasting developed in a particular way.[2]

The war years, as Silvey asserted, had not only enormously increased the population's appetite for news, but also had seen unprecedented shifts of population. Furthermore, and importantly for broadcasting, the black-out had caused fundamental changes in the public's leisure habits. The important process of differentiating the audience also began during the war. The *General Forces Programme* was the first attempt by the BBC to cater for a particular category of listener. As Paddy Scannell and David Cardiff have argued:

> Reluctantly at first, the BBC came to accept that, as one of its major contributions to the war effort, it must make its programmes more acceptable and pleasing to the tastes of ordinary men and women both on the fighting front and on the home front.[3]

After the war the BBC provided for a differentiated audience and fulfilled its promise to introduce three radio services, the Home, Light and Third Programmes, all of which were operational by October 1946. BBC Television transmission resumed in June 1946 and the Independent Television services were introduced in September 1955. Television set ownership went from 20,000 in 1946 to 11 million in 1959. In 1955 when the monopoly was broken BBC transmissions could reach 94 percent of the population and there were over 5 million licence holders (although only 200,000 sets were capable of receiving the new programmes).

The 1950s are often dismissed as a featureless interlude between the war and the 'swinging sixties'. Yet the 1950s are crucial to any understanding of contemporary Britain in that they saw the complete 'mediatisation' of the country. The unprecedented growth in the medium of television distinguishes the period. After the 1945 general election the question was asked: 'What influence, for example, has been exerted by the nightly electoral broadcasts, in which radio technique may have counted for as much as merit of argument.'[4] The year 1951 saw the first televised Party Political Broadcast (PPB), and in 1959 the general election was dubbed 'the television election'. In a mere 14 years, radio was superseded by television as the medium for political communication.

The Conservatives believed their 1945 election defeat was caused not by anything that happened in the election campaign, nor by any desire on the part of the electorate for a more egalitarian society, but by the persistent use of the propaganda machinery by the socialists throughout the war, when the Conservatives had been observing the political truce. Socialist talk of an overwhelming mandate was nonsense as the vote was approximately equal. What the Conservative Party needed was a strengthening and reorganisation of the party machine to enable a persistent and ably conducted propaganda campaign to reverse the verdict.[5] Whether or not one agrees with this interpretation of the 1945 defeat, the Conservative Party was convinced that publicity and propaganda were now the key to political success.

The Labour Party, perhaps flushed with their 1945 success, continued to concentrate on pamphlets and the press. The Party maintained a negative attitude to television throughout the 1950s, but in 1946, Patrick Gordon Walker asserted the importance of radio as both a form of publicity and a means of accessing the upper classes. He produced notes for the appointment of a Labour Party Radio Officer. He argued that the Labour Party must:

> make full use of indirect publicity of a sort valuable to us. It would be particularly undesirable whilst Labour is in power to get or try to get a marked increase of direct Labour talks, etc. Moreover the nature of the BBC allows a much wider scope for indirect publicity. There are two main fields for indirect publicity:
> 1.   It pays to get certain subjects discussed.... We should pay particular attention to the new highbrow programme that the BBC is to run. Serious political discussions, reviews of political books, etc will appeal to a class of people it is not easy to reach in the normal way.
> 2.   The BBC likes debates and discussions about topical matters in which opposed views are presented.[6]

Indeed, throughout the 1950s the professional broadcasters were striving to find new ways of presenting politics to the public, not least through debates and discussions. The politicians had to learn new skills and develop new forms to transfer political practices, first to the microphone, then to the screen; radio differed from the public meeting, and television differed from both. The politicians negotiated with each other and with the professional broadcasters. The broadcasters did likewise.

It is in these everyday negotiations that the relationship between broadcasting and the changed character of political public life is embedded. The broadcasters' desire to attract politicians, and the politicians' desire for ably conducted propaganda campaigns coincided in the 1950s to change the character of political public life.

Competition and negotiation

To understand the negotiations it is first necessary to distinguish the two main types of political broadcasting that existed in the postwar era – formal and informal. For formal political broadcasting, PPBs, ministerial and budget broadcasts, politicians chose the subjects and the speakers, and the broadcasters merely provided the means for them to be transmitted. Informal political broadcasting consisted of those programmes in which politicians appeared or in which political issues were raised – precisely those programmes which Gordon Walker suggested could provide indirect publicity. For these the broadcasters had editorial control and could thus select speakers and content. The better broadcaster a politician proved to be, the more likely he was to be chosen to appear. In order to exploit these opportunities politicians had to develop appropriate skills.

The second necessary prerequisite for an understanding of the postwar negotiations is the necessity of situating them in the context of competition. Until 1955 there was competition between the radio and television broadcasting professionals at the BBC, and after 1955 between the BBC and Independent Television Authority (ITA).

Laurence Gilliam, BBC Head of Features, suggested that radio slowly developed its own forms:

> Once broadcasting had got over its initial intoxication with its own existence, it started to wonder what it was for...slowly, obstinately and with growing success, a group of writers and producers insisted on exploring the possibilities of the radio medium itself.[7]

Television, too, had slowly and obstinately to develop its own forms, and in competition with radio. Radio broadcasting had gained such kudos for the BBC throughout the war that it was thought to be unassailable as the medium for education and information. The Light Programme was to entertain, and though most popular, was thought of as the most trivial by the professional broadcasters at Broadcasting House. Maurice Gorham fostered the first few months of the new Light Programme and was then appointed to take charge of the reinstated television service at Alexandra Palace. This appointment was significant in that it demonstrated that television was also perceived as a light entertainment vehicle. Those professionals working in television actively encouraged politicians to embrace the new medium, not only as an alternative to political meetings and radio broadcasting, but also to improve the image of television and to enable television to compete with radio as a medium for education and information.

The most vocal expression of the competition between sound and vision is located in the arguments for the control of news output, not least because it was principally on the news that the BBC's wartime reputation was built. But news was also a major source of political information.

As early as 1946 negotiations were under way to produce *News in Vision*. Gorham wrote to the Director General, William Haley, suggesting that the prewar practice of recording the Nine O'clock News and transmitting it at the end of the evening's television programmes, in sound only, whilst the test card appeared on the screen, should now be discontinued. Film newsreels were not sufficient as they did not constitute news broadcasts but rather they were topical programmes. Gorham then gave a detailed account of proposals to develop television news so that it would be an explicit news of the day.[8] Haley replied:

> I doubt whether the implications of completely visual news bulletins have still been fully comprehended. There is all the difference between a news bulletin and a news reel. The first is a vital public service charged with responsibilities of all kinds. The second is in essence an entertainment.[9]

The light entertainment medium of television would have to content itself with newsreels.

In 1947 Tahu Hole was appointed Controller of News. Hole's attitudes, coupled with Haley's attitude to television, were largely responsible for keeping news from the television screens until 1954. His policy was one of caution: by eliminating the opportunity for mistakes the reputation of the BBC could be protected. No news item could be reported unless verified by two independent sources. Furthermore, Hole unquestioningly implemented the BBC policy that newsreaders did not participate in writing or presenting the news, they merely announced it. Innovation and interpretation were anathema to BBC Radio News. The lengths to which Hole was prepared to go to protect and isolate news were demonstrated in 1948. The Talks Department was seeking to produce a daily 5-minute radio talk to follow the 15-minute news bulletin at 10 o'clock on the Light Programme. George Barnes, who was at this time Director of the Spoken Word, wrote to Hole:

> The purpose of this five minute programme . . . is to interpret an item in the news in terms which will interest, and seem relevant to the experience of, the average Light Programme listener who probably left school at 14 or 15 and whose ideas on economics and politics are nebulous and parochial. The vocabulary and the amount of knowledge which can be assumed are matters for close study before the programme begins.[10]

Barnes was reiterating the broadcasters' perception of the Light Programme listener, who was also assumed to constitute the bulk of the television audience, as lacking the sophistication and education of listeners to the Home and Third Programmes. Despite the inherent elitism in this view, an attempt was to be made to include the Light Programme audience in the political discourse of the day.

Hole's objection was not to the inclusion of the less educated in political discourse, but to the attempt to connect a Talks Department Programme to the News Division. The original title suggested for this programme was *Tonight's News Topic*. Hole insisted that it must be made clear that the talks were not associated with the News Division, because news did not make comment or attempt interpretation. Thus, Hole argued, the word 'News' must be dropped from the title and the talks should not be trailed in news bulletins under any circumstances. Eventually, the title *Topic for Tonight* was agreed. Hole was still not satisfied and suggested that if the programmes were billed as *News* and *Topic for Tonight*,

> the impression created in the public's mind would be that the two separate programme items were related. . . . I think it would invite criticism on the grounds that it tended deliberately to mislead listeners into thinking that the topic would be springing directly from the News.[11]

Hole succeeded in keeping comment and news entirely separate. The programme did go on air but the subjects of the talks were broadly topical rather than based directly on the day's news. *Topic for Tonight* was not billed with news in the *Radio Times*, nor trailed in news bulletins.

Hole, with Haley as an ally, prevented any innovation in BBC news. In 1952, Ian Jacob replaced Haley as Director General. George Barnes was at this time Director of Television and Harman Grisewood was Director of the Spoken Word. In 1953 they reported to the General Advisory Committee that:

> The institution of a visualised news bulletin has long been regarded as necessary... and in view of the likelihood of commercial television in 1955 it is proposed to start such a service in the first quarter of 1954.[12]

Cecil McGivern, Controller of Programmes, Television, was fighting to get Hole to relinquish his stultifying hold on news. Hole's elitist attitude not only served to isolate news from all other forms of broadcasting, but also his prevention of a visual news service led the politicians to doubt that television was an appropriate medium for serious political communication. John Green, Head of Radio Talks, described the period thus:

> Television was a frippery, speech was the communicating medium. In the hassle between Hole and McGiven things came to a complete standstill. They were not on speaking terms. Jacob asked me to reconcile them. Using his military experience he wanted to put the two protagonists with two others to get to the bottom of it. He asked who would be as detached as me. Frank Gillard (Head of West Region) was decided upon. Frank and I spent two years reporting, it was an appalling waste of time.[13]

Nevertheless, the first television *News and Newsreel* went on the air in July 1954. Hole had done little more than to attempt to transpose his sound policies to the screen. When no film was available, the announcer read the news out of vision against a caption. Hole insisted that seeing the reader's face would introduce personality to the hitherto anonymous news. Public and press reactions to these first attempts at television news were so negative that, a few weeks before the start of ITN, Hole relented and allowed the newsreader to be seen on BBC Television News. However, Aiden Cawley, the first Editor-in-Chief of ITN, had publicised his intention of using news-casters, who would both write and present the news, in a style natural to the spoken word. The newscaster was to inject something of his personality into the ITN news bulletins, to give them added meaning and vitality.[14]

Reginald Bosanquet described the early days of ITN as successful in jolting the BBC out of their complacency about news coverage by taking viewers away from them with the fresh approach. Then along came the Suez crisis, when Bosanquet asserts:

> Our newly won viewers deserted us in hordes. Why? The reason was simple. During World War II, then still very vivid in people's minds, the BBC had built itself a tremendous reputation across the globe for its factual reporting and integrity of its treatment of news. Could this new service ITN, although much livelier in its presentation, be relied on in the same way?[15]

Viewing figures slumped and it took some years to reach the point where viewers had the same confidence in ITN as they had in the BBC. Nevertheless, the advent of Independent Television was a turn-ing point in the development of television. To meet the challenge of the new competitor, BBC sound and vision had no option but to co-operate in developing the news in vision.

Competition also made it harder for the BBC to maintain an air of deference to politicians. For instance, in 1956 Grace Wyndham Goldie, Assistant Head of Television Talks, was refused permission to send Aiden Cawley to Cairo to interview Nasser in the wake of the Suez crisis. The Prime Minister considered it unwise to give Nasser a platform. Yet, in 1957, the Robin Day interview with Nasser for ITN was proclaimed as innovative television of the highest calibre. The BBC could only take comfort in the fact that the Day interview went out at the off-peak time of 11.05 p.m. and was thus seen by a rela-tively small audience. Eden's attempt to appropriate the BBC during the Suez crisis, coupled with the breaking of the monopoly, led the BBC to ask if they should continue to serve the wishes of parliament when there was no such onus on the independent services.

The Conservative Party, which had broken the monopoly, also realised that there was no such onus on the new services. In 1957, the Party's General Director pointed out that the ITA could reduce audience figures for PPBs:

> It was absolutely vital that the (ITA) programme companies should be persuaded to take the broadcasts at least for the coming year, otherwise we shall have an alternative programme which may mean losing three quarters of our viewing audience.[16]

The dilemma was resolved by all parties insisting that the ITA broadcast the complete series of PPBs, at exactly the same time as the BBC transmissions. The audience could turn off, but no alternative viewing was to be offered.[17]

Competing for the audience, and the now differentiated sections of it, was a key factor for both broadcasters and politicians. The early radio PPBs on the Home Service had to compete with the programmes being provided on the Light and Third programmes. In 1947, the London Labour Party wrote to the Party Chairman, Morgan Phillips, indicating that their 'friends' at the BBC had voiced some concern about the arrangements for the forthcoming political broadcasts.

> Namely, the PM follows immediately after a session of *The Brains Trust*, which has a low listening figure, while on the Light Programme there is a peak listening item – a Boxing broadcast – with which the PM will have to compete. In the case of Mr Eden there is apparently no substantial attraction on the Light, while he follows immediately after *ITMA* which of course has the largest listening figure of all items. Our friends are very much concerned that this sort of thing may be repeated unless a suitable amount of care is taken.[18]

As BBC television had the monopoly, the situation did not arise until 1955, and then the politicians pre-empted the position by the insistence, discussed above, that the ITA adhere exactly to the BBC's schedules.

Thus the timing of programmes was seen as a crucial element in securing an audience. In the absence of competition, politicians vied to get the Thursday evening slot for their televised PPBs. The theory was that greater numbers of the working classes would watch the broadcasts as they would lack the money to seek entertainment outside the home, Friday being the traditional pay day of the weekly paid. The timing of programmes was not the only factor in attracting the audience. Popularity was also an issue.

Jacob wrote to the Conservative Party Office in 1957, discussing the popularity of PPBs, and asserted that the Corporation did not wish to convey that they found PPBs consistently unpopular. They were not unpopular broadcasts of their kind.

> What we did want to make clear was the deterrent effect of placing these broadcasts at a time when the public expects to be entertained; this deterrent effect is still greater of course when a PPB is substituted for a popular entertainment item which thereby has to be dropped.[19]

The average audience for a PPB was classed against those for programmes like *In the News* and *Press Conference*, which were designed to be popular and did attract larger audiences. Jacob suggested that the BBC could advise on improvements in technical production, but to go further than this and attempt to make these broadcasts rival the attraction of popular entertainment would be unreal and moreover harmful to political broadcasting. Jacob was thus both complaining that the politicians were seeking to override the BBC schedule and force popular items to be dropped, and stressing that it was professional broadcasters not politicians who excelled at producing popular entertainment. Politicians may not have wanted to be confused with entertainers but they could see the advantages of being on the air at a time when the audience expected to be entertained and would therefore be gathered in larger numbers. Presumably, like many of today's critics of the media, they assumed the 'passive' audience would attend to what ever it was given.

However, in 1959 a Conservative PPB cut short an extremely interesting scientific programme on the BBC and the audience demonstrated its activity rather than passivity by complaining in large numbers. The Party was urged to take steps to avoid a Party programme suffering damage by unsympathetic programming:

> It does bring out the risk that one of our programmes may fail to get across simply because, through no fault of its own, it appears to displace, or cut short, a very popular programme.[20]

Politicians not only competed with the broadcasters for sympathetic programming and popularity of programmes, they were also competing with broadcasters to maintain the primacy of parliament as the forum for debate.

In 1944, the BBC enshrined their deferential attitude to parliament in the introduction of the 14-day rule or – as Frank Gillard described it – 'the BBC's ludicrous own goal'.[21] The rule forbade discussion of matters to be discussed in parliament during the following fortnight. Television was not to compete with parliament by simultaneously debating issues. As time passed broadcasters pointed out the idiocy of the rule, which they themselves had introduced. Often it was not possible to know, 14 days in advance, what was to be debated. Further, issues for debate were just those topical issues on which the public should be informed. The rule effectively prohibited the BBC from carrying out the duty to inform. In 1955 Jacob noted:

> As time went on it became more difficult to operate the rule, and the Governors felt that it was not one which should be perpetuated. For some time past they have been doing their utmost to get rid of it.[22]

The live programme *Any Questions?*, produced by Gillard, was instrumental in removing the rule. In 1956 the programme went out in the same week as the Budget. Freddie Grisewood, the question-master, pointed out that the rule prohibited the panel from discussing Budget issues, or any other matter, such as housing, which would have financial implications. Despite the warning, Conservative MP, Ted Leather, began the programme by thanking the questioner, who had asked about the cost of living, 'for blowing this iniquitous and stupid foruteen day rule out'.[23] The panel pursued the matter to the embarrassment of Grisewood and the amusement of the audience.

Noting that the Budget ruled out almost every topic for political debate as most had some pecuniary implications, a compromise was sought. Anthony Eden was given assurances that the BBC and ITA would not usurp the supremacy of parliament if the rule were suspended. An initial six-month suspension led to the rule never being re-introduced. However, the BBC's annoyance with parliament for breaking the monopoly may well have lessened their deference to the institution and strengthened their desire to be rid of a rule that perpetuated its supremacy.

Woodrow Wyatt, writing in 1955, argued the necessity for the 14-day rule. Simultaneous parliamentary and television debates were to be resisted, for they opened the way to the televising of parliament itself. The grave implication was that putting parliament on the screen was to put MPs permanently on the election platform. Speeches would be made not to convince parliament, but to harangue voters. He also argued that 'The House of Commons works smoothly because it is informal.... You cannot be intimate with several millions of viewers watching. Relaxing with feet upon the table would vanish.'[24] Perhaps to prevent MPs haranguing voters, or to allow them to keep their feet on the table, the politicians resisted the televising of parliament for nearly 40 years. The cameras entered the House of Lords in 1985 and the House of Commons in 1989. Prime Minister's Question Time was an unknown phenomenon to the 1950s audiences. Conversely, the relaxed, untelevised House of Commons of the 1950s, where MPs were not electioneering, is an unknown phenomenon today. The cameras did not simply enter and record parliament, they became an integral part of the parliamentary process, and consequently parliamentary practices changed.

The Conservatives' belief in the supremacy of parliament was also evident in the extraordinary action by Winston Churchill, as Prime Minister, in banning government ministers and junior ministers from informal broadcast debates. In 1952, the BBC suggested a series of radio debates between junior ministers and their predecessors. Churchill at first agreed in principle but, having giving the matter consideration, wrote the following memo to Lord Swinton (Chancellor of the Duchy of Lancaster):

On second thoughts I am rather shy about these Junior Ministers' broadcasts. Why should they be given precedence over the departmental chiefs? Why should the Socialists have the advantage of putting up quite irresponsible people to cross examine our Under Secretaries? It is not a fair contest anyway. Their people can say anything that is popular, and ours in reply will be limited not only by Government policy but by how far they are entitled to be exponents of it. The first case that came along was for an Under Secretary of the Foreign Office to have a duel with Aneurin Bevan on Foreign Affairs. Do we really want this? Are we not giving Bevan an advertisement which he does not deserve? I am afraid I did not see all the difficulties when you put up the proposal. Please do not go any further with it until after we have had a talk.[25]

Lord Swinton replied:

The whole understanding was that this would be a series of matches between our second eleven and their second eleven; and the BBC are not playing the game if they put up leading ex-Ministers. If the operation can be worked on the lines we originally agreed, I still think it a good plan, for I see no other way of getting good Government speakers on the air, and of having speakers on our side who can be relied upon to put over our policy.[26]

Lord Woolton then wrote to Churchill, agreeing that:

On reflection I am increasingly doubtful whether ministers should take part in this activity, either on television or the BBC. They could certainly explain their policies through either medium. But I am sure that they should not debate them with their predecessors except in Parliament. The United States may be an awful warning to us. Some of us think that respect for politics is reduced by the political discussions between back-benchers, which are built along the lines of entertainment; in short they are a sort of political knockabout turn which adds little of information and dignity to political life. We think the BBC political debates should be confined to PPBs, and that in addition to these there should be the reports of Parliamentary proceeding given each night and at the weekend. So far as the BBC insists on having other discussion these should be conducted by men who are not ministers of Cabinet rank in the current Government and who were not Ministers in the previous Government.[27]

The matter continued unresolved until Churchill decreed, some months later: 'It would be unwise for Ministers to take part in this sort of activity; they should not debate their policies with their predecessors except in Parliament.'[28]

The spirit of the time is seen in Lord Woolton's interesting distinction not between television and radio, but between television and the BBC. In 1952 radio was still the BBC, and vice versa. Churchill was keen to keep the parity of the status quo: ministers were not to appear in informal broadcast debates. Politics and entertainment were not yet to be fused. In the light of this ban, the difficulty the Conservatives had in matching the Labour Party's success in the broadcasting of informal political debates could, in some part, have been of their own making. In 1953, Lord Brand asked Jacob to explain how speakers were chosen by the BBC, as a left-wing bias was apparent, but conceded that the ban on ministers broadcasting, made the bias 'particularly difficult to deal with when the Party is in power and when seventy of its leading lights are thus largely immobilised'.[29]

In 1956, the Party Chairman was asked to seek a modification of the ruling. Not only did the ruling deprive the Party of some of its ablest minds, but resulted in failure to make known to the public the personalities from whom, in the course of events, future Conservative administrations would be drawn. Whilst these potentials were banned, 'lively back-benchers with little capacity but with engaging personalities, are able to win widespread publicity. Some may have developed egos potentially dangerous to party unity.'[30]

The Conservatives continued to query the socialist bias in BBC broadcasts, and in 1956 William Clark felt it necessary to point out that:

> On the subject of Ministers and Junior Ministers appearing in television and radio Mr Grisewood said the BBC had no objection to their appearance by invitation on such programmes as *In the News*. The only reason that they had not been invited in recent years was because of a ruling by Sir Winston Churchill that Ministers were not to appear.[31]

Thus the ban may have been instigated by Churchill, but it lasted throughout the Eden administration and into that of Macmillan. No evidence of the date on which the ban was lifted could be found, but in 1958, Sir Toby Low wrote to Lord Hailsham, indicating that some back-benchers were less than happy with the situation. Low had appeared in *Under Fire*, produced by Granada in their Manchester studios. He argued that he was bullied into appearing in a half-hour programme on employment and neglect in Wales – in which he did not do well. He said:

> The real point is this – why do Ministers, junior or senior, not take the opportunity of these programmes to stand up for their policies and explain them thoroughly and get themselves known. I know the risks and can well understand why Winston Churchill made rules about ministerial television broadcasts four or five years ago but though the risks may not have decreased the advantage to ministers appearing on television – indeed the vital importance of it – have increased enormously. Front bench Labour men do not miss these opportunities.[32]

Thus, it seems, the Conservatives were, to a large extent, hoist by thier own petard. In keeping their leading lights off the air the Conservatives gave Labour the advantage in informal radio and television debates in which they faced government back-benchers who were often not in a position to know all the answers. Unsurprisingly, the general consensus of opinion between the parties and the BBC was that Labour were winning televised debates.

Thus, throughout the 1950s, no senior government ministers were permitted to debate issues with the Opposition in informal political broadcasts. This position, like the absence of scenes from the House of Commons, is almost impossible to comprehend today when both are virtually nightly occurrences. Nevertheless, the fact remains that Conservatives, whilst losing the battle for the airwaves, were winning at the ballot box and remained in power during the 1950s. This begs the question long asked by sociologists of the media: what is the precise connection between listening, viewing and behaviour? No convincing answer has yet been given to this question. However, the Conservatives' experience of the 1950s may well give credence to today's argument that public disillusionment with politics is fostered by overexposure to politicians.

Government ministers may not have been allowed to appear in cross-party debates but they could face journalists. The first *Press Conference* was broadcast on 11 July 1952 – Mr Butler had accepted Grace Wyndham Goldie's invitation to be the first personality to face a panel of four journalists. Mrs Goldie had particularly sought eminent politicians for the first broadcasts in order to establish the seriousness of the programme and to give it status. The BBC Press Officer made the following statement on 9 July 1952:

> This is not only the first time Mr Butler has ever appeared in television, but the first time that a Chancellor of the Exchequer in office has ever taken part in a BBC television programme, other, of course, than in Newsreels.[33]

Mrs Goldie wrote to her superior, Leonard Miall, after the Butler programme:

> I felt the programme lacked pace and sharpness. I hope that we shall get this into later ones...in discussion afterwards Mr Butler said extremely forcibly...that this first programme was in a style which would have 'sold' television to the Cabinet.[34]

Indeed, the press reports indicated that television was making history, and the Chancellor's appearance was impressive. The programme may well have 'sold' television as Herbert Morrison agreed to appear next, but Mrs Goldie was aware that improvements in the broadcast could be made, and Morrison was aware that he would be using a new medium. Thus an experimental session was arranged, the main purpose of which was:

> to test Mr Morrison, who will be appearing in *Press Conference* of August 7th as the main speaker. Mr Morrison is conscious that he may be rather difficult to light and is anxious to see himself on the monitor and find out how he is likely to come over and get all possible help from us about technique and so on.[35]

The experimental session paid dividends and the Controller of Television Programmes, McGivern, wrote to Mrs Goldie the day after Morrison's programme and clearly stated the importance of her pioneering work in political television. He said:

> Again congratulations. Overall, excellent. If you make this series succeed you will not have created a new television programme – it existed in America – but by the Lord, you will have altered the political habits of professional politicians in these islands.[36]

Press Conference was but one of many innovations in informal political broadcasting instigated by Mrs Goldie. Hole may have had control of the news, but Mrs Goldie, along with other gifted producers, established informal political broadcasting on television. The informal broadcasts were the locus of much of the innovation in political broadcasting. In 1946 Gordon Walker had acknowledged the importance for the Labour Party of indirect publicity on radio, and in 1959 the Conservative Central Office noted that informal political broadcasts were more important than PPBs – not only were there more of them but they were more popular than the formal broadcasts.[37] It was largely due to the pioneering spirit of the producers of informal political broadcasts, not least because they were seeking to improve the status of television as a serious medium of education and information, that the new political practices developed and the politicians' habits were reformed.

The news practices

The overriding principle which guided the postwar development of new political practices was that political public life was now being conducted in the home, around the fireside, on an intimate personal level. The old practices which were successful at a public meeting, addressing large numbers of electors, had to be reformed to practices appropriate for the individual in the informal privacy of the home.

The development of the electronic media enabled the time/space distanciation of modernity[38] which extended to all areas of life including politics. In the prewar era political public life, as public life in general, was more rooted in place. The public meeting was the key political activity – at such meetings politicians generally preached to their particular converted (with the odd heckler). Yet by 1954, Philip Goodhart, in a *Daily Telegraph* article aptly entitled 'Fireside Politics', reported that:

> Since the 1950–51 period both parties report a drop of up to 50% in the average attendance at their meetings.... It may be significant...that attendance at lunch-time meetings – when there is no competition from television – has remained as high as it was in the pre-election period.[39]

The popularity of television may have killed the political meeting, but it also offered the parties a way of restoring contact with the electorate. Broadcasting offered politicians the chance to reach not only much larger audiences, but also differing sections of the public including the supporters of other parties, and those previously politically ignorant or uninterested. Politicians of any party were no longer restricted to preaching to the converted, or subjected to heckling from the opposition. Conservatives now sought to show the appropriateness of their policies to the 'cloth cap brigade' and Labour sought to attract the higher classes. Before the 1951 election Labour attempted to get the more aristocratic members of their Party to broadcast whilst John Profumo urged Edward Heath, the Opposition Chief Whip, to

> Carefully select speakers, advise them, and remove all other duties from them . . . . One of the broadcasts in the next campaign should come from a Conservative working man or woman, a nation-wide search for someone possessing all the qualities should begin.[40]

Paradoxically, differentiating the audience had a levelling effect on the two main political parties, which may go some way towards elucidating the historians' dilemma with postwar consensus. Each was trying to attract the other's votes and to demonstrate that their policies were applicable to all citizens. The electronic media provided the means to access the opposition's voters and the floating voters *en masse*.

Prior to political broadcasting, the public meeting attracted the politically active, but elections 'were won on the doorstep'. Canvassing was the means by which the electorate were enticed to use, or change, their vote. The political broadcast had the potential to do both: to consolidate the views of the faithful and to persuade the floating voters.

Of course, canvassing did not disappear – it, too, was reformed. Goodhart in 1954 reported:

> Television looms as a threat to canvassing. As one senior Labour Party official said to me: 'I would certainly never send canvassers to call on an evening when *What's My Line?* is on, and soon we may not have the canvassers even if we wanted to send them out.

We in the Labour Party have a lot of hard thinking to do about television.'[41]

Goodhart pointed out that the Labour Party's thinking on television was largely negative. Whilst Gordon Walker had asserted the importance of indirect radio publicity in 1946, the Labour Party did retain a negative approach to television throughout the 1950s. In 1953, Anthony Wedgwood Benn telephoned the Conservative Party Office to discuss the future policy for televised PPBs. Astonishingly, Benn said:

> I would like to know what is in your mind because I find it very difficult to get our Chief Whip to think about the problem, and if I could go to him knowing what your people are going to bring up I think he would be more progressive in his dealings with this matter.[42]

The unidentified recipient of the call reported that he was very cagey in what he said. Benn then asked the very ingenuous question as to whether there would be any objection to his sending a minute to the Labour Chief Whip as to what he thought should be done! The Conservative recipient made a rather mild joke to the effect that of course he had no objection because he was not employed by Transport House. Benn may, of course, have been being mischievous, but there was clearly a need for the Labour Party to be more progressive. The Labour Party had opposed independent television, the televising of the party conferences, and had approached PPBs with caution. They were now concerned that the popularity of television was deterring canvassers and making their reception on the doorstep more difficult.

In contrast, the Conservative Party believed television could be a bonus to canvassers. On 17 April 1953, the Radio and Television Section of the CCO produced the first *TV and Radio Newsgram*. This was a fortnightly letter to all constituency agents. Its object was to help constituencies make full use of the political influence of broadcasting. The first issue said:

> Television opens an enormous new field of political activity. Potential scope is incalculable at this early stage.... To keep ahead of our political opponents, members of the party must be TV minded... *TV and Radio Newsgram* will serve its purpose if it

stimulates ideas to meet the new challenge of TV to political organisations.

The new medium was also changing constituency activities, and the first *Newsgram* acknowledged this: 'TV is affecting attendance at meetings and reception of the canvasser. It opens up opportunities for new and different activities.'[43]

The point to note was that political programmes opened up a common ground for discussion 'on the doorstep'. Canvassers could now expect the electorate to be better informed. Party activists ignored political broadcasts at their peril. The electorate would want questions raised by political broadcasts answered. The *Newsgram* for March 1954 advised:

> The BBC Programme *Panorama* is developing in popularity, it is very fairly objective and frequently introduces such hotly controversial subjects as raised rents and slum clearance. Regular viewers may find useful talking points when canvassing television owners, by reference to this independent and objective evidence.[44]

In the same year, 1954, the Conservative Party also produced a short film, *TV Can Tell It*. Its purpose was to educate party workers in co-operating in the construction of PPBs for television, and to train canvassers. Once again the Conservatives were taking a more progressive and positive attitude to television than their Labour counterparts. The demise of the public meeting and growth of television led to new political practices for all political activists, from the PM to the canvasser. The CCO set about assisting both party activists and politicians with the new techniques.

In 1952, Lord Woolton sent a letter to all Conservative Members of Parliament, informing them of the facilities Central Office had to offer for tuition and practice in sound and television broadcasting. The aim was for Conservative MPs to receive more invitations from the BBC to appear in controversial broadcasts and to give talks on both political and non-political matters. Woolton pointed out that the BBC had the right to choose speakers but they were influenced by broadcasting ability and tended to repeat successes. It was therefore desirable to excel in broadcasting technique. To this end radio and television facilities were available. For sound:

> Brigadier Hinchcliffe maintains a close liaison with Broadcasting House. In addition he has here a small fully-equipped studio with a tape machine on which voices can be played back immediately. He also has at his disposal an expert broadcast producer who has many years experience with the BBC and is available for tuition. Assistance can be given in the composition of scripts.

For vision:

> We have recently set up a television studio equipped with a television set, mock camera, lights, etc. Mr. Wyndham Goldie, who has considerable knowledge both as actor and producer, will be available at this studio for advice on television technique and production. The studio will be staffed by Mrs Crum-Ewing.[45]

It was not only Labour who had friends at the BBC. Grace Wyndham Goldie's husband was running the Conservative television studio, they had the assistance of a BBC producer and in 1952, the Chief Publicity Officer interviewed Gilbert Harding, after which he reported:

> It was known that Harding was 'a violent anti-socialist'. I told him that we were very worried by the fact that so many of our Party representatives in controversial broadcasting always appear to be on the defensive, and that the Socialists appear to have a much better technique or argument than we have. I asked him whether there was anything we could do to encourage the 'hostile mind' attitude.... What he would like to do is to come to our studio, when we know a certain person has been selected for a controversial broadcast and assume the role of the Socialist and encourage our people to take the initiative and show them how to obtain the maximum amount of the time allowed.[46]

Harding did not require a fee but required that his involvement should be kept secret. It is not clear whether the Conservatives availed themselves of the service, but hostility was not the key to a successful television campaign.

The key to a successful television campaign, as broadcasters knew, and politicians soon came to realise, was 'sincerity'. Ways of appearing sincere had to be incorporated into the new practices, from eye movement to clothing, and from notes to teleprompters.

The Conservative politician was instructed that, when appearing on television, he must:

> behave as a guest; he must seem at ease; he must be friendly; he must be courteous; he must not lecture; he must not condescend; above all he must not bore. For though he is a guest he can be dismissed at will by the turning of a knob.[47]

The Conservative Central Office produced two booklets on *Talking on Television*, one in 1951 and one in 1957. The contrast in style of the two booklets in itself suggests a change in methods of communication. The formality of the first contrasts with the relaxed style of the second. The first relies on text alone whereas the second includes cartoons to illustrate the points being made.

The second was compiled by Mrs Crum-Ewing and stated that preparation for appearance on television fell into two categories, physical and mental, the latter being the more important as, contrary to popular belief, it is the mind that is 'telegenic'. According to her, the mental preparation required knowing what you wanted to say, being well briefed on it and saying it within the time allowed.

The key physical points were the eyes, spine, hands, voice. The eyes were the most important for success on the screen. The potential broadcaster was advised always to look at the person they were addressing in the studio, not at the camera. It was disagreeable to be talked at instead of to. Avoid looking down, it appears nervous and tends to be both unfriendly and unconvincing. Avoid looking up – it makes the speaker look slightly lunatic. Avoid looking around – it conveys an impression of shiftiness. Allow the eyes to express friendliness and use them as you would in everyday contacts. Sit upright; to relax by sitting back in the chair, so the camera slightly looks up the nose, gives the impression of superiority. Leaning forward can be very distorting. Hands should not be artificially controlled as this reveals tension. The voice should be kept at an agreeable level and will only be successful if used as if talking to one person.

Finally, the would-be broadcaster was advised on dress. Sharp contrast of colour must be avoided. A stiff white collar could have a devastating effect. Women should go for a medium colour and avoid spots or stripes, and remember that viewers watching from their fireside are used to seeing women lightly dressed. It looks very stodgy to be too much muffled. The booklet concluded: 'Don't be frightened of television – study it. This is a new art form and no art was ever mastered without the will to study.'

The booklet is both fascinating and amusing because it is an attempt to unpack the everyday world we all take for granted, to indicate how the assessment of friendliness, conviction, sincerity and intelligence operate in daily encounters. Codifying the everyday is an amusing endeavour, as Garfinkel's breaching experiments proved.[48] There was nothing new about the everyday, but as Mrs Crum-Ewing asserted, television was a new form. The art to be mastered was the replacement of the old styles of public oratory with the relaxed styles of private, everyday conversations. The Conservatives clearly perceived this new art to be a more problematic exercise for their members than for members of the Labour Party. Possibly, they considered the socialist more versed in talking to the working classes, and thus more able to adapt to the necessity to address them in their home, in a style and language to which they could relate. Hence in 1957, Bromley Davenport wrote to the Conservative Research Department suggesting that for television:

> Conservative Party Political Broadcasts should really be on the level of the average working class man and put over in language he understands in pounds, shillings and pence, not statistics. So many speakers in Conservative broadcasts seem to speak over the heads of the people and not to them. I think this is a valuable suggestion as it is to this class of people we want to get home our policy and counteract the very simple but effective propaganda of the Socialists.[49]

Politicians also needed to learn new techniques of mental preparation, knowing what had to be said, and saying it within the allotted time. In 1950, Profumo rightly asserted that radio was a medium quite different from public speaking. The approach has to be simple, quiet and homely. He also noted:

> It is quite clear that before long election broadcasts will have to be televised ... viewers are not by any means confined to the higher

money group electors. In fact, rather the reverse. This is a completely new medium requiring special attention. The maximum effect of such transmissions will be spoiled if the speaker appears to READ everything from a script or looks tired or ill at ease.[50]

For radio broadcasting the politician could read his script; the new medium required new techniques. In 1954, Churchill was asked by Woolton to give the next Party Political broadcast. He had not broadcast for some time and was advised that an appearance would greatly encourage the country. He replied to Woolton, saying:

Before I commit myself I should like to know what it is thought would be involved in my case. Principally I am concerned with having notes which I can follow without looking down or wearing spectacles. Much has been tried in this direction in America.[51]

Churchill was informed that the American technique was the teleprompter. The script went from left to right in large letters on a ribbon directly under the camera, and gave the impression that the speaker was speaking without notes. It was not as good as it sounded, as the regular speed of the ribbon did not allow for normal variations of conversational talking. The CPO concluded 'I don't think you would like it much in any case.'[52] Churchill was urged to answer questions instead.

Clearly, even the PM was somewhat frightened of television. Michael Cockerell noted that Churchill had perceived television as having no part to play in the political process, until the Coronation of 1953 changed his mind. In 1954, Churchill arranged for a secret screen test, on which he would judge whether to appear on television or not. Having 'descended to this level', Churchill ordered the test be destroyed but, fortunately, Winifred Crum-Ewing had preserved it. The test demonstrated that Churchill in fact had a good understanding of the nature of television but was dismayed by his aged appearance and believed he would have come over better if he were younger.[53] As the dates coincide, it is reasonable to assume that Churchill undertook this test in response to the request to give the next PPB. Fear and suspicion of the new medium, failure to produce the teleprompter, dismay at his elderly appearance, or a combination of all three, may well have resulted in Churchill's decision never to address the nation on television.

In 1956, Mrs Crum-Ewing produced a report on party political television. The report said that generally it was the interesting rather than the handsome face that charmed the viewer. The important thing was that the participant should:

> look the viewer in the eye and speak from his own heart and mind, not from a piece of paper. The teleprompter may be a comfort, but it requires many hours of practice, otherwise the face assumes the rigid expression of reading, which is most disconcerting. We do NOT recommend its use in political television. An easier and simpler method of prompting is the 'idiot board'. Single words conveying the substance of a paragraph are put on an easel.[54]

Thus the teleprompter was not used in PPBs, but the question-and-answer format was not without its critics. Lord Hailsham wrote to Heath in 1958 protesting that the use of this format was a retrograde step. He said:

> Television broadcasting is a highly complicated and important medium of propaganda and I believe it to be of first importance that we should think straight about it. The ultimate element in all advocacy is, in the last resort, integrity of presentation . . . Of all the media where integrity is vital, Television is that where it counts more than in any other. This consideration involves not merely the sincerity of the actual person presenting the message. It also involves the presentation of him in a *mise en scène* which is seen to be genuine and not seen to be – or believed to be – phoney. Oddly enough the old fashioned radio 'talk', though applied in its original form to Television was almost laughably archaic, had this integrity . . . the trouble is that it represents a technique so slow that it wholly fails to retain the *interest* of the audience. If the first quality is integrity, the second is *interest*.[55]

Hailsham argued that the question-and-answer format applied to PPBs was intrinsically false and suggested a documentary format instead. However, many politicians sought to maintain the question-and-answer format, possibly because it more closely resembled the old practices of the political meeting – which Hailsham saw as a retrograde step. The political broadcast was an entirely new form which required new practices. In the event, all three formats, straight talk, question-and-answer and documentary were utilised in the new practices developed for television. Political broadcasters chose the style with which they felt most relaxed and in which they could most easily adopt an everyday conversational manner. The tele-prompter promoted neither and was therefore excluded from the new practices. The Conservatives' desire to utilise radio and televi-sion and the mammoth effort they devoted to utilising it successfully appeared to be unrewarded as Labour was achieving greater success with far less effort. A contributory factor was Churchill's ban on ministers, appearances but it was suggested that the real difficulty lay in the nature of the parties' policies.

In 1953 Lord Brand asked Jacob how speakers were chosen by the BBC, and said:

> I have often thought that too much latitude is given to people like A. J. P. Taylor and Co. Probably they have friends in the BBC who were at Oxford with them and who naturally therefore get in touch with them. I think I told you that the MPs I met had as almost their greatest grudge against the BBC that fact that it built up people like Beverley Baxter and Bob Boothby, but I do not see how this is to be entirely avoided.[56]

Jacob replied that both sides did not notice statements with which they agreed, but seized on those with which they disagreed and assumed propaganda was being put out. He suggested that BBC staff recruited in the 1930s may have grown up with a left-wing ethos, but it was rare for speakers to be chosen without several people having a say.

> A more real difficulty is that it is much harder to find Conserva-tives who are good performers at the microphone than it is to find socialists. Moreover some of the Conservatives who are capable of broadcasting are not thought by their party to be representative. Boothby is a case in point. . . . Whatever we do we shall always be open to criticism by somebody, and I think MPs are only too ready to be annoyed unless they are used themselves.[57]

Lord Brand replied that the answer to the left-wing staff bias was that Socialists proselytise more ardently and are drawn to the BBC as a means of spreading the gospel, and asked

> is it really true to say that it is harder to find Conservatives who are good performers at the microphone than it is to find Socialists? Doubtless it is easier to broadcast a demagogic sort of appeal that it is to explain Conservative principles.[58]

In 1956 a report on the Conservative Broadcasting Committee suggested that some members took the negative attitude that:

> Conservatism as such did not lend itself particularly readily to the medium of television, and therefore our best line was to protest to the BBC against any programme which had a suspicion of Socialist bias. I [Bellairs] must say that I was rather appalled that so many members should consider that it was difficult to put over the Conservative viewpoint on television. I cannot for the life of me see why. Personally I think it most important that before the next general election we have a team of experienced TV personalities ready. After all, we have to face the fact that we are living in a television age, and it is no good trying to put the clock back.[59]

Curiously, from this point of view the Labour Party had the advantage simply because it was the Labour Party. The Conservatives did not appear to weigh this advantage against the Labour Party's disadvantage of having lost the 1951 election and failure to regain power throughout the 1950s.

In 1958, the CCO complained to Norman Collins, director of ATV, about socialist bias in the Granada programme *Under Fire*. Collins gave a further possible explanation of the Labour Party's advantage in his reply:

> So far as the appearance of Government speakers, both back benchers and Ministers, is concerned, the Government has had a disproportionately high use of ITV time. On the other hand the Left with less time has made far more conspicuous use of it. This is not surprising. The opposition is always free to range over the whole field of the offensive, and the Government spokesman is

bound, the more highly that he is placed to be cautious and therefore uninteresting in his reply . . . irrespective of the Party in power, the Government in this sort of exchange is always bound to come off worse.[60]

From this point of view, paradoxically, the Conservatives were disadvantaged by being the party in power. The government was in a catch-22 situation: back-benchers were often not in a position to answer and the more senior ministers were restrained by policy. Perhaps, unlike today's politicians, they had learnt the lesson of the devastating effect of the Bevanite split on the previous Labour government, and ministers were thus at lengths to ensure that any party divisions did not get a public airing. In 1950 Marjorie Maxse wrote to David Maxwell-Fyfe because she understood that George Barnes was an old friend of his. The point of her letter was:

> that we are very worried about the selection of Conservative members and representatives in the television programme 'In the News'. Greville watched (the programme on November 17th) and tells me it was absolutely appalling and that Michael Foot and Barbara Castle just rode rings round Boothby and Lady Astor. This seems to be the general opinion and we have had many letters of protest . . . I am afraid they did let down the Party rather badly.[61]

She requested that Barnes be contacted to see that more balanced teams were put on the air. Maxwell-Fyfe replied that he had often discussed the matter with Barnes in connection with sound broadcasts, and the answer was always 'all right, tell me who?' Maxwell-Fyfe made some suggestions of his own and asked Miss Maxse to do likewise, so that a list of prospective television broadcasters could be sent to Barnes. He advised: 'Soundness is not enough. One must have personality, spontaneity with some combustibility and, if possible, a name, combined with an inherently Conservative outlook which will come out to our supporters.'[62]

Perhaps in desperation at the lack of success of other strategies, in 1957 Viscount Hinchinbrook, MP, offered Oliver Poole, the Joint Chairman of the Party a possible solution to left-wing bias in the BBC:

> I know that names for the Chairman of Governors of the BBC have been suggested to you and I think that this is one of the best ways over the years ahead of eliminating the general bias in the BBC that undoubtedly exists towards Left Wing idealism.[63]

Paradoxically, the Labour Party with its negative approach to television was winning the battle for the air waves whilst the Conservative Party, despite its positive approach, was losing. The Conservatives believed they were being defeated because the BBC displayed a left-wing bias, the ban on ministers kept their leading lights off the air and as the party in power they were constrained by policy. Furthermore, the Labour Party's demagogic policies were more susceptible to proselytising and the Labour Party could more easily talk to the working class in language they understood.

Morgan Phillips, Chairman of the Labour Party, gave a plausible explanation for the phenomenon. In 1958, six years after the Conservatives had provided their members with a similar service, the Labour Party provided a television studio for coaching their politicians. Phillips stated at the time:

> A democracy thrives on political knowledge so anything which furthers the spread of such knowledge must be encouraged . . . but I see a danger in over-grooming. It would indeed be harmful because in concentrating on technique there is a danger of losing sincerity. And sincerity is the most vital ingredient of any television political broadcast.[64]

If he was right, today's politicians with their plethora of media advisers and spin doctors may well be advised of the danger of over-grooming, and the importance of sincerity – or at least of the appearance of sincerity – in political broadcasting.

Conclusion

After the Labour Party victory of 1945 Lord Woolton wrote to Lord Beaverbrook:

> You asked me about Conservative election issues . . . I have asked myself what an election campaign is for. Obviously it is not

designed to persuade those whose loyalty to a particular party is deeply ingrained to change their part because they won't do it. It is to catch that unstable vote that is found amongst two classes of people – those who are politically ignorant and those who are highly intelligent. Propaganda ought to be directed at them.[65]

In a democracy, it is self-evident that a primary objective of all politicians must be to attract votes. Without votes there is neither power for politicians nor scope for implementing policies. But, as Carolyn Marvin suggested, new technologies make old practices irrelevant:

> Old practices are then painfully revised, and group habits are reformed. New practices do not so much flow directly from tech-nologies that inspire them as they are improvised out of old practices that no longer work in the new setting.[66]

Politicians, often reluctantly, revised old practices and accepted that they no longer worked in the new setting. Put simply, politicians were slowly, and sometimes painfully, required to develop new prac-tices of electioneering, which reformed group habits and changed political public life. Politics and the media are so closely interrelated today that the postwar era can all too easily be viewed with the modern eye. The politics we recognise today developed in the post-war era. It was a time of negotiation, of both resistance and accept-ance. Politicians interacted with the media to develop new political practices, the media interacted with politics and developed a changed political public life. The politician had to be trained in television and the television producer had to be trained in politics.

Michael Kandiah's detailed analysis of the CCO and political broadcasting from 1945 to 1955 rightly asserts that the CCO was responsive to the electronic media, but fails to address either the politicians' resistance to the media or the professional broadcasters' role in the development of political broadcasting.[67] He thus privil-eges the party machine, and formal political broadcasting, and con-cludes that the CCO was responsible for the politicisation of British television. From this point of view the media were a tool which politicians could employ to further their own ends. It neglects the broadcasters' responsibility for the mediatisation of politics.

Television did not effortlessly enter British politics, or vice versa. Political television was the result of a troublesome combination of two sets of professional practices – which produced a totally new beast. As Alex Kendrick, of American CBS News, suggested:

> Television, partly because it is so conspicuous a thing, and partly because its audience is so enormous, has got itself into the position of being able to change the very nature of the events, which, in theory, it is there merely to record.[68]

Similarly, Maurice Wiggin, television critic for the *Sunday Times* said of *Panorama*: 'its greatest successes were due not to its stalwart and sometimes distinguished corps of correspondents, but to the fact that it began to *make* News, to create events'.[69]

The technologies of radio and television, far from being the tools of politicians, have shaped modern political practices and hence modern history. The television cameras are active participants in politics and history today simply by being there to record events. Politicians and historical actors today both invite and attract the cameras, and history and politics end up in the home, through the television screen, and thus becomes part of the daily lives of the population.

The 1950s saw the beginning of the transformation of social attitudes. Deference was disappearing and the politicians had to move away from a top-down style of electioneering and learn to talk to the electorate on their own terms, in their homes. If one accepts the argument that politics is what politicians do, then clearly the media have had profound effects on 'doing politics'. Throughout the 1950s the oratorical skills of the public meeting were replaced by the conversational skills of 'fireside politics'.

Notes

1. *BBC Year Book for 1946* (1946), p. 26.
2. Whilst the intention was to place equal emphasis on both the BBC and the ITA and on the Conservative and the Labour Parties, the results are inevitably weighted in favour of the BBC and the Conservative Party

because there is no comparable archival material for the ITA or the Labour Party.

3. Paddy Scannell and David Cardiff, 'Radio in World War II', in *The Historical Development of Popular Culture in Britain*, vol. 2 (Milton Keynes: The Open University Press, 1981) pp. 31–78.

4. *The New Statesman*, 30 June 1945.

5. Woolton Papers (Bodleian Library Oxford): MS Woolton, 21, folios 15–16, written by Sir Joseph Bull for Churchill and forwarded to Woolton for comment, 29 March 1946.

6. L(abour) P(arty) A(rchive) (Museum of Labour History, Manchester): General Secretary's Papers, Box 9 Broadcasting 1–100, notes by Gordon Walker, 27 January 1946.

7. Laurence Gilliam (ed.), *BBC Features* (London: Evans, 1950) p. 9.

8. BBC W(ritten) A(rchive) C(entre) (Caversham Park, Berkshire): T16/119/1, Gorham to Haley, 22 July 1946.

9. BBC WAC: T16/119/1, Haley to Gorham, 16 August 1946.

10. BBC WAC: R51/114/1, Barnes to Hole, 19 August 1948.

11. BBC WAC: R51/114/1, Hole to Controller of the Light Programme, 23 March 1949.

12. BBC WAC: T16/119/1 Barnes and Grisewood, Report to General Advisory Committee, G.86/53.

13. Interview with John Green, 7 April 1995.

14. Robin Day, *Television: A Personal Report* (London: Hutchinson, 1961) Chapter 3.

15. Reginald Bosanquet, *Let's Get Through Till Wednesday: My 25 Years with ITN* (London: Michael Joseph, 1980) p. 27.

16. CPA: CCO4/7/348, GD to Karberry, 14 February 1957.

17. Both Bosanquet's assertion of the popularity of ITN and the Conservative's fear that 75 per cent of the audience could be lost must be put in the context of the relatively small number of sets which could receive the new services in the early days.

18. LPA: General Secretary's Papers, Box 9 Broadcasting 1–100, London Labour Party to Phillips, 11 March 1947.

19. CPA: CCO600/3/11/1, Jacob to Karberry, 18 July 1957.

20. CPA: CCO3/5/39, Goldsmid to Lord Hailsham, 2 February 1959.

21. Interview with Frank Gillard, 24 November 1994.

22. BBC WAC: R34/524/3 Jacob, 11 March 1955.

23. BBC WAC: *Any Questions* script, 28 October 1956.

24. Woodrow Wyatt, MP, 'Why I say Parliament should not go on TV', *Evening Standard*, 7 March 1955.

25. CPA: CRD2/20/3 Churchill to Swinton, 5 August 1952.

26. CPA: CRD2/20/3 Swinton to Lord President and Chief Whip, 7 August 1952.

27. CPA: CRD2/20/3 Woolton to Churchill, 7 October 1952.

28. CPA: CRD2/20/3 Churchill, Prime Minister's Minute, 28 November 1952.

29. Jacob Papers (Churchill College, Cambridge): Jacob 2/2 Correspondence A–B 1952–59, Brand to Jacob, 14 July 1953.
30. CPA: CCO4/7/362 Schofield to Poole, 2 March 1956.
31. CPA: CRD2/20/2 Clark to Lord Privy Seal, 13 March 1956.
32. CPA: CRD/2/30/3 Low to Hailsham, 18 February 1958.
33. BBC WAC: T32/283/2 Press Officer's Statement, 9 July 1952.
34. BBC WAC: T32/282/2 Goldie to Miall, 19 July 1952.
35. BBC WAC: T32/283/2 Goldie to Wright, 18 July 1952.
36. BBC WAC: T32/283/2 McGivern to Goldie, 8 August 1952.
37. CPA: CCO120/14 Memo from Chief Publicity Officer, 7 December 1959.
38. For a full discussion see Anthony Giddens, *The Consequences of Modernity* (Cambridge: Polity Press, 1990), and Joshua Meyrowitz, *No Sense of Place* (Oxford: Oxford University Press, 1988).
39. *Daily Telegraph*, 13 February 1954.
40. CPA: CRD2/20/11 Profumo to Heath, 26 July 1950.
41. *Daily Telegraph*, 13 February 1954.
42. CPA: CCO4/5/292 CCO to GD, Hare, Lady Maxwell-Fyfe, 23 February 1953.
43. CPA: CCO4/5/305 *TV and Radio Newsgram*, 17 April 1953.
44. CPA: CCO4/5/305 *TV and Radio Newsgram*, 12 March 1954.
45. CPA: CCO4/4/250 Lord Woolton to all Conservative Members of Parliament including the Liberal Unionist Group, 19 January 1952.
46. CPA: CCO4/5/291 CPO to Chairman, GD, Lady Maxwell-Fyfe and Mr Hare, 21 January 1952.
47. CPA: CCO4/4/260 Introduction to booklet *Talking on Television* (1951).
48. Harold Garfinkel, *Studies in Ethnomethodology* (Polity Press: Cambridge, 1984).
49. CPA: CCO4/7/345 Davenport to Bellairs, Central Research Department, 21 February 1957.
50. CPA: CRD2/20/11 Profumo to Heath, 26 July 1950.
51. Woolton Papers: MS Woolton 22 folio 89, Churchill to Woolton, 21 January 1954.
52. Woolton Papers: MS Woolton 22 folio 90, Woolton to Churchill, 22 January 1994.
53. Michael Cockerell, 'Television Premiers', Chapter 6 of this book (see pp. 119–27).
54. CPA: CCO4/7/303 Crum-Ewing, 1 February 1956.
55. CPA: CCO600/3/11/1 Hailsham to Heath, 20 June 1958.
56. Jacob Papers: Jacob 2/2 Correspondence A–B, 1952–1959, Lord Brand to Jacob, 30 June 1953.
57. Jacob Papers: Jacob 2/2 Correspondence A–B, 1952–59, Jacob to Brand, 3 July 1953.
58. Jacob Papers: Jacob 2/2 Correspondence A–B, 1952–1959, Brand to Jacob, 14 July 1953.
59. CPA: CRD2/20/15 Bellairs to Fraser, 22 June 1956.
60. CPA: CCO600/3/11/1 Collins to Renwick, 9 May 1958.

61. CPA: CCO4/4/260 Maxse to Maxwell-Fyfe, 22 November 1950.

62. CPA: CCO4/4/260 Maxwell-Fyfe to Maxse, 27 November 1950.

63. CPA: CCO3/5/39 Hinchinbrooke to Poole, 2 May 1957.

64. LPA: General Secretary Papers Box 9 201–301, exclusive interview with Morgan Phillips, Party Chairman, printed in *Impact*, May 1958.

65. Woolton Papers: MS Woolton 20, folio 17, Woolton to Beaverbrook, 31 May 1945.

66. Carolyn Marvin, *When Old Technologies were New* (Oxford: Oxford University Press, 1988), p. 5.

67. Michael Kandiah, 'Television Enters British Politics: the Conservative Party's Central Office and Political Broadcasting, 1945–55', *Historical Journal of Film, Radio and Television*, vol. 15, no. 2 (1995).

68. Alex Kendrick, CBS News, quoted in Norman Swallow, *Factual Television* (London: Focal Press, 1966), p. 107.

69. Maurice Wiggin, *This Week, Rediffusion Television Ltd* (London: McCorquodale, 1966), p. 17.

10
When did Postwar Britain End?
Keith Middlemas

Historians relish periods of transition: the media prefer turning points. As an historian, I must believe that no historical phenomenon ever wholly dies, so long as it is remembered. But postwar Britain (or, more precisely, Britain's postwar settlement) hangs tenuously between living memory and the distant past; and can be read like a fading Cheshire Cat, poised somewhere between a discernible outline and the mere shadow of a grin.

In charting the end of postwar Britain there are relatively few dramatic or iconic events to choose from. Even Churchill's state funeral in 1965, though an event of unusual splendour – notable for the deceased's precise instructions, including the staging in front of St Paul's high altar of the magnificent mourning candlesticks last used at the Duke of Wellington's funeral in 1852 – leads mainly to a conclusion that the British still retained a mastery of ceremony. Yet the fact that the Ministry of Public Building and Works had by then neither jettisoned nor auctioned off the baroque relics of a previous century keeps that event within the postwar era. The new right phenomenon which dawned in the early 1980s not only lacked the ability to stage such sombrely confident public masterworks; the near-extinction of public spirit which it apparently bequeathed to the governing parties of the 1990s may indeed represent a crucial element in a long, lugubrious transition.

If a turning point is required, a better choice would be the events of 1973–74. But before examining the loss of innocence and confidence on the part of the postwar meritocracy which that abrupt crisis brought about, it is necessary to define not so much the postwar era as a whole (for it would be absurd to claim that all the characteristics ended together, or even within a given decade) but the apparent settlement brought about between the onset of reconstruction planning in 1942–44 and the climax of the long postwar boom, *c.* 1965. Looking back like Bunyan's Pilgrim from the other side, the postwar settlement appears to have had four facets: an expression of government and state willpower, a body of activity, a state of mind and a serviceable myth.

I

That the *expression of will* took shape before the 1945 general election, on a broadly cross-party basis embodied in principles shared widely among Britain's administrative, political and industrial elites – but much less among the financial ones – owed as much to the process by which memories of the interwar years had been matured in wartime conditions, like Greek retsina in pine casks, as it did to the actual war emergency. However much they differed on detailed remedies, ministers and civil servants planning within government, and academics and other outsiders imported for the duration, could agree that Beveridge had been right to define a litany of remediable evils familiar to all those who had lived through the interwar years. Industrialists and politicians of all parties could agree with the *general* emphasis on fuller employment, social welfare, national insurance, health provision and wider access to secondary education.[1]

They divided on two principal, and in other cases principled, lines. On the role of the state, many in business and the City of London took the line in favour of the free market already marked out by Hayek in *The Road to Serfdom* (1944). They did so again over the extent and cost of the promises of what the state could achieve, from which competitive bidding by political leaders was to develop, not merely in the 1945 election, but in every subsequent election down to 1970. A comparison of Beveridge's published target of 3 per cent unemployment as the measure of full employment (in *Full Employment in a Free Society* (1944)) with the Coalition government's reservations and secretiveness about anything less than 5–6 per cent[2] indicates how views about the state's capacity to fulfil bargains was to develop. Similarly, a comparison of even the 1944 White Paper's less-studied cautious phrases about the conditional basis for 'a high and stable level of employment' with the very different language of the 1985 Employment White Paper (*Employment, the Challenge for the Nation*) reveals how great was the transition from an era when unemployment was still undeniably the greatest evil to one where inflation had become the dragon to be slain, by monetary and fiscal prudence. At a time when unemployment had reached 13.2 per cent, or 3.5 million, on the newly revised (and inevitably lower) statistical basis adopted two years earlier, the 1985 White Paper starkly laid down that jobs lay not in the gift of any government but were made or lost by market forces.

Qualified it may have been, but the 1944 White Paper embodied a statement about the state's willpower, as well as the limits of its capacity and its necessary dependence on conditional responses by economic institutions and the public. The 1985 one sloughed off the state's responsibility almost entirely, replacing the element of political will with a diagnosis of impersonal causes related to demand, supply-side factors and globalisation of markets. Thus the passive acceptance of external reality replaced guarded belief in rational activism.

Two positions about this transition from willpower to realism can be argued. The first is that neo-Keynesian macroeconomic adjustment failed: the initially slow but remorseless rise of unemployment finally proved irresistible against any remedy short of the Heath–Barber reflation of 1971–73 (which was clearly impossible to sustain and was in fact intended only to last until unemployment fell from its short-term peak of one million to 500 000, or until a full counter-inflation programme had been agreed through the tripartite meetings between the government, the CBI and the TUC). The second is that, after the mid-1960s, the modest degree of inflation which even economists such as Robert Hall, (the government's chief economic adviser in the late 1940s and early 1950s) had agreed was an inevitable – and therefore acceptable – element in postwar macroeconomic management,[3] had become intolerable during the same Heath/Barber boom: hence the unfortunate coincidence of two rapidly-devised remedies – the Bank of England's 'corset', and Anthony Barber's tax on property values, which between them at the end of 1973 collapsed the speculative boom in conditions of appalling uncertainty.

The argument cannot be divorced from its wider, OECD (Organization for Economic Co-operation and Development) context as the first oil crisis shook every Western economy, nor from more domestic but equally slow-burning fuses – the ramifying debate about economic decline, Britain's self-exclusion from the EEC, and early stages in the prolonged abandonment of full employment, first signified by the downgrading of the National Plan in July 1966. James Callaghan's celebrated speech to the Labour Party Conference in September 1976, as the IMF (International Monetary Fund) crisis broke, about 'borrowed time, borrowed money, borrowed ideas', and Denis Healey's warning that full employment could only return once inflation had been brought under control,[4] occurred after the watershed, just as Heath's increasingly urgent advice to Barber from December 1971 onwards,[5] to reduce the long-term trend of unemployment, predated it.

On this criterion, the watershed must relate to the 1973 autumn/winter crisis, the failure of both tripartite talks between management and unions, and of the Counter-Inflation Bill – despite Heath envisaging that the strong state would remedy the private sector's political incompetence – as much as the subsequent miners' strike, and the lost election. For Heath himself, the turning point seems to have been the CBI's surrender in the face of the three-day week, which undermined his own determination and threw him into a premature general election.[6] But if one takes political and industrial institutions, the date comes slightly later. At the party political level, the turnabout was achieved under his successor as leader of the party, Margaret Thatcher. The negotiations between her inner group of shadow ministers and the CBI's representatives headed by Sir John Methuen, December 1975 to 1977, pinpoint the period when the CBI, after two decades of neutralism, for a time hooked its wagon to a different, intensely political Conservative leadership, as the only way to reverse the shift in the balance of power which had brought in, largely at the TUC's behest, the new Labour government's Social Contract, a new industrial relations legal order, and even more rapidly rising wage inflation.[7]

Afterwards, although vestiges of the postwar settlement still appeared in the Conservative document, *The Right Approach to the Economy* (1976), the key shadow ministers, together with business and City leaders, clearly accepted supply-side arguments, and the contentious proposition about the balance of industrial power. Most of them realised that these would involve a higher level of

unemployment, while differing on how long this would persist.[8]
Since Labour's leaders in government had already accepted limits to
the restoration of full employment, albeit for different reasons, an
accumulated revelation about the state's declining capacity in this
cardinal area of the postwar settlement collapsed the willpower of
any likely future government to restore or reinvent it.

II

The transition in the *body of activity* appears more marked if one
makes the comparison between 1965 and 1995, rather than 1945
and 1995, because of the 20 years of accretions to what had largely
been agreed in principle by the wartime Coalition. Almost regardless
of the rise in living standards, as measured in Beveridge's terms, or
educational ones in terms of Butler's 1944 Act, government promises
continued to extend the state's duties and its expenditure down to
the mid-1960s. In that sense, the Thatcher years and their sequel can
be seen to have achieved a more limited rolling-back than was
claimed at the time by her and her allies who had no reason to
share credit for cutting back with the Callaghan/Healey administration, 1976–79.

Nevertheless, during the 1980s, something which seemed almost
costless in the ten good years after 1953 (at a time when the Treasury's warnings went largely unheeded or were ignored at the fault
line between senior civil servants' duty to warn and ministers' awareness of their electoral mandate) came to appear both extravagant and
ill-suited to public policy in a very different context.

The case of industrial policy illustrates the argument well, because
it reached its apogee under Heath, once the DTI (Department of Trade
and Industry) had finally been established as the responsible department in 1970–72. Earlier essays such as the Ministry of Technology or
the Department of Economic Affairs had always failed to extract
sufficient authority from the Treasury, within the machinery of government, for industrial policy to develop in a coherent, long-term
way. The French or German models studied at the time of the
National Economic Development Council's (NEDC) foundation in
1960–1 were never fully grafted onto the British postwar compromise
between Treasury and Board of Trade; which explains why Heath's
centralised essays in industrial and regional policy were only briefly

given priority. After 1974, despite the efforts of Tony Benn to use Heath's legacy, including the 1972 Industry Act, to reorganise British industry, the Treasury was able, in conditions of great economic severity, to restore its ancient primacy.

State industrial policy can be seen as a parabola, curving upwards from the sponsorship arrangements in wartime, through the 1947 Economic Planning Board, the 1961 National Economic Development Council, and the Board of Trade's metamorphosis into DTI; then downwards in the 1980s, until NEDC itself was abolished by Nigel Lawson in 1989. Critics like him declared that the gap between state/government and actual performance (taking the measure to be an aggregate of industrial investment, productivity, competitiveness and non-price factors such as design and after-sales service) had increased remorselessly with each new essay in industrial policy. But on the upward curve, it appeared quite differently; each new government, Conservative or Labour, engaged the problem of industry (manufacturing industry of course, rather than services, and barely at all the financial sector) with renewed, if temporary optimism. It was only on the downward curve, and retrospectively, that the performance of British industry was compared with that of other nations, and seen to be ever-declining in terms of share of world trade or the output of qualified manpower. Less noticed was the counterfactual argument about what performance would have been, had there been no industrial policy, although the new right came near to arguing that, in that case, the 1980s readjustment would have occurred a generation earlier. Either way, it is only recently, after 10–12 years of the *absence* of industrial policy, that relative decline in manufacturing has been stemmed.[9]

This is not the place to disparage or praise the essays in sponsorship of specific industrial sectors, or the regional policy which was Heath's own choice as Britain's exemplar to its EC partners in 1973,[10] or sectoral initiatives, or the micro-industrial policy which emerged haltingly (a mere 12 years after NEDC's Orange Book, *Conditions Favourable to Faster Growth*, 1963) disguised as the 1975 Labour government's Industrial Strategy. All these had to fit into an overall macroeconomic policy approved by the Treasury, with the one short exception of 1971–3. Inspite of that, micro-industrial policy should be seen as a link across the watershed, which helped both to mitigate the bankruptcies and unemployment brought about by the Thatcher/Howe/Lawson deflation of 1980–82 and to hold the loss to no more than 17 per cent of the industrial base.

Nevertheless, the record of state failure, as seen thereafter in the self-evident gap between promises and performance, tarnished the whole theme of industrial policy so that a DTI which was still able to utilise it in the IT and high-tech areas in 1983–4 lost ground in the years when Nigel Lawson was Chancellor of the Exchequer, which was barely recovered by Michael Heseltine at the renamed Board of Trade a decade later.

III

It is harder to be precise about the turning point in the third category, *the state of mind*, than it is in the second. Nothing so simple can categorise the whole nation, a whole national opinion, or even the varied opinions of a whole political or economic elite. Too many professional, micro-elites compete within the curtilage of the state, and inside the political system, while the industrial and financial markets beyond 'pure' politics cannot easily be categorised other than by managerial function. But if the focus is put on a single, controversial question, 'the perception of Europe', a trend appears more distinctly as Britain shifted from seeking in EFTA (European Free Trade Association) a powerful alternative to the EEC, into applicant status, then member of the EC, and finally into a curious category of EU membership, that of 'inside-outsider'.

Living in an island off the north-west coast of Europe, the English have throughout the last hundred years had a distinct perception of the continent, often at variance with perceptions in Edinburgh, Glasgow or parts of Wales and Northern Ireland. British governments of the late 1940s and 1950s however, adopted a Frank Sinatra approach ('I did it my way'), first to the ECSC (European Coal and Steel Community) and Euratom, and then to the EEC itself. Records of the TUC and the CBI's predecessor institutions indicate that this line was in general approved by both sides of industry, while the City markets seemed to have interested themselves very little in the European scene until the emergence of the Eurodollar market.

Not until 1960–61 was this consensus widely disrupted. Whether in the immediate postwar attempt to dominate Western Europe through bilateral trading agreements, or in the responses to ECSC and Euratom, it seemed clear that British governments (which for the most part did at that time represent Scottish, Welsh and Northern Irish opinion) wanted different things from those their French, West German, Italian or Benelux counterparts desired. This is not to say that the Treaty of Rome would not have been different had the British representatives stayed on at Messina in 1955, only that it is hard to conceive how the then Conservative government could have requested them to do so.

The European Free Trade Association turned out not to be what the British desired. But the measure of how deeply prejudiced an extra-continental view of what had become the EEC held even by the protagonists of 1959–61, can be read in the pragmatic, cautious and essentially political diplomacy employed by Macmillan himself. For him the important (and still concentric) circles were the cabinet, the party and, more peripherally, the major Commonwealth countries.[11] Very little effort went into consultation with industry and finance, none with the union side; and the question of how to consult the public, and fulfil the government's democratic responsibility, was postponed until all the major decisions contingent on the application had been made at the centre.

Within the core of economic ministers and senior civil servants, of whom Sir Frank Lee, Permanent Under-Secretary at the Treasury, and Sir Richard Powell, at the Board of Trade, were often the inspiration, it was not the Commonwealth, nor the agricultural interest, nor even the Tory party which counted most, but how ministers and civil servants (who seem to have been more closely interwoven in their debates than at any point since 1942–4), reached their definition of Britain's ultimate national interest. Significantly, this inner group did not seek to make alliances with Britain's potential allies, in particular the Netherlands and Italy, nor to influence the West German administration of Konrad Adenauer; above all, probably as a result of misperceptions in Paris by the British Ambassador Sir Gladwyn Jebb, its members made no special effort to counter in advance the likely objections from de Gaulle.

The introspective nature of the decision-making process, in the 18 months before Britain's public application occurred, made it impossible to adopt the only strategy which might have circumvented the General and met West German, Italian and Benelux governments' requirements for some sort of British act of faith or guarantee of commitment, such as an application to sign the Treaty of Rome in principle as it stood, reserving detailed negotiations about the transition for afterwards. In this, as during the second application in 1967, a British government held to the Sinatra theme.

But solipsism stuttered to an end with the Heath administration of 1970, the only one to adopt a truly European view of what was by then the Community. Whether this derived wholly from the Prime Minister himself, or from the Cabinet and a wider range of civil servants than in 1961, will not be clear until the machinery of government documents are opened. At present, it seems to have constituted an integral element of the Heath government, on which he himself (like Lloyd George at the Paris Peace Conference in 1919) spent much of his time and concentration during his first year.

Heath's own rapport with the French President Georges Pompidou, his understanding of the Community built up since he had taken enthusiastic charge of the original application, his admiration for what the French state had achieved in creating the conditions for France's economic regeneration in the 1960s, and his belief that his government could transform the British state into an efficient instrument to back a synoptic industrial and regional policy, without slavishly following German or French examples, all contributed to the exceptional period of three years in which Britain was opened to European examples, and was regarded in turn by continental contemporaries as a late but welcome convert to the Europeanising process.

Heath's view of the Community and this openness were for a time shared widely by financial institutions, many of which had already made their own dispositions in the EC banking and Eurodollar markets. In the brief period when Competition and Credit Control (which was intended partly to induce City markets to respond to the US and Japanese financial challenges) appeared to be working satisfactorily, it seemed that City of London markets were in fact expanding to meet global competition in banking, and rather more tardily in the insurance market (though this was not yet true of the Stock Exchange). Finance was beginning to share some of manufacturing industry's preoccupations, and the leading economic players had lined up again, as they had begun to do in 1961 – but in this case pushed by a more positive government direction.

Something of that enthusiasm, and its surprised reciprocation across the Channel, survived the oil crisis and the deep depression of 1974, to condition public perceptions and affect favourably the outcome of the 1975 referendum on British membership. But the plant, rooted in thin soil at a time of declining living standards and expectations, was not nurtured with any enthusiasm by post-1974 governments. Continuing recognition among financial institutions and the larger national and multinational corporations that there was no credible economic space for Britain outside the EC did not offset the failure or unwillingness of two subsequent Labour governments to recover what was being lost, nor the reversion to the Sinatra theme by the Thatcher administration after 1979. Only the Single European Act won largely uncritical acclaim in her day, and had there been a referendum on almost any other issue in those 20 years, it is unlikely that the result would have been yes, even by a majority as narrow as the French one which endorsed Maastricht in 1992.

This is only to say, adapting Chesterton, that the people of England have not since 1975 been asked the right questions. There is, in contrast, less doubt where the peoples of Scotland, Wales and North-ern Ireland stood, given the efforts their Development Agencies have made and the largesse all regions have gained from Community sources since 1973.[12] But in terms of government's use of the means of state communication, either for or against the Community since 1956, the Heath administration represented no more than an inter-lude in the trend of defining national interest from an often aggres-sively offshore standpoint. Heath's government was an exception, rather than a turning point.

On the other hand, from the point of view of export earners in industrial and financial markets, there was no reversal matching that in public opinion after 1975, only something close to withdrawal from the increasingly one-sided public political and press debate at home, in favour of a determinedly self-interested policy of ensuring government support for British national and Euro-champion firms wherever possible, within Community institutions and via the Brit-ish national representation in Brussels.

Returns from these informal endeavours have been considerable, especially since the Thatcher government signed the Single European Act (SEA) in 1986, even if the SEA's promissory note about EMU (Economic and Monetary Union) remains highly problematic. But what can be seen as a tacit bargain, institutions' non-interference in public debate at home, the pursuit of national and global advantage in private across the Channel, has helped to impose another sort of limitation on public perceptions about where Britain's overall advantage lies in the European Union. This continued under the Major government, in spite of the more overt line taken by the CBI, the British Bankers Association and the British Insurers Association once the Maastricht Treaty embroiled a government with an exiguous majority in the early 1990s.

IV

As it recedes, the fourth element of *mythology* in the postwar settlement, like the received version of what the British did in the Second World War, appears much larger than it did at the time. It suited the politicised elite in the good years 1953–65 to believe that unemployment and the rest of Beveridge's five giants were remediable, and to hold that what the Labour government had done to effect remedies after 1945 was to pick the best available solutions, to be implanted by the state and the local state according to government priorities, at what was for a time relatively low cost. Whatever questioning followed in the later 1960s failed fundamentally to disrupt that consensus, or its two cardinal assumptions, firstly that what had been done was intrinsically correct, needing therefore only detailed amendment, and secondly that if there *were* a crisis (like 1961, 1966 or 1971), reversion to the wartime method of doing things by agreement, in concert with an increasing range of non-governmental players, would be sufficient to invoke a workable reinterpretation of the original canon.

The fact that competitor nations across the Channel had developed their own distinctive postwar settlements, some of which could by the 1960s be demonstrated statistically to be more efficient than the British version, as well as equally effective in meeting national needs, made surprisingly small impact. Systems in Scandinavia or Austria could be ignored, except by the left, as inappropriate, those in Germany and France treated disparagingly as derivatives from a primal British initiative. Until the new right onslaught on 'New Jerusalem',[13] itself partly an offshoot of the republican/ new right nouvelle vague in the United States, no fully fledged alternative existed; Enoch Powell's mid-1960s critique being too idio-syncratic and austere for more than a handful of pre-1975 Conserva-tives.

But, in fact, the cardinal assumptions in the 1944 Employment White Paper, which had been intended as a tacit bargain underpin-ning relations between the state, industry and labour, as well as the state and civil society in the postwar world, had already fallen into desuetude by the time the long boom began around 1953, and could not easily be revived afterwards. The crux that demonstrated this came, not with the eccentric revolt against the Macmillan tendency in public spending by Peter Thornycroft, Nigel Birch and Enoch Powell, but after 1969 with Harold Wilson's retreat over *In Place of Strife*, when Roy Jenkins' fiscally prudent chancellorship was ended by an electorally driven *sauve qui peut*.

Yet the myths survived for another decade, challenged only by the confluence of new right thinkers and Conservative politicians in opposition. The newly styled Thatcherites then weaned themselves from the centre after 1975 sufficiently to capture a still-divided party – whose clear numerical majority in 1979 nevertheless remained centre right, if not universally One Nation in style. Political direction by the Prime Minister herself and key economic ministers in 1980–2 was therefore required, in addition to the new right philosophy, before the myths were effectively challenged.

In chronological order of implementation by the Thatcher govern-ments, these were: the neo-Keynesian orthodoxy of macroeconomic management; the tripartite approach to industrial relations, together with the practice of informal bargaining between governments, industry and unions; the necessity of state ownership of 'natural monopolies' in the transport, communications and energy infra-structure; and the self-government by professions and professional bodies of financial markets, the civil service, universities, the established church and the legal and medical professions, which had persisted largely unchallenged since the late nineteenth century.[14]

Not all these battles were won. An important distinction should be made between the wars of movement (such as the 1981 budget and the dramatic curbing of strikes and trades unions' political activities of the early 1980s, culminating in the miners' strike of 1984–85), and the wars of position which rumbled on into the 1990s. But, debilitated over so long a period, the postwar myths suffered terminally and were in many cases abandoned even by their 'natural defenders' on the left and centre left. The idea of a tacit contract continually bargained between state and governments, on one hand, and on the other informal players with continuous access to both, almost disappeared at the institutional level, though it repaired and replaced itself lower down at the level of industrial or financial sectors and the larger firm – not least because this was a precondition for the latter's advancement in the European Community political marketplace.

If one asks, when did political parties, civil servants, media, industrial and financial and even trade union elites wake up to this process, the answer must lie in the mid-1970s crisis. The new right capture of the Conservative Party, following the change of leadership in 1975, had been prefigured by the comparable Bennite new left assault on the Labour Party in 1970–3; and although that was partially finessed by Harold Wilson, the ferment continued well into the 1980s. Real political antagonism over issues of the legal order and the balance of informal power erupted between the CBI and the TUC in 1974–7, focusing on the Social Contract and the Bullock Report. City markets did not escape the consequences of the crash at the end of 1973: Conservative as well as Labour ministers were to use the law to set the boundaries of banking supervision, and to challenge ancient myths about self-regulation, whenever malpractice, fraud or incompetence occurred.

In a much more general way, the mid-1970s crisis ushered in an era when financial considerations and the accountancy ethos supervened, for governments wrestling with the cost of public services, as much as for firms responding to global and European competition by shedding labour and cutting costs. Finally, with the state's limits exposed to a remarkable degree in the early 1970s, and its pretensions challenged, the myth of centralised government based on a metropolis which had once been the centre of an empire was also questioned, by local authorities in new right hands resentful of central power, and by regions for whom the results of elections in an English majority of constituencies no longer carried quite the same legitimacy, especially since most of their own domestic economic levels of decision-making had been sucked south into the London orbit.

V

During the late 1970s, and much more obviously in the adversarial decade after 1979, it ceased to be convenient, and eventually ceased to be credible to pretend that the postwar settlement myths retained their validity or that the memory of how things had been done in the Second World War could still be relevant. Irreverent television commentators, journalists and cartoonists had begun to assault the myths in the mid-1960s. Thereafter, bitterness wore away what laughter had already begun to erode. But the turning point itself came within a relatively short period of a year after the oil crisis in the autumn of 1973, when the assets, values and property-based outlook of Britain's elites suffered more severely than at any time since the Great Depression. The very sharp recession destroyed far more than inflated commercial property values. For nearly a decade the prices of houses, agricultural land, antiques, paintings, and decorative art objects had spiralled upwards, outstripping even the rate of inflation (as they were to do again in the period 1985–90, the Thatcher–Lawson boom paralleling that of Heath and Barber). So did share prices, dividends and managerial salaries.

The crash took the *Financial Times* Thirty Share Index from its peak of 543 in May 1972 to 146 in January 1975, a fall more serious and prolonged than in 1929, and three times worse than that experienced at the same time by the Dow Jones Index in the United States. As the values of all assets fell, from house property to fine wines, salaries and dividends were frequently frozen. Yet professional people's costs – above all of school fees, house repairs, cars – rose rapidly at a time of 20–30 per cent inflation.

Responses to this organic shock naturally differed. They frequently included an overt political dimension which foreshadowed the 1979 electoral swing, accompanied by portentous fears of left-wing authoritarianism and middle-class decline.[15] Sufficient elements of unreason and panic existed to justifying portraying the two years 1973–5 as the climax of a long-brewed crisis within the extended state and the political nation, if not entirely in society at large. Afterwards, there would be no more attempts to revive the postwar settlement, or to depict it other than in the lambent colours of nostalgia.

The state being constituted by individuals drawn from several such elites, it is hardly surprising that it should have been riven by the aggression and polarisation demonstrated in the political arena. Over the next ten years, individual senior civil servants who retained faith in its directive power, on lines hallowed in the postwar era, were either silenced or marginalised. As Hugo Young has pointed out, one characteristic of the Thatcher governments was a reassertion of the primacy of political mandates, and of party government over the state.[16] Once willpower altered course, the state's capacity was naturally reduced; and even if this, being a product of a small mandarin elite, is not easily equated to the parallel geographical and functional limits imposed on the civil service during the Thatcher decade, the two phenomena are closely linked.[17]

It did not help the postwar settlement's defenders that under a Labour government with an exiguous majority in 1975, carrying a heavy burden of obligation to the trade union section of the labour movement, Britain like Italy failed to respond to the 1973–5 crisis, so that most other Western countries, led by Germany and Japan, followed rather later by the United States and France, took the harder but more successful road to economic recovery. Continued rapid economic decline accelerated the comparative gap; and also the political gap between government and the economic players who were already preoccupied with the evolution of the European market. Those who in the Second World War had been prepared to accede to a tacit bargain with the state, should be seen after the late 1970s much more as harbingers of liberalisation, deregulation and, finally, privatisation.

VI

During the postwar era, defined here as the 30 years after 1944, the states of Western Europe possessed sufficient willpower, competence and motivation to try to shape their domestic contexts, and through them the external world, first to implant, then to expand and improve their individual variations on the postwar settlement theme. In some cases, of which Sweden, Austria, Germany and France were until recently the leading exemplars, the process lasted until at least the late 1980s. Whatever the form of welfare state, industrial policy or macroeconomic management chosen, the idea that there had come into being a settlement of the prewar discontents and evils gave an extra dimension of legitimacy to states which were, with the possible exceptions of Italy, and of course Spain and Portugal before 1975, fully re-established well before the new West German state's Basic Law, 1949.

Begun earlier than theirs, in the gloomiest years of the Second World War, the matching process was completed in Britain in two stages, the first by 1944, the second by 1949, although some of the details remained to be decided. It was, however, increasingly put at risk by relative economic decline, and by the fading capacity of much of British industry and some of its services to remain competitive in what were becoming global markets. But until 1974–5 it was not threatened, except by the Powell faction in the Conservative Party; which in Heath's first two years seemed to have been dispersed. There was no ideological explosion in the interior comparable to the volatile compound of new right economics, fundamentalist Christianity, right-wing nationalism and populism in the United States, whose ferments have not yet petered out within the Grand Old Party.

In the United States it was the New Deal, the *prewar* settlement, which came to be seen on the Republican right as an aberration. For all the activity in Britain of the IEA (Institute of Economic Affairs), the CPS (Centre for Policy Studies) and the later new right exponents' attempts to unpick the postwar settlement's assumptions, the 1980s wars of position stopped short at fundamental change in the basic health, welfare and educational elements of the postwar settlement (i.e., those sections established in principle by 1944); with the significant exceptions of the state as owner/manager, and the state as guarantor of full employment. Both these latter roles, had, in any case, to a large extent been economically undermined before 1979. The Thatcher governments did indeed roll back the state and open up the postwar settlement to question; but to a point level with 1944, not, as in the United States under Ronald Reagan, 1924.

The phenomenon that the Thatcherite wars of movement, being easier, were won, while those of position led to Pyrrhic battles which are in many cases still unresolved, underlines the fact that the new right *revanche* lacked momentum, especially once its chief protagonist had been ousted in 1990 by a party she had never wholly succeeded in capturing. The double question has then to be asked: would what was done in the 1980s have been possible without the Labour government's turnabout in 1976, and without the earlier turning point which enforced that, the British state's crisis in 1973–4?

Popular memory of a long postwar boom was of course an illusion, as debate even in the 1960s about Britain's relative economic decline revealed. But the illusion acquired a political dimension as the gaps increased between what successive governments promised and the capacity of the state they temporarily controlled to redeem their promises, and between the expectation of a still-credulous public and what a rational outsider could reasonably have expected any British government at the time to have achieved. Heath's administration had the misfortune to be elected just as the tide of public perception finally turned. A prime minister and a government with more willpower to push its policies through, using the state's full resources, than any since 1945 found themselves crippled by inadequate means: externally by the first oil shock and its consequence, the *sauve qui peut* which followed among EC member states; at home by the loss of public good will. A government which could have survived the hostility of organised labour found itself hamstrung by the withdrawal of organised management's support during the three-day week. Yet even so, had the February 1974 election result, held a little earlier or later, been different, Heath might have steered through the eye of the storm to calm on the other side.

At a deeper level, however, the things Heath aimed at – a systematised industrial relations, a tripartite bargain to restore the 1944 compromise, and a collective understanding that productivity, competitiveness, investment and technology were legitimate requirements in return for a state guarantee of full employment – all belonged to a period when the economies and political preconceptions of Western states had been uniquely favourable. Perhaps only his vision of a British developmental state, securely ensconced among European *frères semblables*, belonged to the future. If so, it was a future which, after his fall, British governments determined not to endorse.

The sudden *reversal* can be explained in terms of immediate and wider causes: the 1974 miners' strike, the behaviour of unions, managements and the still-abstracted City markets, and the civil service and the Heath government itself. What this showed was that the postwar state had become arterio-sclerotic in its middle age, as Keith Joseph understood when he and Margaret Thatcher set up the Centre for Policy Studies with Heath's injudiciously given assent, in 1975. The British state had never been as capable of the sort of activity Heath aimed at as its West German and French counterparts. Equally, the British version of the postwar settlement suffered from being implemented earlier than theirs, at a time when Britain was receiving a larger percentage of Marshall Aid than the more devastated continental states, who were therefore compelled to choose different routes: this being a variation on the 'early start' thesis about Britain's nineteenth century industrial revolution.

But the new right critics who steered with the changed tide after 1974 and the deeper, colder current below the surface, were not wrong to focus on the intrinsic gap between the state's aspirations as legislator (in Adam Smith's use of the word) and its effectiveness actually to change individual and collective patterns of behaviour in civil society. The Cabinet's military advisers in the strike-torn quasi-revolutionary years 1919–21 had occasionally pointed out to the politicians that the army they relied on had changed as a result of the First World War: from being a well-trained, politically ignorant force, it had become politically more aware and less reliable as an instrument of domestic discipline. Something similar could be said of post Second World War wage earners, once full employment at well under 3 per cent unemployment had become assimilated in the mid-1960s, as if it had been a natural and permanent phenomenon. Until the mid-1970s crisis, governments had assumed that they could still trade benefits for conformity in the labour market, but the experience of *In Place of Strife*, and the 1972–3 tripartite talks suggested that in both the labour and the industrial–political markets, the tacit obligations of the mid-1940s had ceased to operate.

New levers would be needed, new inducements. Since it was not open to government to change its public, the temptations of an outlook that eschewed such complex bargains, and in their place welcomed deregulation, liberalisation and the entry of foreign competitors as the best solvent of domestic cartels and restrictive practices, grew steadily after 1974. Flight from the state did not really become an ideology on its own in the Thatcher years, for the state remained as the guardian of a territorial view of sovereignty, internal order and discipline, public social values, and international status. But its apparent failure in that central crisis, and again in 1979's 'winter of discontent', established what was then a new insight: the state's weakness signified that foolish governments ought not to have committed it to such an expanding set of guarantees in the first place.

Unfortunately for the politicians at the time, the state was the only instrument they possessed, and its apparently proven weakness in one set of markets debilitated their endeavours, if not their electoral promises, in the spheres of social values and social behaviour – a phenomenon which the 1940s makers of the postwar settlement might have understood better than they.

Notes

1. See the Federation of British Industry (FBI)'s wartime pamphlets *Reconstruction* (London, 1942), and *A National Policy for Industry* (London, 1944).
2. Keith Middlemas, *Power, Competition and the State*, vol. 1: *Britain in Search of Balance, 1940–61* (Basingstoke: Macmillan, 1986), p. 90.
3. Ibid., p. 266; but see also p. 297 for Hall's revised position (1960–1).
4. LPAC Report 1976, p. 188, NEDC (78), 3 December 1977.
5. Edward Heath, letter in *The Times*, 1988. As late as October 1971, indeed, Leslie O'Brien, Governor of the Bank of England, was still in public deploring a level of 700,000 out of work (Lord Mayor's Dinner, 21 October 1971, *Bank of England Quarterly Bulletin*, December 1971); see also Keith Middlemas, *Power, Competition and the State*, vol. 2: *Threats to the Post-war Settlement, 1961–74* (Basingstoke: Macmillan, 1990), pp. 330–3.
6. Interview with Edward Heath, September 1993.
7. CBI Archives, D/DG files 1975–7, Modern Records Archive, Warwick.
8. Keith Middlemas, *Power, Competition and the State*, vol. 3: *The End of the Post-War Era* (Basingstoke: Macmillan, 1991), pp. 237, 247–8.
9. Walter Eltis, 'How Much of the UK Competitiveness Gap has been Closed?' (London: Foundation for Manufacturing and Industry, 1995).
10. Interview with Edward Heath, September 1993.
11. Alastair Horne, *Macmillan* (London: Macmillan, 1989) and Jackie Tratt, *The British Government and the Problem of European Trade, 1958–61: A Study in Policy Development* (unpublished PhD, University of Sussex, 1995).
12. For an illustration of just how much British regions gained from the European Community's regional structural funds, see Keith Middlemas, *Orchestrating Europe: The Informal Politics of the European Union, 1973–95* (Fontana, 1995), diagram on p. 391.
13. Heralded by Corelli Barnett, *The Audit of War* (Basingstoke: Macmillan, 1986).
14. Harold Perkin, *The Rise of Professional Society* (London: Routledge and Kegan Paul, 1989).
15. Middlemas, *Power, Competition and the State*, vol. 3, chapter 1, esp. pp. 38–41.
16. Hugo Young, *One of Us* (London: Macmillan, 1989), p. 521.
17. Peter Hennessy, *Whitehall* (London: Secker & Warburg, 1989).

Index